Another Encyclopedia

of Theme Activities

for Young Children

edited by
Kathy Charner,
Stephanie Roselli,
and
Brittany Roberts

Also by Gryphon House:

Another Encyclopedia
of Theme Activities
for Young Children

edited by
Kathy Charner,
Stephanie Roselli,
and
Brittany Roberts

Illustrations by Kathi W. Dery

Lewisville, NC

Copyright
© 2012 Gryphon House
Published by Gryphon House, Inc.
PO Box 10, Lewisville, NC 27023
800.638.0928; 877.638.7576 (fax)

Visit us on the web at www.gryphonhouse.com.

Library of Congress Cataloging-in-Publication Data

Another encyclopedia of theme activities for young children / edited by Kathy Charner, Stephanie Roselli, and Brittany Roberts.
    pages cm
  ISBN 978-0-87659-394-3
1. Early childhood education--Activity programs. 2. Creative activities and seat work. I. Charner, Kathy, editor. II. Roselli, Stephanie, editor. III. Roberts, Brittany, editor.
  LB1139.35.A37A55 2012
  372.21--dc23
                          2012017531

Bulk Purchase

Gryphon House books are available for special premiums and sales promotions as well as for fund-raising use. Special editions or book excerpts also can be created to specifications. For details, contact the director of marketing at Gryphon House.

Disclaimer

Gryphon House, Inc., cannot be held responsible for damage, mishap, or injury incurred during the use of or because of activities in this book. Appropriate and reasonable caution and adult supervision of children involved in activities, and corresponding to the age and capability of each child involved, is recommended at all times. Do not leave children unattended at any time. Observe safety and caution at all times.

Table of Contents

Introduction

Another Encyclopedia of Theme Activities is a book written by teachers for teachers, just for you! Incorporate these easy-to-use activities into your curriculum, use the activities to support teachable moments or the emerging interests of the children in your class, or integrate the activities into your daily, weekly, or monthly plans.

You also can use the activities in *Another Encyclopedia of Theme Activities* to meet the developmental needs of the children in your class. If, for example, a few children need to develop their counting skills, you can select activities that address these skills, or if you need to scaffold the fine motor skills of one or more children, you can select activities to address that need.

The activities in this book have been organized by age within each theme to make it easy to incorporate into daily classroom activities. Many activities can be done in large group, small group, or center settings and can be repeated to reinforce the development of a skill. Some activities, once introduced, can also be repeated independently by the children, while other activities can be used as transitions.

Each activity provides the following:
- Learning objectives
- Key vocabulary that supports children's language learning
- Children's books that support the activity
- Materials needed to complete the activity
- Any preparations that need to be completed by the teacher prior to the activity
- Simple, easy-to-follow directions
- Assessment questions to ensure that children acquired the skills supporting the objectives of the activity

Some of the activities also include teacher-to-teacher tips with practical information from someone who has already done the activity with children, or fingerplays, songs, and poems that support the activity.

Whether you are using this book to support your classroom curriculum, to focus on a specific topic, or to address the emerging interests of the children in your class, *Another Encyclopedia of Theme Activities* provides fun, educational activities for any early childhood classroom.

Fun with Feet

AGES
3+

Learning Objectives

Children will:

1. Learn that feet are an important part of the body.
2. Learn that their feet can do many good things.

Vocabulary

feet	tiptoe	walk
jump	toes	

Children's Books

Mouse Paint by Ellen Stoll Walsh
My Feet by Aliki
One Foot, Two Feet by Peter Maloney and Felicia Zekauskas

Materials

2 colorful "toe socks" stuffed with tissue paper
pictures cut from magazines of people using their feet in different ways (walking, jogging, biking, and so on)
string or colored masking tape
tape

Preparation

- Place a piece of string or colored tape along the floor that leads to a variety of places in the classroom.
- Display pictures of people using their feet on the floor along the path.

What to Do

1. Invite the children to talk about how our feet help us. Share these comments with the children during their discussion: Our feet help us to walk, run, balance, jump, ride a bike, climb, tiptoe, and so on.
2. As you talk about the different ways that children use their feet, allow the children to practice those movements with you on the carpet.
3. After your discussion, invite the children to stand and follow you as you visit different places in the classroom, walking along the string or piece of tape affixed to the floor.
4. Suggest that the children play a game of Follow the Leader along the string behind you as you tiptoe, jog, balance, march, leap, and move around the room.

Assessment

1. Can the child name at least two ways to use his feet?
2. Can each child tiptoe, jog, hop, jump, balance, march, leap, and so on?

Mary Murray, Mazomanie, WI

Can You Tie Your Shoes?

Learning Objectives
Children will:
1. Learn how to tie their shoes.
2. Develop math and oral language skills.

Vocabulary
shoelaces shoes tie

Children's Books
Dominic Ties His Shoes by Etta Sare
Red Lace, Yellow Lace by Mike Casey and Judith Herbst

Materials
card stock
chart paper
picture of a child tying his shoes (use a search engine to find a picture on the Internet)
pictures of the children in the class or name cards
pocket chart (optional)
tape

What to Do
1. On chart paper, write, "Can you tie your own shoes?" and make two columns (yes and no).
2. Show the children a picture of someone tying a pair of shoes, and model how to tie shoes for children. Let the children talk about who ties their shoes for them.
3. Ask the children to tape or place their picture or name card in the correct column or color in a spot on the chart/graph. Count the number in each group.

Assessment
1. Does the child want to learn to tie her own shoes?
2. Can the child count and compare the number in each column on the graph?
3. Can the child tie his own shoes?

Jackie Wright, Enid, OK

Have You Ever Had an X-ray?

Learning Objectives
Children will:
1. Learn about their bodies.
2. Develop math and oral language skills.

Vocabulary
accident	doctor	operation
bones	left	right
cast	inside	X-ray
crutches	nurse	

ALL ABOUT ME

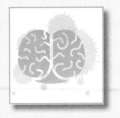

Children's Books
Jessica's X-Ray by Pat Zonta
The Skeleton Inside You by Philip Balestrino

Materials
card stock or index cards
chart paper or magnetic board
picture or name cards
sample or picture of an X-ray
tape or magnet

Preparation
Collect materials for the activity. Some materials may take time to receive (for example, the sample of an X-ray), so prepare a few days in advance.

What to Do
1. At group or circle time, show pictures or samples of real X-rays, and involve the children in a discussion about X-rays. Talk about X-rays being a photo of the inside of your body, and ask the children how it is different from a regular photo.
2. After the children have had a chance to contribute to the conversation, write, "Have you ever had an X-ray?" on chart paper. Make two columns, labeling one "Yes" and labeling the other "No."
3. Have each child answer the question by placing his picture or name card in the appropriate column. Complete the activity by counting how many people are in each column.

Assessment
1. Is each child able to participate in this activity?
2. Did the child add to the discussion?
3. Can the child count how many children answered yes and how many children answered no?

Jackie Wright, Enid, OK

I Am Unique

AGES 4+

Learning Objectives
Children will:
1. Identify their unique characteristics.
2. Identify how they are the same as other children.

Vocabulary
characteristics
self-portraits
unique

Children's Books
I Like Myself by Karen Beaumont and David Catrow
I'm Like You, You're Like Me by Cindy Gainer
Marvelous Me: Inside and Out by Lisa Bullard
The One and Only Special Me by Rozanne Lanczak Williams

Materials
3–4 mats or sheets of chart paper
3" x 5" index cards and pens (for labeling groups)
crayons, markers, paint, or colored pencils for each child
paper

What to Do
1. Pass out paper and drawing utensils. Ask the children to draw self-portraits (pictures of themselves). When they are finished drawing their pictures, ask the children to bring their self-portraits to the carpet.
2. Have the children share their self-portraits with their neighbors. Tell the children that another word that means different is *unique*. Ask, "What makes you unique or different from your friends? How are you the same as your friends?"
3. After the discussion, read a book about characteristics, such as *I'm Like You, You're Like Me* by Cindy Gainer. Pause as needed to discuss and answer questions.
4. After reading the book, choose several characteristics (eye color, hair color or length, skin color, height, and so on) by which to group children. Identify one characteristic at a time and label the mats or chart paper with the options presented by the class (for example, if you choose eye color, label one mat "Blue," one mat "Brown," and one mat "Green").
5. Have the children identify which group they belong to by placing their self-portrait on the appropriate mat.
6. Repeat with another characteristic.

Assessment
1. Can the child identify ways he is unique?
2. Can the child identify characteristics she has in common with the other children?

Kathryn Hake, Lebanon, OR

> **Teacher-to-Teacher Tip**
> It may be helpful to have some mirrors available for children to use before or while they create their self-portraits.

Growth in Me

AGES 5+

Learning Objectives
Children will:
1. Understand how physical appearances change with age.
2. Talk about what makes them unique.
3. Develop oral language skills.

Vocabulary
age	fat	straight
big	grow	tall
chubby	long	thin
curly	small	

Children's Books
I Like Me! by Nancy Carlson
Just the Way You Are by Marcus Pfister

Materials
two photographs per child (one full-length
   baby photo, one full-length current photo)
Note: The children may bring in baby photos
   even if they are not full-body photos.

What to Do
1. Prior to passing out the pictures, talk about what the children did when they were little versus what they do now. If some children have younger siblings, you might want to talk about things their younger siblings do and things that they do. How do they look and act differently from their younger siblings?
2. Discuss how parts of our bodies keep changing and growing.
3. Pair each child with a partner and give each pair their pictures. (Each group should have their four pictures.) Let the children look at the photographs and discuss how they have grown since the time they were babies.

Assessment
1. Can the child look at his photograph and assess how much he has grown over the years?
2. Can the child point out two or three changes in her friends since they were babies?

**Shyamala Shanmugasundaram,
Annanagar East, Chennai, India**

Preparation
A few days prior to the activity, ask the children to bring their two photos from home.

baby photo   current photo

Make Your Own Journal

AGES 5+

Learning Objectives
Children will:
1. Make a journal and learn about keeping a journal.
2. Draw or write about their lives.
3. Use creative expression to design a book.

Vocabulary
diary
journal
personal

Children's Books
Franklin and Me: My First Record of Favorite Things, Personal Facts, and Special Memories by Paulette Bourgeois
It's All About You: Writing Your Own Journal by Nancy Loewen

Materials
2 pieces of cardboard per child (approximately 5" x 7")
blank sheets of paper the same size as the cardboard (fold 8" x 10" sheets of typing paper in half to fit 5" x 7" covers)
card stock or construction paper
glue
hole punch
paper clip (optional)
ribbon or yarn
stickers (optional)

Preparation
Make enough blank "books" to use in the writing center during center time.

What to Do
1. Read books to the children about keeping a journal. Discuss what could be kept in a journal.
2. Ask the children to decorate the front of the books with stickers or markers. Help the children write their names on their books.
3. Tell the children that these books will be all about them, and allow them to personalize the covers and the pages within however they wish.

Assessment
1. Did each child understand the concept of journal keeping?
2. Did the child personalize the book for himself?

Donna Alice Patton, Hillsboro, OH

> **Teacher-to-Teacher Tip**
> For five-year-olds doing this activity, give them the materials to create a small book, and guide them through the process of putting the books together themselves.

The Amazing Alphabet

Learning Objectives

Children will:

1. Identify letters of the alphabet.
2. Improve fine motor skills.

Vocabulary

alphabet   letters   read

Children's Books

Alphabet Soup by Abbie Zabar
Chicka Chicka Boom Boom by John
    Archambault and Bill Martin, Jr.
The Handmade Alphabet by Laura Rankin

Materials

alphabet letter cards *a* to *z*
bold line marker
colored copy paper
plastic letters *a* to *z*
tape
white copy paper

Preparation

- Print one letter of the alphabet on each sheet of colored paper.
- Display the letters randomly around the floor of the room.

What to Do

1. Introduce the topic of our amazing alphabet. Invite the children to sing the traditional alphabet song with you:

   A–B–C–D–E–F–G
   H–I–J–K–L–M–N–O–P
   Q–R–S–T–U–V
   W–X–Y and Z.
   Now I know my ABCs.
   Next time won't you sing with me?

2. Draw the children's attention to the alphabet letters on the floor.
3. Take a Letter Walk around the room, and name the letters on the floor as you find them.
4. Invite the children back to the circle area, and hand out the plastic alphabet letters.
5. Stack 3–5 letter cards facedown on the floor. Turn over one letter at a time. Each time you display a new letter, the child holding the matching letter places her letter next to your card. Continue until all the letters have been matched.
6. For a fun extension, teach the children the letters of the alphabet in sign language.

Assessment

1. Does the child recognize the letters she comes across?
2. Can the child match the letter cards with his pair?

Mary Murray, Mazomanie, WI

Teacher-to-Teacher Tip

Focus on no more than three to five letters at a time, or focus on a letter that relates to a topic of interest to the children, such as seeing a spider in the classroom (S), noticing that it is raining outside and everyone is wearing boots (B), or that there is red paint at the art center (R).

Letter Dough

AGES **3**+

Learning Objectives
Children will:
1. Improve fine motor skills.
2. Identify letters of the alphabet.

Vocabulary
alphabet
letters
shapes
spell

Children's Books
Alphabet City by Stephen T. Johnson
Chicka Chicka Boom Boom by John
    Archambault and Bill Martin, Jr.
The Graphic Alphabet by David Pelletier
LMNO Peas by Keith Baker

Materials
modeling dough
plastic letters

What to Do
1. Read a book about the alphabet with the children, such as *LMNO Peas* by Keith Baker.
2. Provide modeling dough and no more than five plastic letter shapes.
3. Invite the children to flatten out the modeling dough, press plastic letters into the dough, and then remove them.
4. Encourage the children to make "snakes" from the dough and to form letters from their dough snakes to match the plastic letters on their table.
5. Ask the children to name the letters they are making.
6. For a fun extension at the sand and water table, add water to the sand at the table to create wet sand that will keep its form. Invite the children to press plastic alphabet letters into the sand to form letter imprints or to spell their names or other words.

clay

plastic shape

clay letter

Assessment
1. Did each child identify correctly the letters he made?
2. Can each child make the dough letters?

Mary Murray, Mazomanie, WI

Animal Alphabet

AGES
4+

Learning Objectives
Children will:
1. Learn animals that begin with each letter of the alphabet.
2. Identify animal pictures.

Vocabulary

alligator	iguana	rabbit
bear	jaguar	seal
cat	koala	turtle
dog	leopard	unicorn
emu	monkey	viper
fox	newt	wolf
frog	owl	yak
goose	penguin	zebra
horse	quail	

Children's Books
The Alphabet Tale by Jan Garten
Ape in a Cape by Fritz Eichenberg
Creature ABC by Andrew Zuckerman

What to Do
1. Show the children the animal alphabet book you created. Some children might be able to recognize the first letter in the animal's name from the print.
2. Give all the children an opportunity to guess the animal that is behind the flap and make predictions about what animal, or letter, might come next in the alphabet. After several guesses, lift the flap and expose the picture.
3. Continue with the next page in the book.

Assessment
1. Is the child able to recognize the letters of the alphabet?
2. Can the child name the animals in the book?
3. Can the child name additional animals that begin with the same letter?
4. Can the child tell you what sound the letter makes?

Jackie Wright, Enid, OK

Materials
construction paper
glue stick
laminating materials
marker
pictures of animals, one for each letter of the alphabet
tape

Preparation
Create an interactive, lift-the-flap animal alphabet book before the children arrive by following these steps:
1. On each page, glue a picture of an animal.
2. Cut 26 construction paper squares large enough to hide the animals. These will be the flaps to cover the animals.
3. Label the flaps with the animals' names.
4. Laminate the pages and flaps separately for durability.
5. Bind the pages between the covers.
6. Tape the flaps at the tops to hide the pictures.

My Alphabet Book

AGES 4+

Learning Objectives
Children will:
1. Identify letters of the alphabet.
2. Improve fine motor skills.

Vocabulary
alphabet   book
author   write

Children's Books
Alphabet Adventure by Audrey Wood
Eating the Alphabet by Lois Ehlert

Materials
construction paper
copy paper
glue sticks
hole punches
magazines
scissors
stickers
yarn

Preparation
- Create an alphabet booklet for each child. For each booklet, fold 13 pieces of copy paper in half, and staple them together down the center fold. (Alternatively, use a hole punch to make three holes along the folds. Tie the pages securely together with yarn.)
- Write one letter of the alphabet on each page.
- Make a cover from a piece of construction paper. On it, write, "_____'s Alphabet Book."

What to Do
1. At the beginning of the year, give each child an alphabet book. Tell the children that they will be authors and will create their own books as they learn the letters of the alphabet.
2. Help each child print his name on the cover of the book.
3. Give the children access to a wide variety of collage materials that they can glue into their books. Throughout the year, each time the child learns a new letter, he can add a page to his book. For example, the A page may have a picture of an ape and of an ant cut from a magazine, an apple shape, the word *art* cut from a newspaper, a sticker of the letter *A*, and a drawing by the child of the letter *A*.
4. Each time the child adds to a page, review with her the pages that she has already created.

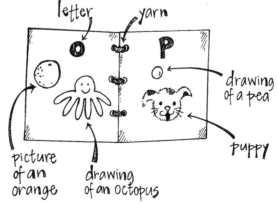

Assessment

1. Can the child name the letters?
2. Can the child tell you the sound a specific letter makes?
3. Can the child draw or cut pictures of things that begin with that letter sound?

Rachael Partain, Mechanicsburg, PA

Newspaper Letter Search

AGES 4+

Learning Objectives

Children will:
1. Identify letters of the alphabet.
2. Develop fine motor skills.

Vocabulary

alphabet   letters
book   write

Children's Books

The Alphabet Book by P. D. Eastman
Dr. Seuss's ABC: An Amazing Alphabet Book by Dr. Seuss

What to Do

1. Work with a small group of children.
2. Invite each child to turn over an alphabet letter card and pick up a colored highlighter and a sheet of newspaper. Instruct the children to search the sheet of newspaper for the letter on their letter cards and to highlight each letter that they find on the sheet of newspaper.
3. After each child has highlighted several of the selected letters, she may turn over a new letter card and select a new highlighter. She can search for the new letter and highlight it with the new color.

Fingerplays, Songs, and Poems

"The Alphabet Song" (Traditional)
"ABC Rock" by Greg and Steve, *We All Live Together*, Volume 1

Materials

alphabet cards
highlighter markers in a variety of colors
pages of recyclable printed material, such as newspaper, magazines, and so on

Preparation

Place a few alphabet cards (no more than five) on each table, along with pages of the newspaper and a variety of colors of highlighter markers.

Assessment

1. Can the child name the letter that she was looking for?
2. Can the child find the letter and highlight it on the paper?
3. Did the child follow directions?

Mary Murray, Mazomanie, WI

Bath Time

Learning Objectives
Children will:
1. Improve fine motor skills.
2. Learn about dogs.

Vocabulary
back	rinse	water
head	scrub	wet
leg	soap	
paw	tail	

Children's Books
Bathtime for Biscuit by Alyssa Satin Capucilli
Dogs by Emily Gravett
Harry the Dirty Dog by Gene Zion

Materials
6"–12" plastic toy dog
deep plastic tub
large beach towel
sponge
towel
water bottle (without a lid) or plastic pitcher
   containing water

Preparation
Fill the plastic tub with 1"–2" of soapy water, and set the tub on a large beach towel.

What to Do
1. Talk with the children about caring for dogs. Talk about food, shelter, exercise, cleaning, veterinarian visits, and so on. Read one or more books about dogs.
2. Invite the children to take turns giving the toy dog a bath. Have the children scrub the dog with the sponge in the soapy water. The children can use the water bottle or pitcher to rinse the dog and then dry the dog with the towel.

Assessment
1. Are the child's fine motor skills improving?
2. What did the child learn about dogs?

Mary Murray, Mazomanie, WI

> **Teacher-to-Teacher Tip**
> Have the children try this activity at the water table instead. Simply add the following items to the water table learning center: soapy bubbles, miniature sponge pieces, mini towels, and small plastic toy dogs.

Bear Hunt

Learning Objectives

Children will:

1. Participate in a "bear hunt."
2. Develop descriptive language.

Vocabulary

around	find	over
bear	hunt	read
between	next to	under

Children's Books

Bear Wants More by Karma Wilson
Bears: Polar Bears, Black Bears, and Grizzly Bears by Deborah Hodge
Brown Bear, Brown Bear, What Do You See? by Bill Martin, Jr.
The Little Mouse, the Real Ripe Strawberry, and the Big Hungry Bear by Audrey Wood and Don Wood
Otto the Book Bear by Katie Cleminson
Panda Bear, Panda Bear, What Do You See? by Bill Martin, Jr.
Polar Bear, Polar Bear, What Do You Hear? by Bill Martin, Jr.
The Three Bears by Paul Galdone

Materials

bear books (see suggestions)
blankets
snack: bear cookies and juice boxes
stuffed bears, one per child (Ask the children to bring a bear from home or use bears from your school. If stuffed bears are not available, use paper cutouts of bears.)
We're Going on a Bear Hunt by Michael Rosen and Helen Oxenbury

Preparation

- Right before the activity, have a volunteer (parent or assistant) hide all the bears on the playground area (or an outdoor classroom).
- Bring blankets and fiction and nonfiction books about bears outside.

What to Do

1. Before going outside, sing and read *We're Going on a Bear Hunt* to the class. Build anticipation by telling the children that they are going on a bear hunt, just like in the story!
2. Once outside, tell the children to find one bear and then describe where they found it.
3. Encourage the children to take their bear to a blanket and "read" a bear book to their bear.
4. Once reading is over, have a snack with the bears!

Assessment

1. How well was the child able to participate in a bear hunt? Did he find a bear or did he need help to do so?
2. Did the child incorporate positional language, using words such as *beside*, *under*, or *next to*, in her description of where she found the bear?

Fingerplays, Songs, and Poems

"Goin' on a Bear Hunt" by Greg and Steve, *Kids in Action* CD

Tracy Parson, Lilburn, GA

Teacher-to-Teacher Tips

● This is a special day activity that you can make as elaborate or as simple as suits the needs and resources of your class. It gets children responding to the literature, dramatizing, and enjoying the great outdoors!

● This activity can also be done inside the classroom by hiding teddy bear counters before the children arrive or while the children are outside playing.

Book Bag Fun

AGES 3+

Learning Objectives
Children will:
1. Improve language skills.
2. Develop an appreciation for literature.

Vocabulary
book
book bag
pet
read

Children's Books
Caring for Your Pets: A Book About Veterinarians by Ann Owen
Ferret Fun by Karen Rostoker-Gruber
Peek-a-Pet! by Marie Torres Cimarusti
The Perfect Pet by Margie Palatini
Pet Show! by Ezra Jack Keats
Wanted: The Perfect Pet by Fiona Roberton

Materials
beanbag or small toy pets
gallon-size resealable plastic zipper bags
storybooks about pets

What to Do
1. Select a book about pets to read to the class. After the story, encourage class discussion by asking simple questions about the book.
2. Place the book inside a resealable bag along with a related toy pet. Display the book bag in the library corner.
3. Invite children to open the bag and "read" the book to the pet on their own. Encourage children to tell about the story as they turn the pages for the pet to see.
4. For several days, read another pet story to the class and create another book bag for the library corner.

Assessment
1. Are the child's language skills improving as he listens to and "reads" books?
2. Is the child developing an appreciation for books as a source of interesting stories and information about a topic (in this case, about pets)?

Teacher-to-Teacher Tip

Add some fun pet-themed pillows to the library corner for added appeal.

Mary Murray, Mazomanie, WI

Animal Egg Surprise!

AGES
4+

Learning Objectives
Children will:
1. Develop fine motor skills.
2. Identify a variety of animals.
3. Improve oral language skills.

Vocabulary
animals   egg
close   open

Children's Books
Birds, Nests, and Eggs by Mel Boring
Miles and Miles of Reptiles by Tish Rabe
The Yucky Reptile Alphabet Book by Jerry
    Pallotta

Materials
10 assorted small plastic toy birds or reptiles
10 plastic eggs (that open and close)
basket
pictures of reptiles and birds

Preparation
- Place a miniature toy reptile or bird inside each plastic egg.
- Place the ten eggs in a basket.

What to Do
1. Read books about birds and reptiles with the children. Talk with the class about how some animals hatch from eggs.
2. Explain how birds and reptiles lay eggs on land, and their baby animals hatch from each egg.
3. Show the pictures of various reptiles and birds as you talk about each one that hatches from an egg.
4. Display the basket, and invite small groups of children to come forward to open each egg and find out what animal is hiding inside.
5. Encourage the children to name the animals as they remove them from their containers.

Assessment
1. Is the child able to open and close the eggs?
2. Is the child able to identify the names of animals that hatch from eggs?

Mary Murray, Mazomanie, WI

Teacher-to-Teacher Tip
If you do not have animals small enough to fit inside the plastic eggs, simply attach an animal sticker to a small square of card stock and use that in place of the toy animal.

Animal Pass

Learning Objectives
Children will:
1. Develop gross motor skills.
2. Learn about animals.

Vocabulary
animal	over	under
ask	pass	
high five	question	

Children's Books
Brown Bears by Marcia S. Freeman
A Forest Habitat by Bobbie Kalman
In Arctic Waters by Laura Crawford

Materials
stuffed toy or beanbag animals

Preparation
Gather the toy animals you are going to use for this activity. Look up facts about each animal's habitat and what they eat. Find information about animals in books or on websites such as National Geographic or the San Diego Zoo.

What to Do
1. At small group time, show the children one of the toy animals. Share with the children a few facts about the animal you are holding up.
2. Instruct the children to form a line. Encourage them to pass the object over their heads or under their legs to the person behind them.
3. When the object reaches the end of the line, the last child holds the animal high in the air and shouts its name aloud.
4. Ask the child to place the animal on a table or shelf and move to the front of the line.
5. Before moving on to the next animal, repeat one or more of the animal facts related to that animal.
6. Repeat the activity with the other animals.

Assessment
1. Does the child have the coordination to pass the animal over his head or between his legs?
2. What did the child learn about animals?

Mary Murray, Mazomanie, WI

Animal Path

Learning Objectives

Children will:

1. Follow directions.
2. Learn about animals.

Vocabulary

animals   step
pathway   walk

Children's Books

Animals: A Visual Encyclopedia by DK
  Publishing
Encyclopedia of Animals by DK Publishing
Kingfisher First Encyclopedia of Animals by
  Kingfisher Books
National Geographic Encyclopedia of Animals
  by Karen McGhee and George McKay
Smart Kids Animal A–Z by Roger Priddy

Materials

5–10 carpet squares
10 or more stuffed or beanbag animals or
  pictures of animals

Preparation

- Display the carpet squares in a row leading
  from one area of the classroom to another.
- Arrange the toy beanbag animals randomly
  about the border of the carpet squares,
  creating an "animal path" to walk on.

What to Do

1. Read one or more books about animals to the children, and then talk with them about
   different animals.
2. Walk with the children along the animal path and talk about the animals along the path.
3. Help the children identify the animals as they walk along the path to another area of the
   room.
4. Encourage the children to look at the books about animals.
5. After the children have learned about the animals on the path, ask the children a different
   question as they walk on the path. They can think or whisper their answers as they walk.
   Suggested questions include the following:
   - Where does each animal live?
   - What does the animal like to eat?
   - Where could you see each animal today?
   - What letter of the alphabet does each animal name start with?
   - Which animal would be the biggest in real life?

Assessment

1. Can each child follow directions?
2. What did the child learn about the animals
   on the path?

Mary Murray, Mazomanie, WI

Teacher-to-Teacher Tips

● Give specific instructions and observe the children as they follow the given directions, such as "Crawl along the pathway"; "Put your hands on your head as you walk along the pathway"; and "Put your hands on the shoulders of the person in front of you as you walk along the pathway."

● Invite a child to identify each animal as she walks along the pathway. Ask this child to walk along the pathway and pick up the animal as you give specific directions such as pick up the animal that has the longest tail, or the smallest animal, or the animal that might eat other animals, and so on.

B–U–N–N–Y

AGES
4+

Learning Objectives

Children will:

1. Identify pictures.
2. Sing a new song.

Vocabulary

bee	chick	frog
bird	cloud	sun

Children's Books

Home for a Bunny by Margaret Wise Brown
The Runaway Bunny by Margaret Wise Brown

Materials

box or other container
card stock
glue stick
pictures of ordinary objects and animals, including one of a rabbit with pink ears (use a search engine to find pictures on the Internet)
scissors

Preparation

● Cut card stock into card-size pieces.
● Create a set of animal picture cards to use in a game. Glue pictures of animals on most of the cards, and on at least four of the cards, glue a picture of a rabbit with pink ears.
● Shuffle the cards and place them facedown in a box or other container.

What to Do

1. Teach the children the following song:

"B–U–N–N–Y"
(Tune: "Bingo")
I know a rabbit with long pink ears
And Bunny is his name-o!
B–U–N–N–Y
B–U–N–N–Y
B–U–N–N–Y
And Bunny is his name-o!

2. Pass the container around the circle of children.
3. Each child draws a card and identifies the animal on the card. If he draws a rabbit, he hops around the circle as the group sings the song.

Assessment

1. Is the child able to identify the animals in the pictures correctly?
2. Is the child able to sing along with the rest of the class?

Jackie Wright, Enid, OK

Cats and Dogs

AGES
4+

Learning Objectives
Children will:
1. Identify dogs and cats.
2. Develop oral communication skills.

Vocabulary

cat	fur	love	tail
dog	legs	pet	

Materials
chart paper
marker
stuffed or toy dogs and cats, or pictures of dogs and cats

Children's Books
Cat and Dog by Else Holmelund Minarik
A Cat and a Dog by Claire Masurel
Dogs by Emily Gravett
Harry the Dirty Dog by Gene Zion
How to Be a Good Cat by Gail Page
How to Be a Good Dog by Gail Page
I Am the Dog, I Am the Cat by Donald Hall
National Geographic Readers: Cats vs. Dogs by Elizabeth Carney

What to Do

1. Introduce the topic of cats and dogs by reading one or more books about dogs and cats.
2. Show the children the toy dogs and cats (or pictures of dogs and cats) and help them identify each as a dog or cat.
3. Encourage group discussion about dogs and cats, comparing the two animals as you and the children talk about how they are alike and different.
4. Make a Venn diagram on a piece of chart paper as you discuss how cats and dogs are alike and different.

Assessment

1. Is the child able to determine which animals are cats and which are dogs?
2. Is the child able to describe the characteristics of each animal and to help develop information for the Venn diagram?

Mary Murray, Mazomanie, WI

Cows

Learning Objectives

Children will:
1. Learn that milk comes from dairy cows, and identify milk products.
2. Improve oral language skills.

Vocabulary

butter	cow	milk
cheese	cream	yogurt

What to Do

1. Read one or more books about dairy cows.
2. Ask the children to tell the group what they learned from the books about cows and where milk comes from.
3. Teach the children the following poem:

   Brown Cow (author unknown)
   Brown cow, brown cow, what do you see?
   I see a farmer looking at me.
   Brown cow, brown cow, what do you see?
   I see a young calf looking at me.
   Brown cow, brown cow, what do you see?
   I see a pink pig looking at me.
   Brown cow, brown cow, what do you see?
   I see a billy goat looking at me.
   Brown cow, brown cow, what do you see?
   I see a milk machine looking at me.

4. Tell the children that you will put the books about cows in the library area so they can look at them to learn more about dairy cows, how milk is produced, and the products that are made with milk.

Children's Books

Cow by Jules Older
The Cow Loves Cookies by Karma Wilson
The Cow That Went Oink by Bernard Most
Milk: From Cow to Carton by Aliki
The Milk Makers by Gail Gibbons

Materials

books about dairy cows

Assessment

1. What has the child learned about dairy cows and about the products made from milk?
2. Can the child name products that come from dairy cows?
3. Was the child able to learn the poem?

Mary Murray, Mazomanie, WI

Eloquent Elephants

AGES
4+

Learning Objectives

Children will:
1. Learn about elephants.
2. Develop gross motor skills.

Vocabulary

elephant
trumpet
trunk
tusks

Children's Books

But No Elephants by Jerry Smath
Elephant by Jinny Johnson
Elephants Can Paint Too! by Katya Arnold
"Stand Back," Said the Elephant, "I'm Going to Sneeze!" by Patricia Thomas
Tara & Bella: The Elephant and Dog Who Became Best Friends by Carol Buckley

Materials

4 stuffed toy or beanbag elephants, or 4 pictures of elephants

What to Do

1. Designate a portion of the group or circle time area as the elephant movement area. Ask the children to sit in four groups, in single file lines.
2. Invite one person from each group to enter the elephant movement area and role-play an elephant. The children may swing their arms downward like a trunk and lumber around the open area moving about like an elephant.
3. Recite the following elephant poem as the children move about. Then call out, "Elephants sit down." Those four children return to their line and the next four children enter the elephant movement area. Recite the poem again as the children observe the new elephants moving about.

Elephants
Elephant big, elephant round
Elephant walks and shakes the ground.
Elephant trunk, elephant ears
Elephant far and elephant near.
Elephant drink and elephant eat,
Elephant tail and elephant feet.
Elephant gray, elephant tall;
Favorite animal of them all.

4. Continue the activity, allowing all the children an opportunity to move like an elephant.
5. Sit in a circle and share these elephant facts with the children:
   - Elephants have a long trunk and large floppy ears.
   - Elephants eat, drink, and smell with their trunks.
   - Elephants can pick things up with their trunks.
   - Female elephants live in family groups; adult males live on their own.
   - There are two kinds of elephants: Asian and African.
   - Elephants eat grass, leaves, twigs, roots, and plants.
   - Elephants have tusks, which are like long teeth.
   - Elephants have thick wrinkly skin with a tuft of hair at the end of the tail.

Assessment
1. What did the child learn about elephants?
2. Was the child able to act and move like an elephant?

Mary Murray, Mazomanie, WI

Find the Matching Bird

AGES 4+

Learning Objectives
Children will:
1. Identify bird names.
2. Improve oral language skills.

Vocabulary
bird	feathers	wings
birdhouse	fly	

Children's Books
About Birds: A Guide for Children by Cathryn Sill
Birds by Kevin Henkes
Flap Your Wings by P. D. Eastman

Materials
5 brown lunch bags
pictures of birds from magazines, catalogs, or from the Internet, two of each bird
Note: Select birds that are distinct, such as a robin, bluebird, hummingbird, cardinal, and blackbird.

Preparation
- Create five lunch bag bird nests as follows. Open the lunch bag and stand it up. Grab the top of the lunch bag, and roll the sides outward and downward until the rolled brown paper bag is formed into a nest shape.
- Place one picture of a bird in each nest, and place the nests randomly about the room. Keep one set of pictures to show the children.

What to Do

1. Show a group of five children the pictures of birds. Tell the children the name of each bird, and ask the children to describe the birds.
2. Tell the children that there are five birds that match the birds in the pictures in nests in the classroom.
3. Give the five pictures of the birds to five children, and ask them to find each bird in a nest in the classroom.
4. Ask one child at a time to "fly" around the room, find the matching bird, and bring it back to the group.
5. Help the group of children determine if the two bird pictures match.
6. When the group of five children is finished, the children make the birds "fly away" (back to their nests) so the next set of children can play the game.

Assessment

1. Did the child learn the names of the birds?
2. Is the child able to describe the characteristics of each bird?

Mary Murray, Mazomanie, WI

Good Morning, Pets!

AGES 4+

Learning Objectives

Children will:
1. Improve memory skills.
2. Develop oral language skills.

Vocabulary

good morning
greet
pet names according to family pets

Children's Books

The Best Pet of All by David LaRochelle
The Perfect Pet by Margie Palatini
Pet Show! by Ezra Jack Keats
Wet Pet, Dry Pet, Your Pet, My Pet by Dr. Seuss

Materials

animal or pet stickers
paint stir stick
photos of children's pets

Preparation

● Send home a note two weeks in advance, asking families to send pet photos. Children who don't have a pet can bring in a picture of a pet they'd like to have or a picture of a friend or relative's pet.
● Create a "pet pointer" by attaching an assortment of animal or pet stickers to both sides of a wooden paint stir stick.
● Display the pet pictures on a special bulletin board titled, "Good Morning, Pets!"
● Write the pet's name under each pet photo.

What to Do

1. Use the pet pointer to point to the various pets. Say the name of each pet as you point to it on the bulletin board, and then invite the class to say, "Good morning, ____," filling in the name of that pet.

2. Continue the activity until the children have greeted all the pets displayed.
3. After the children have greeted all the pets, ask one child to tell the class about her pet.

Assessment
1. Can the child name any of the pets on the bulletin board?
2. Is the child able to describe and talk about the pet in the photo he brought to class?

Mary Murray, Mazomanie, WI

Teacher-to-Teacher Tip
This is a great activity to do after your usual good morning routine.

AGES

Home for a Pet

Learning Objectives
Children will:
1. Improve word-picture association skills.
2. Improve oral language skills.

Vocabulary
bird	ferret	house
cat	guinea pig	mouse
dog	home	snake

Children's Books
Caring for Your Pets: A Book About Veterinarians
    by Ann Owen
Dogs by Emily Gravett
Ferret Fun by Karen Rostoker-Gruber
Ferrets by June McNicholas
I Am the Dog, I Am the Cat by Donald Hall
Peek-a-Pet! by Marie Torres Cimarusti
The Perfect Pet by Margie Palatini
Pet Shop Follies by Mary Ann Fraser
Pet Show! by Ezra Jack Keats
Wanted: The Perfect Pet by Fiona Roberton

Materials
5 different stuffed or plastic toy pets
5 pictures of pets (to match the toy pets)
5 sheets of colored, 8" x 11" card stock
basket or shoebox
black marker
glue

Preparation
● Fold each piece of card stock width-wise so it stands up like a tent. Print the name of each pet on the side of each card stock "house." Attach a picture of the animal above the word on each animal house.
● Place the toy pet animals in a basket or shoebox.
● Stand the animal houses on a table.

What to Do
1. Show the children the animal houses.
2. Ask one child to remove one animal at a time from the basket and match it to its home. Continue with the remaining pets.
3. Help the children name each animal and read the word on each home.
4. For a fun extension, add more animal toys so the children can sort them by type into larger homes. For example, ask the children to put all of the dogs together, all of the cats together, and so on.

Assessment
1. Can the child use the photos to match each animal to its home?
2. Can the child sort the animals by type?

Mary Murray, Mazomanie, WI

Peek at a Pet

AGES 4+

Learning Objectives
Children will:
1. Follow directions.
2. Recognize and name various animals.

Vocabulary
box   name   pet
lift   peek   say

Children's Books
Fish by June Loves
The Perfect Pet by Margie Palatini
Pets by Liz Gogerly

Materials
decorative gift bag
masking tape
small stuffed toy pet or plastic pet

Preparation
- Make a line on the floor with masking tape.
- Secretly place a pet inside the bag and place it at the end of the masking tape line.

What to Do
1. Use this fun activity when it's time to transition from one activity to another.
2. Tell the children to line up at the end of the line and to quietly step along the line toward the box.
3. Invite each child to peek inside the bag to see the pet that is hiding there.
4. Then the children quietly move on to the next activity.
5. Place a different pet inside the bag each time you transition to another activity. Children will look forward to walking quietly to peek inside the bag.

Assessment
1. Can the child follow directions?
2. Can the child recognize and name the pet in the bag?

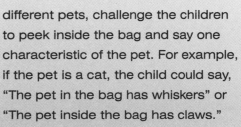
Teacher-to-Teacher Tips

- Create a zigzag line of masking tape leading up to the box. Instruct the children to walk along the line heel to toe as they move toward the box.

- After the children have learned about different pets, challenge the children to peek inside the bag and say one characteristic of the pet. For example, if the pet is a cat, the child could say, "The pet in the bag has whiskers" or "The pet inside the bag has claws."

Mary Murray, Mazomanie, WI

Pet Accessories

AGES
4+

Learning Objectives

Children will:

1. Improve their sorting skills.
2. Develop critical thinking skills.

Vocabulary

birdcage	exercise	pet food
birdseed	wheel	salt lick
catnip	fishbowl	tag
cedar	food dish	water
bedding	guinea pig	water bottle
collar	hamster cage	
dog biscuits	leash	

What to Do

1. Invite the children to explore the pet accessories.
2. Ask the children to figure out which items belong with each pet and to verbalize their thinking as they work.
3. Ask the children to place each pet accessory near the picture of the pet that uses that accessory.

Assessment

1. Can the child match the accessories with the correct animals?
2. Is the child developing improved thinking skills as he thinks through which accessories are used with the pets that are pictured?

Mary Murray, Mazomanie, WI

Children's Books

The Best Pet of All by David LaRochelle
How Do Dinosaurs Love Their Dogs? by Jane Yolen
The Perfect Pet by Margie Palatini
Pet Care for Kids series by Kathryn Stevens
Pet Show! by Ezra Jack Keats
Wanted: The Perfect Pet by Fiona Roberton
Wet Pet, Dry Pet, Your Pet, My Pet by Dr. Seuss

Materials

pictures of common household pets to correspond with the pet accessories
variety of pet accessories

Teacher-to-Teacher Tip

Display the pet pictures and pet accessories in the science area for the children to explore independently.

Pet Toss and Pass

AGES 4+

Learning Objectives
Children will:
1. Develop gross motor skills.
2. Learn the names of pet animals.

Vocabulary

bird	catch	fish	pets
carry	crawl	hamster	toss
cat	dog	lizard	

Children's Books
The Best Pet of All by David LaRochelle
Children Make Terrible Pets by Peter Brown
The Perfect Pet by Margie Palatini
Pet Show! by Ezra Jack Keats
Wet Pet, Dry Pet, Your Pet, My Pet by Dr. Seuss

Materials
5 or more beanbag or stuffed animal pets

What to Do
1. Do this activity with a small group of children.
2. Help the children form a line.
3. Stand three feet from the line of children.
4. Toss one of the beanbag animals to the first child in line and say the animal's name.
5. The child who catches the animal names the pet and tosses it back to you.
6. Continue tossing the pet and identifying each animal as you move down the line of children.
7. After all children have tossed the pet, repeat the activity with another pet.

Assessment
1. Is the child able to catch and toss the beanbag pets?
2. Did the child learn the names of the pet animals she caught and tossed back?

Mary Murray, Mazomanie, WI

Roar like a Lion

AGES 4+

Learning Objectives
Children will:
1. Identify pictures of animals.
2. Learn creative expression.

Vocabulary

cub	lion	loud	roar
fierce	lioness	quiet	sound

Children's Books
African Lions by Joelle Riley
The Happy Lion by Louise Fatio
If I Were a Lion by Sarah Weeks
The Lion and the Mouse by Jerry Pinkney
Lions by Beverly and Dereck Joubert
Lions (Amazing Animals) by Valerie Bodden
Lions (Big Cats) by Don Middleton

Another Encyclopedia of Theme Activities

Materials
books about lions
glue stick
index cards
marker
pictures of lions, lionesses, and lion cubs
scissors

What to Do
1. Talk to the children about how lions roar.
2. Read the children books about lions and their behavior.
3. Show the children the lion cards you created.
4. Ask the children to roar like the lion depicted on the picture card—for example, a small roar for lion cubs and a large roar for a male lion.

Assessment
1. Can the child tell the difference among the three types of lions pictured—male lions, lionesses, and lion cubs?
2. Does each child roar like a male lion, lioness, or lion cub when he sees the appropriate card?

Jackie Wright, Enid, OK

Preparation
Create a set of lion picture cards by gluing pictures of male lions, lionesses, and lion cubs on several index cards.

Teacher-to-Teacher Tip
Encourage the children to use their bodies as they roar to act like a lion.

Which Arctic Animal Would You Rather Be?

AGES 4+

Learning Objectives
Children will:
1. Learn about arctic animals.
2. Learn about graphs.

Vocabulary
arctic dog (such as Siberian Husky or Alaskan Malamute)
polar bear
reindeer
walrus

Children's Books
Here Is the Arctic Winter by Madeleine Dunphy
In Arctic Waters by Laura Crawford
Over in the Arctic by Marianne Berkes
Polar Bears by Gail Gibbons

ANIMALS

Materials
chart paper and marker
crayons, markers, paper
pictures of four different arctic animals (use a search engine to locate pictures on the Internet)
tape or glue

Preparation
- Draw a horizontal box across the top of the chart paper and print, "Which arctic animal would you rather be?" on the box.
- Draw four columns with four boxes, one box at the top of each column. In each box, tape or glue one picture of an arctic animal, such as an arctic dog, walrus, polar bear, puffin, or reindeer.

What to Do
1. Read one or two books about arctic animals, and then engage the children in a discussion about arctic animals.
2. Show the children the animals on the chart. Ask each child to select his favorite arctic animal and indicate his choice by making a mark under the animal he prefers.
3. Compare the results in each column. Help the children count the number of marks in each column. Which animal received the most marks? Which animal received the fewest marks?
4. Suggest that the children draw a picture of their favorite animals.

Assessment
1. What did the child learn about arctic animals?
2. Is the child able to understand and compare the results of the graph?

Jackie Wright, Enid, OK

Teacher-to-Teacher Tip
You can also do this activity with a pocket chart instead of chart paper and a marker.

Animal Cup Concentration

AGES 5+

Learning Objectives
Children will:
1. Name animals and the beginning sounds of their names.
2. Participate in a classroom game.

Vocabulary
various animal names, such as *zebra, lion, monkey, panda, bear, tiger*

Children's Books
Edward the Emu by Sheena Knowles
Going to the Zoo by Tom Paxton
If Anything Ever Goes Wrong at the Zoo by Mary Jean Hendrick
Sam Who Never Forgets by Eve Rice

Materials
12 disposable cups
card stock
glue
marker
pictures of 6 different animals

Preparation
- Cut the card stock into cards that are the same size.
- Create two sets of cards—six in each set. On one set, glue pictures of animals. On the other set, write the letter representing the beginning sound of each animal name.
- Make a card stock gameboard large enough to hold all the cards, with four cards across and three down. Space the cards several inches apart to leave room for the diameter of the 12 cups.

What to Do
1. Place the gameboard on a table.
2. Randomly place the animal cards and the letter cards on the gameboard, and cover the pictures and letters with cups turned upside down.
3. Work with one child or a small group of children.
4. Let one child turn over two cups at a time, trying to match an animal to the letter representing the beginning sound of its name.
5. Continue playing until all matches are made.
6. Rearrange the animals and letters on the gameboard and play again.

– animal cards –

Assessment
1. Was the child able to match the beginning sound of the animal's name with the correct letter?
2. Did the child show improvement in visual memory skills as she played the game?

Teacher-to-Teacher Tip
Add Velcro sticky dots to the cards and the gameboard to keep the cards in place as the children turn over the cups.

Fingerplays, Songs, and Poems

"Animal Fair" (Traditional)
I went to the animal fair.
The birds and the beasts were there.
The old baboon by the light of the moon
Was combing her auburn hair.
The funniest was the monk;
He climbed up the elephant's trunk.
The elephant sneezed and fell on his knees,
And what became of the monk,
The monk, the monk, the monk?

Jackie Wright, Enid, OK

Animal Rescue

AGES 5+

Learning Objectives
Children will:
1. Identify which animals belong in water and which animals belong on land.
2. Follow directions.

Vocabulary
animals
drown
float
land
sink
swim
water

Children's Books
The Antarctic Habitat by Molly Aloian
The Arctic Habitat by Molly Aloian
Backyard Habitats by Kelly Macauley and Bobbie Kalman
Beavers and Their Homes by Deborah Chase Gibson
A Grassland Habitat by Kelly Macauley and Bobbie Kalman
A House for Hermit Crab by Eric Carle
I See a Kookaburra! Discovering Animal Habitats Around the World by Steve Jenkins and Robin Page
A Rainforest Habitat by Molly Aloian
Water Habitats by Molly Aloian

Materials
plastic animal toys (include animals that live in or near the water and animals that live on land)
towel
water table or tub of water

Preparation
Place the toy animals in the water.

What to Do
1. Read books about animals and their habitats to the class.
2. Invite one or two children to work at the water table for this activity. Explain to the class that some animals live on land, while others live in or near the water. Encourage the children to talk about how some animals swim or drink from water while others live beneath the water or on the water's edge.
3. Invite the children to observe as you "rescue" the animals from the water that belong on land. Ask the children if they can identify the animals and where they live as you pull them from the water. If the animal lives on the land, set it on the towel. If the animal lives in or near the water, set it back in the water.
4. After your demonstration, invite two children to try the activity. Allow time for all children to have an opportunity to work at the water table with the various land and water animals.

Assessment
1. Can the child identify which animals belong in water and which animals belong on land?
2. Is the child able to follow the directions to do the activity?

Fingerplays, Songs, and Poems

Teach the children this short song sung to the tune of "I'm a Little Teapot." Invite children to chant the song as they work at the water table.

"Animals on Land"

Look in the water.
Come and see.
I see animals looking at me.
Does the animal live on the land?
Then—pick it up
and make it stand.

Recite this short poem aloud and then teach it to the children. At a later time, allow small groups of children to recite the poem for the class.

"Animals in Water"

A beaver swims and splashes.
A duck will drink and float.
A fish swims back and forth.
A cow prefers a boat.

Mary Murray, Mazomanie, WI

Good Morning Animal Hop

AGES 5+

Learning Objectives

Children will:

1. Improve gross motor skills.
2. Follow directions.

Vocabulary

animal   good morning   leap

Children's Books

Don't Wake Up the Bear! by Marjorie Dennis Murray
Good Morning, Chick by Mirra Ginsburg
Good Morning, Good Night by Michael Grejniec
Good Morning, Little Polar Bear by Carol Votaw
Hello Baby! by Mem Fox

Materials

4 or 6 beanbag or stuffed animal toys

Preparation

Display the animals in two rows on the floor. Leave about three feet of space between the animals and at least five feet of space between the two rows.

What to Do

1. Begin your good morning routine with this small group movement activity.
2. Help the children form a single-file line behind one row of animals. Demonstrate how to play leapfrog as you hop over each animal in the first row.
3. As you come to each animal, greet the animal by saying, "Good morning, Mr. ____," or "Good morning, Mrs. ___," naming each animal. Invite the children to follow along, leaping over each animal and bidding it good morning.
4. After you come to the end of row one, walk over to row two and continue down the line, back to where you started.
5. After each child completes the good morning routine, ask the children to collect the animals as the class begins its day.

Assessment
1. Can the child leap over the animals?
2. Is the child able to wait his turn and to copy your directions?

Mary Murray, Mazomanie, WI

Hatched or Born?

Learning Objectives
Children will:
1. Develop observation skills.
2. Learn to classify animals.

Vocabulary
born   egg
classify   hatched

Children's Books
Animals Born Alive and Well by Ruth Heller
Chickens Aren't the Only Ones by Ruth Heller
An Extraordinary Egg by Leo Lionni
From Tadpole to Frog by Wendy Pfeffer

Materials
2 paper bags
glue
index cards
clear contact paper or laminating machine
marker
pictures of animals (birds, lizards, snakes, puppies, kittens, chicks, mice, horses, dinosaurs, and so on)

Preparation
- Draw or attach pictures of the animals to index cards and laminate for durability.
- Label one paper bag "Hatched" and the other "Born." Draw or attach a picture of an egg on the "Hatched" bag and a picture of a baby animal on the "Born" bag.

What to Do
1. Read to the children books about animals that are hatched and animals that give birth to live babies.
2. During circle time or group time, talk with the children about animals and how some come from eggs and others are born like human babies.
3. As a group, help the children classify each card, and discuss what they know about the animal.
4. Once the group does this a few times, place the materials in the center of your choice so the children can repeat it independently to reinforce what they have learned.

Assessment
1. Can the child recognize different animals?
2. Can the child classify the animals?

Sandy L. Scott, Meridian, ID

Hop like a Bunny

Learning Objectives

Children will:

1. Identify pictures of objects and animals.
2. Learn about rhyming.
3. Develop gross motor skills.

Vocabulary

card   hop   rabbit
directions   move

Children's Books

The Bunny Book by Richard Scarry
Home for a Bunny by Margaret Wise Brown
Let's Make Rabbits by Leo Lionni
The Runaway Bunny by Margaret Wise Brown

Materials

2 colors of index cards
glue stick
marker
rhyming pictures of animals and ordinary objects that rhyme with the animals' names, such as cat and hat, goat and coat, fish and dish, duck and truck, fox and box, frog and log, mouse and house, pig and twig, rat and mat, seal and meal, and snake and cake
scissors

Preparation

- Create two sets of picture cards, one of animals and one of objects that rhyme with the animal names. Glue pictures of animals on one color of cards and pictures of objects that rhyme with the animals on the other color of cards. Write the names of the animals and the objects on each card.
- Draw or glue pictures of a rabbit on at least four cards, two of each color.

What to Do

1. Talk to the children about how rabbits move. Tell the children that the object of this game is to match two words that rhyme, an animal and an object.
2. Place all the cards facedown on the floor, keeping each color separate.
3. Ask one child to flip over one of the animal cards and then to turn over the rhyming cards until she finds an object that rhymes with the animal's name.
4. If the child turns over a rabbit card, everyone jumps up and hops around like a rabbit.
5. Continue until the child has turned over an object card that rhymes with the animal on her card.

Assessment

1. Is each child able to name the pictures correctly?
2. Is the child's rhyming skills improving as she does this activity?
3. Is the child able to hop around the room?

Fingerplays, Songs, and Poems

Here Is a Bunny (Traditional)
Here is a bunny
*   With ears so funny,*
And here is a hole in the ground.
When a noise he hears,
*   He pricks up his ears*
And jumps in the hole in the ground.

Jackie Wright, Enid, OK

Teacher-to-Teacher Tip
Instead of rabbits, you can use different animal pictures and movements: slithering snakes, swimmy fish, and so on.

I Am an Octopus

AGES 5+

Learning Objectives
Children will:
1. Learn about octopuses and other sea creatures.
2. Improve gross motor skills.

Vocabulary
clam	lobster	sea
crab	octopus	tentacles

Children's Books
The Amazing Octopus by Bobbie Kalman
How to Hide an Octopus & Other Sea Creatures by Ruth Heller
Octopus (A Day in the Life: Sea Animals) by Louise Spilsbury
An Octopus Is Amazing by Patricia Lauber
Tickly Octopus by Ruth Galloway
Welcome to the World of Octopuses by Diane Swanson

Materials
hats
pictures of sea creatures (clams, crabs, lobsters)
scissors
crepe paper streamers
tape
wiggle eyes (2 for each child)

Preparation
- Cut out 20 pictures each of shrimp, crabs, and lobsters. Cut streamers into pieces that are 10"–15" long.
- On the day before you plan to do this activity, send a note home with the children asking the families to bring a hat the next day. (Provide extra hats for children who do not have hats at home.)

What to Do
1. Read the children books about octopuses and other creatures that live in the sea.
2. Describe to the children how octopuses living under the sea move with their tentacles to catch fish, clams, crabs, and lobsters.
3. Show the children the pictures of shrimp, crabs, and lobsters.
4. Ask the children to stick eight pieces of streamers around their hat with tape and then add two wiggle eyes.
5. Scatter the pictures of shrimp, crabs, and lobsters on the classroom floor.

6. Tell the children to wear their hats and pretend to be octopuses in the sea. They "catch" their food (shrimp, crabs, and lobsters) with their tentacles by moving their hats with their heads. When they touch their food with their tentacles, they can pick up the food with their hands.

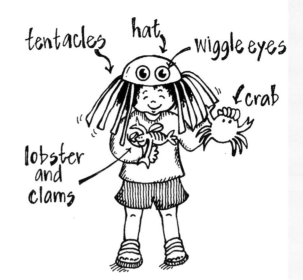

tentacles   hat   wiggle eyes

crab

lobster and clams

Assessment

1. What did the child learn about octopuses and other sea creatures?
2. Does the child have the coordination to move his head so the tentacles on his hat touch one of the pictures of shrimp, crabs, or lobsters?

Shyamala Shanmugasundaram,
Annanagar East, Chennai, India

I Like Me!

AGES 5+

Learning Objectives
Children will:
1. Learn about the characteristics of different animals.
2. Develop oral language skills.
3. Develop self-confidence.

Vocabulary
animal   puppet   talk

Children's Books
Animals: A Visual Encyclopedia by DK Publishing
First Animal Encyclopedia by DK Publishing
Kingfisher First Encyclopedia of Animals by Kingfisher Books
Nat Geo Wild Animal Atlas by National Geographic
Not All Animals Are Blue by Beatrice Boutigon
Oodles of Animals by Lois Ehlert

Materials
2 animal puppets
2 chairs

Preparation
- Set two chairs facing each other in a quiet corner of the room.
- Place one puppet on each chair.

What to Do

1. In addition to reading books about animals to the children, place a few reference books about animals in the library area for the children to look at independently.
2. Select two children to sit on the chairs and face one another.
3. Tell each child to place an animal puppet on his hand.
4. Ask the children to take turns making the animal puppets talk to each other about what makes each animal special and unique.
5. Encourage the children to begin their sentences by saying, "I like me because . . ." or "I'm special because . . ." (I have shiny scales, I have a furry tail, I live in the jungle, I have a long neck, and so on).
6. When the children have each had a turn, ask them to place the puppets back on the chairs for the next children.

Assessment

1. What did the child learn about animals?
2. Does the child use descriptive words to describe the animal?
3. Can the child use a puppet to participate in a conversation?
4. Is the child's self-confidence improving by talking with another child?

Mary Murray, Mazomanie, WI

Teacher-to-Teacher Tips

- Display a new pair of puppets on the chairs each day. The children will want to try this activity again and again.
- If you don't have any animal puppets, let the children use stuffed toys, beanbag animals, or pictures of animals.

Pet Park

AGES
5+

Learning Objectives

Children will:

1. Build a park for pets.
2. Develop spatial reasoning skills.

Vocabulary

blocks	path	run
build	pet	walk

Children's Books

Just Me and My Puppy by Mercer Mayer
Wet Pet, Dry Pet, Your Pet, My Pet by Dr. Seuss

Materials

8" x 11" blue pond-shaped piece of paper
building blocks
pictures of pet parks (use a search engine to find images on the Internet)
plastic toy pets
variety of building materials, such as cardboard, canning-jar rings, pipe cleaners, and so on

What to Do

1. Show children pictures of pet parks.
2. Engage the children in a discussion about the purpose of pet parks and how they are used.
3. Invite the children to use the blocks and other materials to create a pet park. Encourage children to use the pond as part of their creation, and to create walking paths and other structures for the pets to walk and run along, jump over, and so on.
4. Invite the children to manipulate the toy pets within the park setting and verbalize as they build, explore, and play.
5. As they work, ask the children questions about their structures.

Assessment

1. Does the child understand how pet parks are used, and is she able to work with the other children to build a park for pets?
2. Is the child developing spatial reasoning skills as she builds a pet park?

Mary Murray, Mazomanie, WI

Pet Talk

AGES
5+

Learning Objectives

Children will:

1. Develop oral language skills.
2. Enhance social development.
3. Improve critical thinking skills.

Vocabulary

alike	different	same
animal	fish	special
bird	pets	
both	reptile	

Children's Books

The Best Pet of All by David LaRochelle
Buying, Training, and Caring for Your Dinosaur by Laura Joy Rennert
Children Make Terrible Pets by Peter Brown
Every Buddy Counts by Stuart J. Murphy
The Perfect Pet by Margie Palatini
Pet Show! by Ezra Jack Keats
Wet Pet, Dry Pet, Your Pet, My Pet by Dr. Seuss

Materials

large sheet of construction or butcher paper (for the "pet mat")
stuffed toy pets, plastic animals that are pets, or pictures of pets

Preparation

- Lay the butcher paper on the floor to act as a "pet mat."
- Display an assortment of pets along one edge of the pet mat.

What to Do
1. Select two children.
2. Invite the children to sit outside the border of the pet mat.
3. Each child picks up a pet from the border of the mat.
4. Ask the children to have a conversation with their partner about the pets, including how the two animals are alike and how they are different.
5. After several minutes of conversation, ask the two children to return the pets to the border of the mat.

Assessment
1. Can the child compare and contrast the pets?
2. Can the child participate in a conversation about the pet?
3. Can the child ask and answer simple questions about the pet?

Mary Murray, Mazomanie, WI

Shadow Animals

AGES 5+

Learning Objectives
Children will:
1. Cultivate their individual creativity.
2. Improve fine motor skills.
3. Play cooperatively with each other.

Vocabulary

animal	finger	light
beam	(middle,	rabbit
bird	ring,	shadow
dark	index,	thumb
dog	pinkie)	torch
	hand	wrist shape

Materials
flashlights (with spare batteries)

Preparation
- Clear space for pairs of children to stand in front of a flat, light-colored stretch of wall, ideally with several feet between each pair so their flashlight beams don't overlap.
- Lower overhead lights or blinds so the room is as dimly lit as possible while remaining safe.

Children's Books
Nothing Sticks Like a Shadow by Anne Tompert
Shadow by Suzy Lee
Shadows and Reflections by Tana Hoban
What Makes a Shadow? by Clyde Robert Bulla

What to Do

1. Give each pair of children a flashlight and let them experiment to find the best distances between hands, wall, and light source.
2. Show them how to make the shadow animals listed below, taking turns to hold the flashlight. Once the children know how to make shadow ears, eyes, mouths, heads, and wings, allow children to invent their own animal shapes.

To make a bird:
Hold your hands out in front with palms facing up. Cross wrists so your right hand is on the left side and left hand is on the right side. Link your thumbs, then point them upward. Flap your fingers to move the wings.

To make a rabbit:
Hold one hand out in front with palm facing the wall. Curl your ring finger and pinkie finger in toward your palm. Rest your thumb on top to hold them down. The gap between your fingers, thumb, and palm becomes an eye. Make a V shape between your index and middle fingers. Wave them around to make rabbit ears.

To make a dog:
Put your hands together, palms facing. Point fingers away from you. Move your pinkie fingers downward to give the dog a mouth. Open and close it by moving fingers in and out of position. Curl your left index finger round and rest it on top of the right one. This makes a tiny gap, which becomes the dog's eye. Cross your thumbs to make ears.

Assessment

1. Is the child expanding his creativity as he creates shadows?
2. Is the child improving his fine motor skills as he makes shadow puppets?
3. Is the child able to work cooperatively with the other children to create group shadow puppets?

Kirsty Neale, Orpington, Kent, UK

> **Teacher-to-Teacher Tip**
> Take things a step further by grouping more children together and seeing what sort of shadow shapes they can make using four or six hands, instead of just two.

Artsy Art

AGES 3+

Learning Objectives
Children will:
1. Participate in the visual arts.
2. Engage in active play using fine motor skills.
3. Understand that pictures and symbols have meaning and that print carries a message.

Vocabulary

art	draw	paints
brushes	glue	paper
colors	markers	pencils
crayons	mixing	scissors

Children's Books
The Art Box by Gail Gibbons
Harold and the Purple Crayon by Crockett Johnson

What to Do
1. Read *The Art Box* and talk about art with the children. Show pictures of art.
2. Discuss the rules for the art center. Have the children put on painting smocks if they choose to paint. Allow other children to choose their art materials, and let them produce art.

Assessment
1. Can each child utilize the different materials in the art center?
2. Did each child create something during the activity?

Carol Hupp, Farmersville, IL

Materials
brushes
crayons
glue
markers
paint smocks
paints
paper
pencils
pictures of art
scissors

Preparation
Put out art materials.

Teacher-to-Teacher Tip
To focus this activity more, give the children suggestions of which mediums to use or what to create.

Another Encyclopedia of Theme Activities

Bookmark It!

AGES **3+**

Learning Objectives

Children will:

1. Learn about the love of reading.
2. Use fine motor skills to create a bookmark.

Vocabulary

book   library   read

Children's Books

The Best Book to Read by Debbie Bertram and Susan Bloom

The Best Place to Read by Debbie Bertram and Susan Bloom

The Best Time to Read by Debbie Bertram and Susan Bloom

Book! Book! Book! by Deborah Bruss

Lola at the Library by Anna McQuinn

Wild About Books by Judy Sierra

What to Do

1. Give the children the precut bookmarks.
2. Place materials that the children can use to decorate the bookmark in the art center. Encourage them to decorate their bookmarks however they like.
3. After the bookmarks are dry, share with the children a book about reading, and demonstrate using a bookmark. Tell them that the next time they are reading a book, they can use a bookmark to save their place!

Assessment

1. What did the child learn about the love of reading by listening to the books you read?
2. How well did the activity develop the child's fine motor skills?

Donna Alice Patton, Hillsboro, OH

Materials

art materials to decorate the bookmarks, such as glitter, fun foam shapes and letters, sequins, and stickers
glue
markers, crayons, colored pencils
paper, fun foam, or fabric
scissors

Preparation

To make this super fast and simple, cut 2" x 6" paper, fun foam, or fabric bookmarks.

A R T

Teacher-to-Teacher Tip

For older children, include child-safe scissors in the materials and encourage the children to cut out their own bookmark.

Colors Make Scents

Learning Objectives
Children will:
1. Experience sensory awareness through aromas.
2. Practice color mixing.

Vocabulary
color
color names: *red, orange, yellow, green, blue, purple, brown, black, white*
paint
smell

Children's Books
Elmer and the Rainbow by David McKee
I Ain't Gonna Paint No More! by Karen Beaumont
Mouse Paint by Ellen Stoll Walsh

What to Do
1. Pour the white paint into the plastic plates or pie tins, and add the selected food extract to the paint. To avoid sensory overload, choose no more than two different kinds of extract.
2. Drop a little food coloring onto each plate, and let children stir in the food coloring, noting the changes that occur. Add more food coloring for darker colors. Use two different colors so children can enjoy mixing yellow and green to make blue, blue and red to make purple, or yellow and red to make orange.
3. Let children paint with the aromatic paints, making new colors from the original ones. Children never seem to tire of this activity.
4. Leave the paintings to dry overnight before hanging them up or taking them home.

Assessment
1. Can the child describe what happens when the food coloring is added?
2. Can the child identify the colors?

Kay Flowers, Summerfield, OH

Materials
fingerpaint paper or butcher paper
food coloring
food extracts (for example, vanilla, lemon, raspberry)
newspapers
plastic plates or pie tins
small paintbrushes
white paint

Preparation
Cover art table with newspapers and have all materials handy.

Teacher-to-Teacher Tip
This activity is also fun as fingerpaint art, and the children will be able to smell the wonderful aroma on their hands for a long time afterward.

Give Me a Brush, Any Brush

Learning Objectives

Children will:

1. Use different kinds of paintbrushes.
2. Develop fine motor skills.

Vocabulary

bristles   paintbrush
canvas   smock
drop cloth   tray
paint roller

What to Do

1. Examine the types of paintbrushes. Allow the children to feel the bristles of each one, and discuss what each brush is designed to do.
2. Discuss the various colors of paint on the walls of their home, classroom, or center.
3. Allow the children to use the different brushes to "paint" water onto the brick, block, or outdoor wall surface.

Assessment

What fine motor skills did the child exhibit?

Tina R. Durham-Woehler, Lebanon, TN

Materials

large brick or block wall (outdoors)
small buckets
various types of wall/surface paintbrushes
water
water smocks

Preparation

- Locate different types of paintbrushes.
- Fill each bucket halfway with water.

Teacher-to-Teacher Tip

If desired, a mural can be done with tempera paint on butcher paper instead of water. With the paint, each child can see what they contributed to the artwork. When the mural is dry, display anywhere in the classroom.

A R T

Tropical Play Clay

AGES **3+**

Learning Objectives

Children will:

1. Make play clay using ordinary ingredients.
2. Create a variety of fun shapes—even letters and numbers—with their clay.
3. Have fun outdoors using fine motor skills.

Vocabulary

clay   knead   tropical

Materials

flour
measuring cup and spoon
mixing bowl
plastic resealable bag per child (optional)
salt
small saucepan to boil water
unsweetened flavored drink mix
vegetable oil
water

Preparation

If children are too young, prepare recipe ahead of time and divide into plastic resealable bags. This recipe can be mixed and allowed to cool; after it cools, children can then knead the dough. This recipe can be doubled.

    1¼ cups of flour
    ¼ cup of salt
    1 package of unsweetened flavored drink mix (Use it dry, do not mix with water. Use tropical flavors—cherry makes red, and so on.)
    1 cup of boiling water
    1½ tablespoons of vegetable oil

What to Do

1. Allow the children to mix the dry ingredients in a bowl. After they are finished, have the children bring their mixtures to the front of the classroom.
2. **This step is for teachers only:** Stir in the hot water and oil. Allow mixture to sit until you can put your hands in comfortably. Knead with your hands. **Warning:** The mixture will still be warm.
3. After the mixture cools down more, allow the children to mix it for about five minutes or until it forms a ball. Play clay can be stored in a plastic bag for up to two months of play.
4. Let the children create!

Songs, Fingerplays, and Poems

(To the tune of "Here We Go 'Round the Mulberry Bush")
This is the way we knead the dough,
Knead the dough,
Knead the dough.
This is the way we knead the dough
In pretty, pretty colors.

Assessment

1. Was each child able to follow the recipe?
2. Did each child use creative expression in using the clay?
3. Was each child able to use fine motor skills to knead the clay?

Donna Alice Patton, Hillsboro, OH

Trunk Painting

AGES **3+**

Learning Objectives

Children will:

1. Improve gross motor skills.
2. Develop artistic and creative skills.
3. Expand listening skills.

Vocabulary

elephant   paintbrush   trunk

mural   smock

Children's Books

Elephants Can Paint Too! by Katya Arnold

Materials

art smocks

canvas, tarp, or drop cloth

mural paper

paintbrushes

tempera paints

Preparation

Set up the art center with mural paper on the wall and a canvas, tarp, or drop cloth on the floor to catch the paint that might fall off the paintbrushes.

What to Do

1. Share the book *Elephants Can Paint Too!* by Katya Arnold with the children.
2. Invite the children to paint like an elephant. Have them extend an arm out in front of themselves like a trunk and use large movements to paint designs on large sheets of mural paper.
3. Be sure children wear art smocks for this fun activity.

Assessment

1. Can each child use a paintbrush at arm's length?
2. Did each child follow along with the book?

Mary Murray, Mazomanie, WI

art smock   mural paper   drop cloth

I'm an Artist

Learning Objectives

Children will:

1. Develop an appreciation for art.
2. Develop oral language skills.

Vocabulary

easel	palette	water
paint	paper	
paintbrush	smock	

Children's Books

The Artist Who Painted a Blue Horse by Eric Carle

Hands: Growing Up to Be an Artist by Lois Ehlert

I Am an Artist by Pat Lowery Collins

Leonardo and the Flying Boy by Laurence Anholt

Materials

art smock

markers, crayons, chalk, paint, and paintbrushes

paper

pictures of artwork (the Internet is a good source)

Preparation

Display one or two pictures of artwork in the art area.

What to Do

1. Invite the children to put on an art smock to protect their clothing.
2. Suggest that the children describe things they like about the artwork that is displayed.
3. Encourage the children to use the artwork as inspirations for creating their own pictures or to create a picture of their own choosing.

Assessment

1. Is the child developing an appreciation for art?
2. Is the child able to describe what he likes about the artwork that is displayed?

Mary Murray, Mazomanie, WI

Teacher-to-Teacher Tip

Display an assortment of books about painting for additional inspiration.

Kite Fun

AGES 4+

Learning Objectives
Children will:
Follow simple directions to create a kite.

Vocabulary
diamond   kite   wind
fly   string

Children's Books
Kite Flying by Grace Lin
Kites by David Pelham
Kites Sail High by Ruth Heller

Materials
crayons
diamond-shaped stencil
glue
markers
poster board
scissors
streamers in different colors
string
white construction paper

Preparation
Create enough construction paper diamond shapes for the children to create their own kites.

What to Do
1. Share books and pictures about kites. Pass out diamond shapes to the children to decorate.
2. Encourage the children to use crayons and markers to decorate their kites.
3. While children are creating their kites, ask them questions, such as, "If you were a kite, where would you fly?" or "Why do you think it would be hard to fly a kite in the rain or the snow?" or "How do kites fly?"
4. When the children are finished, ask them what kind of tail they would like to put on their kite, and provide them with streamers. Allow the children to glue the kite's tail onto the kite.
5. Assist the children in stapling or taping string to their kites.

Assessment
1. Can each child name any of the steps in making his kite?
2. Can each child name the colors on his kite?

Tracey R. Hill, Trotwood, OH

Little Michelangelos and the "Sixteen" Chapel

AGES 4+

Learning Objectives
Children will:
1. Learn an appreciation for painting and art.
2. Create individual explorations of art.
3. Develop fine and gross motor skills.

Vocabulary
masterpiece   painter   Sistine Chapel
Michelangelo   Renaissance

Children's Books
Art Is . . . by Bob Raczka
No One Saw by Bob Raczka

Materials
markers, crayons, paint, or colored pencils
paintbrushes
paper
pillows or soft mats (optional)
tape

Preparation
- Put tape on the back of a few pieces of paper and place it on the underside of a table.
- Gather materials and make them available for children.

What to Do
1. After reading any book related to the art of Michelangelo Buonarotti, explain to the children that Michelangelo painted the ceiling of the Sistine Chapel while lying on his back on a scaffold.
2. Ask children if they think it would be easy to paint while lying on their backs.
3. Explain to the children that paper has been placed underneath the table so that they can experience painting like Michelangelo.
4. Demonstrate painting like Michelangelo to the children (if you can!).
5. Encourage them to try it after you have finished your demonstration. As they work on their masterpieces, allow them to replace their papers if they mess up.

Assessment
1. Can each child paint or color on the underside of the table?
2. Did each child create her own masterpiece?

Eamonn Fitzgerald, Lexington, KY

Teacher-to-Teacher Tip
Encourage the children to stay on their own papers.

Mixed-Media Weaving

AGES 4+

Learning Objectives
Children will:
1. Identify and describe attributes of materials.
2. Develop spatial awareness.

Vocabulary
over	under	yarn
string	weaving	

Children's Books
The Goat in the Rug by Charles L. Blood
The Weaving Adventures of Edgar and Rita by Frances Iverson

Materials
beads
chart paper or whiteboard
chenille craft stems (also called pipe cleaners)
feathers
ribbons
sticks
strips of fabric
Styrofoam meat tray
variety of sizes and weights of yarn and string
wire

What to Do
1. Read a children's book about weaving with the children.
2. Show various types of yarn, string, and fabric strips. Discuss the attributes of each. For example, yarn can be fuzzy, soft, smooth, flexible, thick, thin, bright, dull, or sparkly. The children will use different adjectives to describe the materials.
3. Write some of the words that children use to describe the objects on chart paper or a whiteboard.
4. Show the beads to the children, and have the children feel and describe the qualities of the beads. Have the children sort the beads by color or shape.

Preparation
- Cut slits on either side of the Styrofoam tray, approximately ½"–1" apart.
- Starting at one end, wrap a large piece of string from the first slit to the slit at opposite side of the tray.
- Leave a tail of string at the end, about 5" in length.
- Wrap the string around the back of the tray and continue to the next slit.
- Continue wrapping back and forth until you have the warp of the loom.
- Tie the two tails together to secure the loom.
- Gather materials for weaving.
- Cut fabric into strips.

A R T

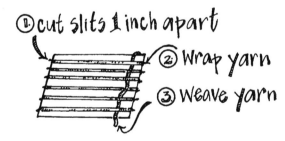

① cut slits 1 inch apart
② Wrap yarn
③ weave yarn

5. Demonstrate how to weave the materials over and under across the loom. Show the children how to thread a bead onto a chenille craft stem, and then weave using the beaded chenille stem.

Assessment

1. Did the child demonstrate the concepts of over and under?
2. Did the child attempt to sort the objects by color, size, or texture?
3. Can the child name adjectives that describe the materials?

Marcia Beckett, Madison, WI

Teacher-to-Teacher Tips

- Set up the looms for all children ahead of time. Give the children assistance as they weave, pushing the materials close together so there are no gaps in the weaving.
- The finished weavings can be displayed on the Styrofoam trays.
- This project is easily adaptable to an older child, and he could probably set up the loom on his own.

Mr. Sun

AGES
4+

Learning Objectives
Children will:
Develop fine motor skills by using fingerpaints.

Vocabulary

cheeks	hot	ray
eyes	mouth	shine
face	nose	sun

Children's Books
Lucia and the Light by Phyllis Root
My Light by Molly Bang
The Sun by Seymour Simon

Materials
child-safe scissors
embellishment materials such as faux jewels
fingerpaint paper (or butcher paper)
glue
newspaper
pink crayons
salt
sun template
yellow fingerpaint

Preparation
Cover the tables with old newspaper and gather the paper and paint. Add salt to the fingerpaint for sparkle.

What to Do

1. Let the children fingerpaint on large sheets of butcher paper with the shiny side of the paper facing down. Allow the paint to dry overnight.
2. The next day, help the children use a template to trace a large sun on the painted paper. Let them cut around the rays themselves if they are developmentally able.
3. Provide a selection of embellishment materials, and glue and help children make faces on their suns. Allow the children to use the pink crayons to put a hint of pink on the cheeks, if they wish.

Fingerplays, Songs, and Poems

"Mr. Sun" (Traditional Song)
Oh, Mister Sun, Sun,
Mister Golden Sun,
Please shine down on me.

Oh, Mister Sun, Sun,
Mister Golden Sun,
Hiding behind a tree.

These little children
Are asking you
To please come out
So we can play with you.

Oh Mister Sun, Sun,
Mister Golden Sun,
Please shine down on me!

Assessment

1. Can the child use the fingerpaint and glue?
2. Can the child identify the colors of the paint?
3. Can the child use the scissors to cut out her sun?

Jackie Wright, Enid, OK

Purple Paintings

Learning Objectives
Children will:
1. Identify the color purple.
2. Learn about different shades of purple.
3. Create purple paintings.

Vocabulary
black
darker
lighter
purple
white

Children's Books
Purple by Melanie Mitchell
Purple by Sarah L. Schuette (Spanish version available)
Purple Pride by Christianne C. Jones
Harold and the Purple Crayon by Crockett Johnson

Materials
paintbrushes
pie tins (5)
tempera paint in purple, white, and black
white construction paper

Preparation
Place the paper, paint, pie tins, and paintbrushes in the art center.

What to Do

1. Ask the children to pour purple paint into one of the pie tins; encourage them to identify the color.
2. After they identify the first color, have the children pour purple paint into a second pie tin, but this time, add a little bit of white paint and stir. Ask the children if this color is lighter or darker than the plain purple paint.
3. Have the children repeat their actions in a third pie tin; however, ask them to add enough white paint so that the mixture is about half purple and half white.
4. Ask the children if the mixture is getting lighter or darker. Explain that when you add more white to a color, it becomes lighter.
5. Next, ask the children to pour purple paint into a fourth pie tin, and this time, add a little bit of black paint and stir. Is this color lighter or darker than the plain purple paint?
6. Have the children repeat their actions in a fifth pie tin; this time, ask them to add enough black paint so that the mixture is about half purple and half black.
7. Ask the children if the mixture is getting lighter or darker. Explain that the more black you add to a color, the darker that color becomes.
8. Have the children use the five shades of purple paint to make paintings.

Assessment

1. Can each child identify the color of the plain purple paint?
2. Can each child tell which shades are lighter and which are darker?

Laura D. Wynkoop, San Dimas, CA

Star Painting

AGES
4+

Learning Objectives

Children will:
1. Examine pictures of stars in space.
2. Create star paintings.
3. Identify colors.

Vocabulary

black
blue
purple
silver
space
star

Children's Books

The Magic School Bus Sees Stars by Nancy White
Stars by Jennifer Dussling
Stars! Stars! Stars! by Nancy Elizabeth Wallace

Materials

black, purple, and blue tempera paint
paint trays
pictures of stars in space
silver foil star stickers
white construction paper

Preparation

Fill the paint trays with tempera paint.

Another Encyclopedia of Theme Activities

What to Do

1. Ask the children if they have gone outside at night to look at stars. Discuss their experiences.
2. Show the children some pictures of stars in space. Ask the children to identify the colors they see.
3. Provide white construction paper and trays of black, purple, and blue tempera paint. Have the children fingerpaint their paper until all the white is gone. This will create a fun and realistic space background.
4. Let the paintings dry. After they are dry, ask the children to add foil star stickers to create space scenes.

Fingerplays, Songs, and Poems

Star Light (Traditional)
Star light,
Star bright,
First star I see tonight.
I wish I may,
* I wish I might*
have the wish I wish tonight.

finger painting

silver foil star

Assessment
Can the child identify the colors she used in her painting?

Laura D. Wynkoop, San Dimas, CA

X Marks the Art!

AGES 4+

Learning Objectives
Children will:
1. Learn to follow a map.
2. Create collage art.
3. Identify their names in print.

Vocabulary
create   follow   think

Children's Books
We're Going on a Bear Hunt by Michael Rosen
We're Going on a Book Hunt by Pat Miller
We're Going on a Leaf Hunt by Steve Metzger
We're Going on a Lion Hunt by Margery Cuyler

Materials
brown lunch bags (one per child)
construction paper and glue for "treasure" art
craft items for the bags (pom-poms, scraps
    of papers, pieces of cloth, cotton balls,
    buttons, and so on)
large box
map that leads to an X

Preparation
- Create a map of the classroom for children to follow to find the treasure. Write children's names on the bags.
- Fill bags with craft items. Place the bags in the box and hide the box in a secret spot. Mark this spot on the map with an X.
- Set activity tables with construction paper and glue bottles to make treasure art.

What to Do

1. Tell the children they are going on a treasure hunt. Provide the children with the map of the classroom.
2. Encourage each child to follow the map to look for the X and the bag with her name on it.
3. Lead the children on the hunt. Sing the following song as the children search, and encourage the children to sing along.

(To the tune of "Mary Had a Little Lamb")

> *We're going on a treasure hunt,*
> *Treasure hunt,*
> *Treasure hunt.*
> *We're going on a treasure hunt;*
> *We're looking for the X.*

4. When the bags have been found, allow each child to take a bag. Have the children open their treasure bags.
5. Tell the children to take their treasure bags back to the activity tables. Instruct them to glue the "treasures" onto the paper. Leave the art to dry.

Assessment

1. Can each child follow the map?
2. Did each child create his own piece of treasure art?

Kara Stokke, Maumelle, AR

Art Smart

AGES 5+

Learning Objectives

Children will:

1. Explore various art mediums.
2. Express creativity.
3. Improve vocabulary.

Vocabulary

chalk	paper
color	pastel
crayon	pencil
dark	rough
light	smooth
lines	thick
oil	thin

Materials

art paper
assortment of art supplies, such as pencils, colored pencils, chalk, pastels, oil crayons, charcoal, markers, colored glue, and glitter glue sticks
pencil cases
still-life display

Preparation

- Place an assortment of various art supplies in each pencil case and zip it shut.
- Display a select group of still-life items on a table in the center of the classroom.

What to Do

1. Assign each child a partner to work with, and provide each pair of children with two sheets of paper and a pencil case containing art supplies.
2. Instruct each pair of children to find their own space in the classroom. Allow children to work on the floor, at tables, or wherever they like.
3. Invite the children to open their pencil cases and use the various art supplies to make marks or designs on their papers. Encourage children to notice the feel, the various textures, lines, and colors that the different art supplies make.
4. Invite children to use the art supplies in more than one way if possible, to form thick or thin lines, pressing harder or lighter to form dark or light color, and so on.
5. Have children talk about their art discoveries as they work with their partners, comparing and contrasting the various art supplies.
6. After several minutes of exploring with the materials, provide children with more sheets of paper and invite them to draw pictures of the still-life display using the various art supplies.

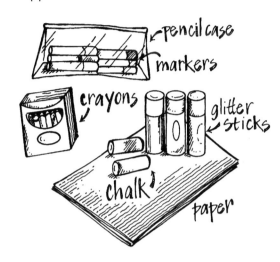

Assessment

1. Did each child explore the different ways to use her art supplies?
2. Did each child share his discoveries with his partner?

Mary Murray, Mazomanie, WI

> **Teacher-to-Teacher Tip**
> Provide children with clipboards and take the class outdoors for this activity. After exploring with the materials, encourage children to draw a scene from nature.

Clay Boy

Learning Objectives
Children will:
1. Make predictions using pictures and content for guides.
2. Retell information from a story.
3. Respond to simple questions about reading material.
4. Engage in active play using fine motor skills.
5. Identify body parts and their functions.

Vocabulary
arms   head   roll
ball   legs
body   pinch

Children's Books
Clay Boy by Mirra Ginsburg and Jos. A. Smith

Materials
clay (½ stick for each child)
pencil to create facial features
plastic bags
scraps of material
wiggly eyes

Preparation
Cut sticks of clay. Collect items to decorate the clay boy.

What to Do
1. Show the cover of the book *Clay Boy* to the children. Introduce the clay to the children and explain the rules for using clay in the classroom.
2. Provide each child with a piece of clay and allow him to begin working it.
3. Read *Clay Boy,* using various strategies to keep the children engaged.
4. After the story, demonstrate how to build a clay boy. Demonstrate to the children how to take some clay and roll it into a ball in your palms; also show them how to pinch more clay and roll lengths to make arms and legs.
5. Finally, show the children how to use the remaining piece to make the body of the clay boy. Show the children how to assemble the clay boy and make depressions with the pencil for his eyes and mouth.
6. Dismiss the children to their tables so they can begin creating their clay boys. As children complete their clay boys, take pictures and add them to a book for classroom display.
7. After allowing the clay to dry, allow the children to take home their clay boys in plastic bags.

Assessment
1. Did each child create his own clay boy?
2. Can each child identify the different parts of her clay boy's body?

Debora Pletzke, Orland Park, IL

Teacher-to-Teacher Tip
Give each child a small piece of clay to hold and soften while you read the story. Explain in detail your expectations—the clay needs to stay in the children's hands, not on the carpet.

Hole-Punch Pictures

AGES 5+

Learning Objectives
Children will:
1. Improve fine motor skills.
2. Learn to differentiate shapes and sizes.
3. Develop visual-motor coordination.

Vocabulary
collage	drawing
design	overlap
dots	

Children's Books
1 2 3 I Can Collage! by Irene Luxbacher
Sunday with Seurat by Julie Merberg

Materials
colored card stock and/or paper
construction paper
glue
hole punch
pencils
small bowls or containers

Preparation

Use a hole punch and colored card stock or paper to create a majority of the scraps the children will use in this activity, separating different colors into small bowls. Save a few extra sheets of paper for each child to punch on his own.

What to Do

1. Encourage the children to draw a simple outline or design onto construction paper to fill with the hole-punch scraps (if you prefer, you can use printed images instead).
2. Tell the children to spread glue over a small area of their picture and press a punched circle on top. Add another next to it (using the same color), so the edges overlap. Keep adding circles, pressing down firmly so they stick to the glue. Overlap them so as little background as possible shows through.
3. When the children have covered the whole glued section, tell them to add some glue alongside it, and continue placing circles in the new section of glue.
4. Have children swap colors when they reach the next part of the picture, and add more circles in the same way. Once the picture is completely colored in with punched holes, set it aside it to dry.

Assessment

1. Did each child successfully create a collage?
2. Did each child demonstrate creative ways to use waste material?

Kirsty Neale, Orpington, Kent, UK

> **Teacher-to-Teacher Tip**
> Simple images such as animals, houses, trees and flowers, people, vehicles, or even names written in block letters are all perfect for filling with this kind of dotted collage.

Stained Glass Animal Pictures

Learning Objectives

Children will:
1. Follow directions.
2. Develop an awareness and appreciation of visual art.
3. Develop fine motor skills and eye-hand coordination.

Vocabulary

art   stained glass
color   windows

Children's Books

Stained Glass Windows: Stories in Art by Richard Spilsbury

Materials

animal pictures suitable for tracing
colorful markers or highlighters
construction paper
thick-tipped black markers
tracing paper

Preparation

Select appropriate animal pictures from the Internet for inspiration for the children's drawings.

What to Do

1. Show the children examples of stained glass windows.
2. Ask the children to draw a picture of an animal.
3. Have the children use a thick-tipped black marker to trace over lines of their pictures onto tracing paper.
4. Encourage children to use colorful markers to fill in their traced pictures.
5. Frame the stained glass pictures with a construction paper cutout frame, and display the children's stained glass works in a sunny window!

Assessment

1. Can the child follow sequence directions?
2. Is the child able to artistically express herself?
3. Has the child developed fine motor and eye-hand coordination skills?

MaryLouise Alu Curto, Mercerville, NJ

Teacher-to-Teacher Tip

Inform the children that pictures with very few details work best.

Park the Trucks!
It's Quitting Time!

AGES
3+

Learning Objectives
Children will:
1. Match and compare sizes.
2. Develop fine motor skills.
3. Identify items by name.

Vocabulary

backhoe	dump truck	small
big	garage	wide
bulldozer	long	
color	park	

Children's Books
Big Machines by Karen Wallace
We Need Construction Workers by Lisa Trumbauer
Whose Hat Is This? by Sharon Katz Cooper

Materials
colored card stock
hard hat
scissors
toy working trucks and machinery in assorted sizes (one per student)
whistle

Preparation
Cut various colors of card stock to size, creating a parking space to match the size of each working truck.

What to Do
1. At the end of the day, put on the hard hat and line the trucks along one side of the carpet in the circle time area. Display the colored card stock "garages" on the opposite side of the carpeted area against a wall, creating a large garage of parking stalls.
2. When children see you lining up the trucks, inform them that it means that it's almost time to go home. Blow the whistle and call out, "It's quitting time," to signal clean-up time.
3. All of the children should gather on the floor for the daily closing activities. Have each child sit near a working truck. (Some will have a small truck, while others will have a large truck.)
4. Invite each child to drive his truck to a garage of the same size and park the truck overnight. Once all the trucks are in their respective garages, the children may pack up to go home.
5. Repeat this activity at the end of each day as you continue the study of building and construction.

Assessment
1. Can the child determine the size of her truck?
2. Is the child able to select a parking "garage" that is similar in size to his truck?

Mary Murray, Mazomanie, WI

Teacher-to-Teacher Tip
For extra fun, in the morning invite children to drive a truck out of the garage and into the building and construction work area.

Tool Imprints

AGES 3+

Learning Objectives
Children will:
1. Improve fine motor skills.
2. Identify tools.
3. Improve their vocabularies.

Vocabulary
clay   shape
imprint   tool
press

Children's Books
Monkey with a Tool Belt by Chris Monroe
Tool Book by Gail Gibbons
The Toolbox by Anne Rockwell

Materials
box containing assorted metal tools and
    related items such as large nails, large and
    small screws, nuts, bolts, and so on
playdough or clay
rolling pins

What to Do
1. Introduce the tools and the related items to the children during group time, and tell them that they will be available to make imprints during centers.
2. Place the playdough, the assorted tools, and other related items at a table. Invite children to roll a piece of dough into a half-inch-thick slab. Encourage children to explore with the various materials in the box.
3. Invite children to use the tools, nails, screws, and so on to make imprints in the clay. Encourage children to verbalize as they work.
4. When children are finished exploring with the materials, have them smash the dough and return it to the container for the next child to use.

Assessment
1. Is the child able to roll the dough and make imprints?
2. Can each child identify the tools and related objects in the box?

Mary Murray, Mazomanie, WI

Teacher-to-Teacher Tip
Try the recipe for play clay found on page 60.

Tools Hokey Pokey

AGES 3+

Learning Objectives
Children will:
1. Recognize and name tools.
2. Enhance their awareness of simple tools.
3. Demonstrate balance and control during locomotor movements.
4. Demonstrate listening and understanding skills.

Vocabulary
hammer
pliers
saw
screwdriver
tape measure
tool
wrench

Children's Books
The Toolbox by Anne Rockwell
Tools by Gail Gibbons
Whose Tools Are These? by Sharon Katz Cooper

Materials
card stock
pictures of various tools
real or toy tools

Preparation
- On card stock, make picture cards of tools such as a hammer, wrench, pliers, tape measure, saw, and screwdriver. Print the names of the tools under the pictures.
- If possible, show children samples or toys of the tools as well.

What to Do
1. Turn the tool cards facedown on a table. Allow the children to take turns drawing a card, and then help the children identify and name the tool pictured on the card.
2. Have the children stand in a circle, facing the inside of the circle, with their tool cards in hand. Sing the song "Tool Hokey Pokey" (see below) using the tool cards as props. Sing the song at least twice.

"Tool Hokey Pokey" (by Jackie Wright)
(Sung to the traditional "Hokey Pokey" tune)

You put your tool in.
You put your tool out.
You put your tool in,
And you shake it all about.
You hold your tool carefully,
And you turn yourself around.
That's what it's all about!

Assessment
1. Can each child identify the tools?
2. Can each child follow the directions in the song?

Jackie Wright, Enid, OK

Teacher-to-Teacher Tip
Repeat the activity on several different days to allow the children the opportunity of selecting and naming more than one tool. Once they have had an opportunity to get up and move around, they are more likely to be able to sit back down again and listen attentively.

The Tool Song

Learning Objectives
Children will:
1. Identify the tools.
2. Learn how tools are used.
3. Sing a simple song with actions.

Vocabulary

board	might	sight
fight	nails	tape measure
hammer	pencil	tight
improve	pliers	tools
level	pound	twist
look	saw	work
measure	screwdriver	write

Children's Books
The Toolbox by Anne Rockwell
Tools by Gail Gibbons
Whose Tools Are These? by Sharon Katz
    Cooper

Materials
card stock
colored pictures of tools to use as song
    props: hammer, saw, screwdriver, tape
    measure, level, pliers
felt
flannel board
scissors
Velcro pieces or magnetic tape

Preparation
- On card stock, make cards with pictures of tools mentioned in the song.
- Place Velcro or magnetic tape on the back of the pictures. (If possible, laminate the cards for durability.)

What to Do
1. Display the tool cards one at a time as you teach the children "The Tool Song."
2. Encourage the children to make the motions used for tools as they sing the song.

"The Tool Song" by Jackie Wright
(Sung to the tune of the first lines of "The Trolley Song" by Hugh Martin and Ralph Blane, from Meet Me in St. Louis)

Pound, pound, pound,
Says the hammer.
Pound, pound, pound
The nails in tight.

Buzz, buzz, buzz
Says the saw.
Buzz, buzz, buzz
Saw the board.

Turn, turn, turn,
Says the screwdriver.
Turn, turn, turn,
with your might.

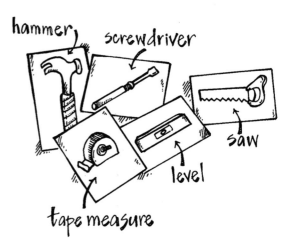

hammer
screwdriver
saw
level
tape measure

Measure, measure, measure,
Says the tape measure.
Measure, measure, measure,
Then use your pencil to write.

Look, look, look,
Says the level.
Look, look, look
With your eyes.

Twist, twist, twist,
Say the pliers.
Twist, twist, twist,
Twist without a fight.

Work, work, work,
Say the tools.
Work, work, work,
Day and night.

Assessment

1. Can each child identify the name and use of each of the six tools mentioned in the song?
2. Does each child demonstrate by his actions that he understands how to use the tools?

Jackie Wright, Enid, OK

Tool Trail

AGES
3+

Learning Objectives
Children will:
1. Compare and contrast tools.
2. Follow directions.
3. Develop analytical thinking skills.
4. Improve gross motor skills.

Vocabulary
carpenter's pencil
hammer
measuring tape
nails
saw
wrench

Children's Books
B is for Bulldozer by June Sobel
Construction Workers by Tami Deedrick
My Little Red Toolbox by Stephen Johnson

Materials
assortment of tools
masking tape
pictures of tools

Preparation
Use the masking tape to create a zigzag line 10'–15' in length on the classroom floor. Display pictures of tools along the length of the line, about 1' away from the tape.

What to Do
1. In small groups, invite the children to line up at one end of the "tool trail." Explain that children are to walk along the tape line as if it's a balance beam.
2. As children walk, invite them to observe and identify the various tools they see along the way.
3. Once children step off the far end of the trail, invite them to talk among themselves about the tools they saw, comparing and contrasting, and discussing each one's use.

Assessment

1. Is each child able to walk along the taped line?
2. Can each child name the tools? Does he know their uses?
3. Does each child follow directions and wait her turn to go along the tool trail?

Mary Murray, Mazomanie, WI

Teacher-to-Teacher Tip
For extra fun, have four wrenches available for this activity. Invite children to carry two wrenches, one in each hand, as they cross the tool trail (for balance). Encourage them to pass the wrenches to the next person in line when they reach the other side.

Big, Bigger, Biggest!

AGES **4+**

Learning Objectives

Children will:
1. Identify items using the terms *big*, *bigger*, and *biggest*.
2. Build with blocks to improve fine motor skills.

Vocabulary

big	build	small
bigger	compare	
biggest	size	

Children's Books

Building a House by Byron Barton
From Cement to Bridge by Robin Nelson
How It Happens at the Building Site by Jenna Anderson

Materials

building blocks
pictures of a birdhouse, a doghouse, a house, and an apartment building

What to Do

1. Explain to the class that people can build things of different sizes. Show pictures of a birdhouse, a doghouse, a house, and an apartment building.
2. Ask children to think of other things that people can build. Allow children to share what it would be like to build one of the items pictured, and ask them to guess what materials they might use to build the item.
3. Invite children to use the blocks to build a small birdhouse, a bigger doghouse, an even bigger house, and then the biggest of all, an apartment building. Have children tell about the four buildings when they are finished.

Assessment

1. Can the child use words to compare the size of the buildings?
2. Can the child tell you how she built her structures?
3. Can the child count the number of blocks used to build the structure?

Mary Murray, Mazomanie, WI

Blueprints

AGES 4+

Learning Objectives

Children will:

1. Role-play being a builder.
2. Express creativity through gross motor skills.
3. Identify numbers.
4. Expand knowledge of planning and technical drawings that builders use.

Vocabulary

blue	draw	white
blueprint pape	house plan	

Children's Books

Houses and Homes by Ann Morris
How a House Is Built by Gail Gibbons

Materials

a real blueprint of any technical drawing
blue copy paper or art paper
hard hat
rubber bands
white crayons, chalk, or white colored pencils

What to Do

1. Display the blueprint, and explain to the children how it is used to help builders and architects have a detailed plan for what they are building. Highlight various interesting points (including numbers) on the blueprint.
2. Ask children to identify what kind of building is planned out on the blueprint.
3. Place hard hats, blue paper, rulers, and chalk or white crayons in the block center.
4. Invite children to create a blueprint for something that they will build in the block area during center time. Once the project is completed, take a picture of the blueprint and the child's construction project.

Assessment

1. Is each child able to create a simple technical drawing?
2. Does each child recognize numbers on the blueprint?
3. Can each child describe and explain his blueprint?

Mary Murray, Mazomanie, WI

Teacher-to-Teacher Tip

Invite a local builder or architect to come in and demonstrate to the class how a blueprint is used in the building process.

Good Morning, Builder!

AGES
4+

Learning Objectives
Children will:
1. Demonstrate higher-level thinking skills by creating structures with a limited number of blocks.
2. Practice counting skills by counting blocks as they build structures.

Vocabulary

| apron | builder | number |
| blocks | hard hat | tool belt |

Children's Books
The Construction Alphabet Book by Jerry Pallotta
One Big Building by Michael Dahl

Materials
builder's apron or tool belt with tools
hard hat
number cards from 1 through 10
set of blocks

What to Do
1. Place the materials in the block center. During center time, children can put on the hard hat and apron or tool belt and use the number cards to build with the blocks.
2. As the child turns over a number card, ask him to identify the number and then count the same number of blocks.
3. Once the blocks have been counted, ask the children to make something using that number of blocks. Encourage the children to count verbally as they place each block in the structure.

Assessment
1. Can the child identify the numbers on the cards?
2. Can the child count the correct number of blocks?

Mary Murray, Mazomanie, WI

Home Improvement Building Store

AGES **4+**

Learning Objectives
Children will:

1. Expand their vocabularies.
2. Improve math skills, such as number recognition and counting.
3. Develop social skills through dramatic play.
4. Identify various tools and building materials.

Vocabulary

build	machines	store
buy	sale	supplies
cash register	shop	tools

Children's Books
Building a House by Byron Barton
The Tool Book by Gail Gibbons

Materials
2 aprons
2 name tags
building and construction catalogs or store flyers
cash register
objects for building and construction, including pieces of lumber or wood
pictures of objects for building and construction
play money
price tags
shopping bags
store sign that reads "Building Supply Store"

Preparation
- Use the materials to set up a home improvement or building supply store in your dramatic play area.
- Display the sign and the selection of materials and supplies in the store. Be sure to include some pieces of lumber or wood.

What to Do
1. Invite children to role-play at the building supply store you have set up. Invite one child to wear the apron and name tag, and pretend to work at the store helping customers. Allow another child to wear an apron and name tag, and work at the cash register.
2. Invite other children to be customers who shop at the store and ask the workers for help finding specific items for building and construction.
3. Encourage the children to have questions for the workers at the store, such as, "What would I need to build a garage?" or "How much wood do I need to build a fence for my dog?" or "Can you show me where the tools are located?" and so on.
4. Allow children to take turns role-playing the workers and customers.

Assessment
1. Does each child interact well with her peers?
2. Does the child discuss prices, sales, measurements of materials, and money?

Mary Murray, Mazomanie, WI

Teacher-to-Teacher Tip
If you make the store elaborate, keep this activity simple. Invite parent helpers to set up the store for you.

BUILDING and CONSTRUCTION

How Many Scoops?

Learning Objectives
Children will:
1. Improve math skills, such as counting.
2. Develop oral language skills.

Vocabulary
count   sand
dump   scoops
estimation   truck
number

Children's Books
The Construction Alphabet Book by Jerry Pallotta
Good Night, Good Night, Construction Site by Sherry Duskey Rinker
A Year at the Construction Site by Nicholas Harris

Materials
2 toy dump trucks
plastic scoops of varying sizes
sand

What to Do
1. Invite the child to select a dump truck and a scoop. Allow the child to drive the dump truck around in the sand.
2. Ask the child to think about how many scoops of sand it might take to fill her truck. Tell her this is called *estimation.*
3. Invite the child to scoop sand and pour it into the dump truck as she counts the scoops. Have the child fill the dump truck until the sand begins to run over the sides. Was her estimation correct?
4. Allow the child to drive the truck a short distance and dump out the sand. Invite the child to repeat the activity using either a different-sized scoop or a different truck.

Assessment
1. Can the child manipulate the dump truck?
2. Can the child predict or estimate how many scoops of sand it will take to fill the truck?
3. Can the child count the scoops of sand as she refills the dump truck with sand?
4. Can the child explain why it might take more scoops of sand to fill the truck if the scoop is smaller?

Mary Murray, Mazomanie, WI

Another Encyclopedia of Theme Activities

In the Yellow City

Learning Objectives
Children will:
1. Improve fine motor skills through building.
2. Develop observation skills.

Vocabulary
block   build   yellow

Children's Books
Block City by Robert Louis Stevenson
The Tool Book by Gail Gibbons
Whose Hat Is This? by Sharon Katz Cooper

Materials
yellow blocks
yellow 1" cubes
yellow strips of paper roads
yellow toy blocks, cars, and trucks

Preparation
Teach the children the song, "I See Yellow."

"I See Yellow"
(Sung to the tune of "Twinkle, Twinkle, Little Star")

I see yellow all around
in the sky and on the ground.
I see yellow in the air.
I see yellow everywhere.
I see yellow all around
in the sky and on the ground.

What to Do
1. Invite children to use the yellow blocks, cubes, and paper roads to build a yellow city including houses, buildings, roadways, and more.
2. Have children manipulate the yellow cars and trucks along the roads as they talk about the people and places in the yellow city.
3. Invite them to sing the song you taught them as they play.

Assessment
Can the child locate and identify objects of a specific color?

Mary Murray, Mazomanie, WI

yellow blocks

yellow strips of paper

yellow car

Build a Zoo

AGES 5+

Learning Objectives
Children will:
1. Develop analytical thinking skills.
2. Improve oral language skills.

Vocabulary
animal   cage   zookeeper
blocks   fence
build   zoo

Children's Books
1, 2, 3 to the Zoo by Eric Carle
I Am a Zookeeper by Cynthia Benjamin
My Visit to the Zoo by Aliki

Materials
4–5 beanbag animals or plastic toy animals
building blocks
canning-jar rings
chenille craft stems (also called pipe cleaners)
recyclable building materials such as paper
    cups, cereal boxes, and so on
several blue pond-shaped pieces of paper
    (approximately 6" x 6")
small cardboard boxes and pieces of
    card stock
small pieces of wood
yarn

What to Do
1. Read a book about zoos to the children, and discuss the children's experiences visiting zoos. If children have not been to the zoo, provide pictures of zoos.
2. Invite the children to use the blocks and other materials to create a zoo. Encourage children to display the ponds, create walking paths, build cages or structures for the zoo animals, and so on.
3. Invite children to manipulate the toy animals in the zoo setting and verbalize as they build, explore, and play.

Fingerplays, Songs, and Poems
Recite this fun poem for the children as they work at building a zoo.

At the Zoo
At the zoo there's lots of fun.
Watch the animals play and run.
Watch the animals sleep and eat.
I think tigers are really neat.
Lions, turtles, rhinos, too,
Sea lions, bears, and cockatoo.
Elephants, hippos, and lots of cats,
At my zoo is where it's at!

Teacher-to-Teacher Tip
For extra fun, invite children to use other building toys as they create a zoo. Plan a zoo field trip or invite a local zookeeper to visit the classroom.

Assessment
1. Can each child put materials together to build a zoo?
2. Does each child use her new vocabulary as she builds?

Mary Murray, Mazomanie, WI

Celebrate with a Winter Picnic!

AGES 4+

Learning Objectives
Children will:
1. Learn the importance of ordinary days as well as holidays.
2. Use creative thought and imagination to plan a winter picnic.

Vocabulary
celebrate moments
celebration
ordinary
winter

Children's Books
It's Winter! by Linda Glaser
Picnic by Emily Arnold McCully
Picnic! A Day in the Park by Joan Holub
Piglet's Picnic: A Book about Food and Counting by Jessica Souhami
When Winter Comes by Nancy Van Laan
Winter by Nuria Roca
Winter Wonderland by Jull Esbaum

Materials
chart paper and marker
food (picnic or finger food)
It's Winter! by Linda Glaser, or another book about winter
tablecloth
We're Going on a Picnic! by Pat Hutchins, or another book about picnics

What to Do
1. Discuss the topic of picnics with children. Read *We're Going on a Picnic!* by Pat Hutchins (or another book about picnics) to the children.
2. Ask the children to share ideas about picnics and create a list of the items you need to have one.
3. Read a book about winter to the children, such as *It's Winter!* by Linda Glaser. Tell the children that they will be having a winter picnic!
4. Explain that a winter picnic takes place inside. Spread a tablecloth on the floor or table, and encourage the children to imagine they are outside by talking about what they see and hear.
5. Supply finger food, allow the children to eat their lunches, or ask them to bring something from home to share during their winter picnic.

Assessment
1. Did each child learn that it does not have to be summer to enjoy a picnic?
2. Did each child use descriptive words and phrases when describing a picnic?
3. Was each child able to use his imagination to create a winter picnic scene?

Donna Alice Patton, Hillsboro, OH

CELEBRATIONS

The Dragon

AGES
4+

Learning Objectives
Children will:
1. Develop gross motor skills through music and movement.
2. Learn about a celebration from another culture.

Vocabulary

celebration	dragon	symbol
Chinese New Year	nobility	wealth
	power	

Children's Books
Bringing in the New Year by Grace Lin
D Is for Dancing Dragon by Carol Crane
Dragon Dance by Joan Holub
Lanterns and Firecrackers: A Chinese New Year Story by Jonny Zucker
My First Chinese New Year by Karen Katz
The Pet Dragon: A Story about Adventure, Friendship, and Chinese Characters by Christoph Niemann

Materials
art materials, such as markers, crayons, paint, and paintbrushes
card stock
green plastic tablecloth
scissors
yarn

Preparation

- Use card stock and art materials to draw and decorate a dragon head mask. Let the children in your class help you to the extent they are able, given the ages and abilities of the children.
- Add yarn on each side of the mask to tie the mask on a child's face.
Note: Be sure the eyeholes in the mask are large enough so the child can see clearly while wearing the mask.

What to Do
1. Read one or more books about the Chinese New Year, and then talk with the children about how a dragon is part of that celebration.
2. Invite several children (no more than six at a time) to become a dragon.
3. Put the mask on the first child. The remaining children line up putting their hands on the shoulders of the child in front of them.
4. Place the green tablecloth on top of the children and encourage them to move carefully about the classroom like a dragon.

Assessment
1. Can the child walk with the other children as part of the dragon?
2. What did the child learn about the Chinese New Year?
3. Did the child work cooperatively with her peers while acting like the dragon?

LuAnn Carrig, Falls Church, VA

Teacher-to-Teacher Tip
If the children get really good at moving around like a dragon, they can participate in a Chinese New Year parade in the school hallways in celebration of the Chinese New Year!

Chinese Lanterns

AGES 5+

Learning Objectives

Children will:

1. Express their individual creativity.
2. Develop and improve their fine motor skills.
3. Learn about another culture.

Vocabulary

celebrate	festival	moon
China	fireworks	New Year
Chinese	holiday	parade
dancing	lantern	party
fair	light	

Children's Books

Bringing in the New Year by Grace Lin
Celebrating the Lantern Festival by Sanmu Tang
Lanterns and Firecrackers: A Chinese New Year Story by Jonny Zucker
Lin Yi's Lantern by Brenda Williams

Materials

felt pens or crayons (optional)
paper or thin card stock (letter size)
pencils
rulers
scissors
sticky tape or glue sticks

Preparation

- Cut a 1" strip from one of the short edges of a piece of paper or thin card stock, and set aside. Fold the remaining paper in half lengthwise.
- Mark lines 1" from each of the short ends and 1½" from the long edge.
- Inside the lines you've just drawn, mark more lines, this time in red, ¾" apart, going from the folded edge down to the long horizontal line.
- Hand a folded, marked piece of paper, plus a 1" strip, to each child.

What to Do

1. The children can decorate their lanterns with felt pens or crayons.
2. Help the children make the lanterns by doing the following steps:
   - Cut along the red lines, starting at the folded edge and stopping at the horizontal line.
   - Cut through both layers of paper.

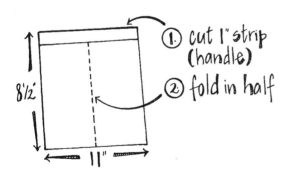

① cut 1" strip (handle)
② fold in half
8½"
11"

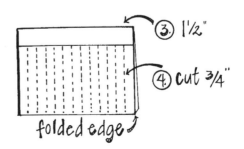

③ 1½"
④ cut ¾"
folded edge

CELEBRATIONS

- Open the paper and curve it around so the short edges slightly overlap. Stick them together with tape or glue to form a lantern.
- Take the extra paper strip and tape or glue the ends to the inside top edge of the lantern on opposite sides, forming a handle.

Assessment

1. Was the child able to follow the directions to make the lantern?
2. What did the child learn about the Chinese New Year?
3. How did the child express his individuality with his lantern?

Kirsty Neale, Orpington, Kent, UK

Teacher-to-Teacher Tip
Share these fun facts with the children: Spring Festival, also known as the Chinese New Year, always starts on the day of a new moon. The festival ends with Lantern Festival on the fifteenth day of the month when the moon is full. Lantern Festival has been celebrated for more than 2,000 years, and people gather with their lanterns at fairs and festivals, where there are fireworks, dancing, special holiday food, and a parade.

Countdown to the Big Day

AGES 5+

Learning Objectives
Children will:

1. Learn how to count down to a big event or special day.
2. Improve fine motor skills by creating a paper chain.

Vocabulary
celebration
countdown

Children's Books
A Birthday for Frances by Russell Hoban
Curious George and the Birthday Surprise by Margret Rey and H. A. Rey
Happy Birthday to You! by Dr. Seuss
Lilly's Big Day by Kevin Henkes
Moira's Birthday by Robert Munsch
Some Birthday! by Patricia Polacco

Materials

bell pattern
construction paper in colors associated with the chosen "big day"
glitter
glue
pencils or markers
scissors
stapler

Preparation

Precut bell shapes and cut the appropriate color(s) of construction paper into 1" x 6" strips.

What to Do

1. Give each child construction paper strips in the color or colors associated with the upcoming special day or holiday. (For example, use red, white, and blue strips for Independence Day in the United States, and pink and red strips for Valentine's Day.)
2. Give each child a precut bell.
3. Encourage the children to decorate the bell using glitter and markers.
4. Tell the children that they are going to make a paper chain that has the same number of loops as there are days until the selected special day, such as Independence Day or Valentine's Day. Show the children how to loop the strips of paper through each previous loop.
5. The children can glue the loops as they link them. Tell them to count to 10 while holding the loop for the glue to dry (you can also use a stapler to speed the process).
6. Help the children attach the chain to the bottom of the bell. For the younger children, create this countdown project when there are less than 10 days until the celebration.
7. Each day the children use their paper chains to count down the days until the big day!

bell pattern

Assessment

1. Does the child understand the concept of counting how many days are left until the big event?
2. Does creating a paper chain improve the child's fine motor skills?

Sandy L. Scott, Meridian, ID

bell

chains

CELEBRATIONS

Happy Chinese New Year!

AGES 5+

Learning objectives
Children will:
1. Learn about the Chinese New Year.
2. Learn how to locate places on a globe.

Vocabulary
China
New Year

Children's Books
Bringing in the New Year by Grace Lin
D Is for Dancing Dragon by Carol Crane
Dragon Dance by Joan Holub
Lanterns and Firecrackers: A Chinese New Year Story by Jonny Zucker
My First Chinese New Year by Karen Katz

Materials
books about the Chinese New Year
chopsticks
forks
globe
paper cups
ramen noodles, rice noodles, or another Chinese noodle (enough for each child to have a small cup)

Preparation
Prepare noodles for the class to snack on while you do this activity.

What to Do
1. Show the globe to the children, and help them locate China.
2. Explain that some countries use a different calendar and celebrate the Chinese New Year, also called Lunar New Year.
3. Read a book about celebrating the Chinese New Year.
4. Encourage the children to share examples of how their families celebrate the New Year.
5. If you are able, cook some ramen noodles in class, or prepare lo mein noodles ahead of time. Give each child a small cup of noodles to taste. Explain that in China, noodles mean long life.

Assessment
1. What did the child learn about the Chinese New Year?
2. Is the child able to locate China on the globe?

Tina Cho, Newton, IA

> **Teacher-to-Teacher Tip**
> Invite parents who normally celebrate this holiday to explain to the children how they celebrate the Chinese New Year.

My Celebration Candle

AGES 5+

Learning objectives
Children will:
1. Learn about the importance of light in celebrations.
2. Develop fine motor skills.
3. Follow directions to make a candle.

Vocabulary
celebrate   joy
festival   light

Children's Books
Festival of Lights: The Story of Hanukkah by Maida Silverman
Happy Birthday, Little Pookie by Sandra Boynton
Happy Birthday Moon by Frank Asch
Holidays around the World: Celebrate Kwanzaa by Carolyn Otto
Just Like Jasper by Nick Butterworth
Lighting a Lamp: A Diwali Story by Jonny Zucker

Materials
glitter
glue
paintbrushes
plain white candles, one for every child
sand
tray

Preparation
- Ask every child to bring a photograph that was taken on their birthday (if they celebrate birthdays).
- Post the birthday photos on the classroom wall.
- Mix the sand with glitter and place it in a tray.

What to Do
1. Talk about how lights play an important role on special occasions like birthdays and festivals (Kwanzaa, Christmas, Hannukah, Diwali, and so on) around the globe.
2. Let the children look at the photographs on the classroom wall, and tell them that they will be able to make their own colorful candle using the following directions:
   - Use a paintbrush to cover the entire candle with glue.
   - Hold the candle at both ends with your index fingers.
   - Place the candle on the tray and quickly roll the candle in the sand and glitter mixture.
   - Grab the wick of the candle and turn the candle upright.
   - Tap the candle a few times to remove extra sand and glitter.
   - Let the candle dry.
3. After the candle has dried, let the children take their candles home.

Assessment
1. What did the child learn about how lights are used in different celebrations?
2. How well did the activity develop the child's fine motor skills?
3. Was the child able to follow directions to make a candle?

Shyamala Shanmugasundaram,
Annanagar East, Chennai, India

Teacher-to-Teacher Tip
Include extra craft materials, such as jewels and buttons, for the children to use to decorate their candles.

CELEBRATIONS

At the Beach

AGES
4+

Learning Objectives
Children will:
1. Develop role-playing skills.
2. Improve oral language skills.
3. Identify objects by color.

Vocabulary
beach	blanket	seashells
beach ball	pail	
beach towel	sand	

Children's Books
Into the Sea by Brenda Z. Guiberson
The Ocean Alphabet Book by Jerry Pallotta
The Seashore Book by Charlotte Zolotow

Materials
beach bag
beach blanket
colorful beach umbrella
other colorful beach items (for example: sunglasses, sun hat, bottle of suntan lotion, sand pail and shovel, water bottle, seashells, water toys, inflated floating ring, and so on)

Preparation
Display the beach blanket, beach ball, and opened beach umbrella. Fill the beach bag with the remaining colored beach items.

What to Do
1. Invite one or two children to sit beneath the umbrella on the beach towel. Encourage them to name the colors on the towel and the umbrella.
2. Invite the children to peek inside the beach bag. Ask them to remove the items one by one. As children remove an item from the bag, have them name the object, describe how it is used, and name its color.
3. Leave the materials for children to use during center time.

Assessment
1. Can the child name the objects?
2. Can the child identify the colors of each object?
3. Can the child describe how each object is used?

Mary Murray, Mazomanie, WI

Teacher-to-Teacher Tip
Attach a word card to each item. Invite children to match the word cards to the correct objects while role-playing at the beach. Provide paper and writing utensils and let children "write" the words.

Basket of Balls

Learning Objectives
Children will:
1. Improve gross motor skills.
2. Enhance color recognition skills.
3. Develop social skills.

Vocabulary
ball	colors	toss
basket	miss	

Children's Books
Color Farm by Lois Ehlert
Dog's Colorful Day by Emma Dodd
Round Like a Ball by Lisa Campbell Ernst

What to Do
1. Have six to ten children gather around the designated space.
2. Invite the children to stand up as you spill out the basket of colorful balls. Have the children pick up one ball at a time, name the color, and then toss it into the basket.
3. Advise the children to stay on the outer edge of the designated area when they toss the ball.
4. Encourage the children to be mindful of those around them as they pick up stray balls and make sure that everyone gets a turn.
5. Have the children toss balls until the basket is full.

Assessment
1. Can the child correctly identify the color of the ball she is tossing?
2. Can the child work together with his peers?
3. Is the activity helping the child develop her gross motor skills?

Mary Murray, Mazomanie, WI

Materials
colored plastic or foam balls of varying sizes (enough to fill the laundry basket)
laundry basket
tape

Preparation
- Use masking tape to designate a space on the floor.
- Place the laundry basket in the middle of the space. Fill the basket with the balls.

different color balls
basket
blanket

Teacher-to-Teacher Tip
For added fun, display the balls randomly around the room. Invite the children to pull a toy wagon around the room and collect all of the balls.

Birdbath

Learning Objectives
Children will:
1. Identify colors.
2. Develop and improve oral language skills.

Vocabulary

bird	fly
birdseed	land
drink	perch
dry	splash
eat	swim
float	wet

Children's Books
Birds by Kevin Henkes
Birds, Nests, and Eggs by Mel Boring
Purple Little Bird by Greg Foley

Materials
hand towels
plastic toy birds in various colors
round, shallow tray of water or water table

Preparation
Purchase an inexpensive bag of plastic toy birds at your local department store, nature store, toy store, or the souvenir shop at your local zoo.

What to Do
1. Display the toy birds and the shallow tray of water on a table or in the water table.
2. Ask the children to identify each bird by its color.
3. After the children have identified each bird, ask them to "fly" the birds to the water for a birdbath.
4. Encourage the children to talk about the birds as they give the birds a bath.
5. Allow the children to use a towel to dry off each bird after its bath.

Assessment
1. Can the child identify the colors of the birds?
2. Can the child correctly describe the birds that he plays with?

Mary Murray, Mazomanie, WI

Bird Watching

Learning Objectives
Children will:
1. Identify colors.
2. Develop math skills, such as sorting.

Vocabulary
bird   cardinal   goldfinch
blue jay   colors

Children's Books
Birds by Kevin Henkes
Birds, Nests, and Eggs by Mel Boring
Purple Little Bird by Greg Foley

Materials
binoculars (teacher-made or real)
bird stickers (optional)
glue or tape (optional)
paper towel tube, cut in half (optional)
pictures of different colored birds
string or yarn (optional)

Preparation
- Display the colorful bird pictures randomly around the room.
- If you like, make a pair of binoculars by cutting a paper towel tube in half, gluing or taping two halves together, and adding a string handle. Decorate the binoculars with bird stickers or other art supplies.

What to Do
1. Invite one child to look through the binoculars and move around the room searching for colorful birds.
2. Each time the child spots a bird, she names the color of the bird.
3. After a child finds all of the birds, have her hand the binoculars to another child. Allow time for several children to go on a bird search by themselves.

Assessment
1. Can the child locate the birds in the classroom?
2. Can the child name the colors?

Mary Murray, Mazomanie, WI

Color Box

Learning Objectives
Children will:
1. Develop color recognition skills.
2. Improve oral language skills by describing objects to their peers.

Vocabulary
box
color
see

Children's Books
Color Dance by Ann Jonas
Color Farm by Lois Ehlert

Materials
10 different colored objects
chair
colorful photo or gift box

What to Do
1. Work with one child.
2. One child sits in the chair with the box on her lap.
3. Encourage the child to remove each object from the box, one by one, and describe the item, including its color, as she looks at it in her hand.
4. The child sets the object on the floor, removes another object, and repeats the activity.
5. Once all the items have been removed, the child places them back inside the colorful box.

Assessment
1. Can the child name the colors of the objects she removes from the box?
2. Does the activity help the child develop her oral language skills?

Mary Murray, Mazomanie, WI

Preparation
Place the colored objects inside the box. Set the box near a chair.

Color Commotion

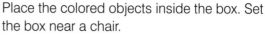

AGES
4+

Learning Objectives
Children will:
1. Develop color recognition skills of the basic colors: black, white, brown, red, orange, yellow, green, blue, purple.
2. Improve gross motor skills.

Vocabulary
color names: *red, orange, yellow, green, blue, purple, brown, white, black*
jump
leap

Children's Books
All the Colors of the Earth by Sheila Hamanaka
Food for Thought by Saxton Freymann and Joost Elffers
My Many Colored Days by Dr. Seuss
Planting a Rainbow by Lois Ehlert

Materials
9 sheets of colored construction paper, one of each basic color

What to Do

1. Invite nine volunteers to come forward and curl up into tight balls on the floor in a row in front of the class. Leave 3'–4' of space between children.
2. Display one colored sheet of paper behind each child, near his feet. Invite the rest of the classmates to leapfrog over each child on the floor and name each color as they leap. (Children place their hands on the back of the child, spread their legs and leap over the child from back to front.)
3. Allow all children to have an opportunity to leap over the children and name the colors.

Assessment

1. Can the child identify the colors of the paper?
2. Does the child have the gross motor skills to leap over his classmates?

Mary Murray, Mazomanie, WI

Go with Green

AGES 4+

Learning Objectives

Children will:
1. Identify specific colors.
2. Develop oral language skills.

Vocabulary

circle   green   hop

Children's Books

The Black Book of Colors by Menena Cottin
Brown Bear, Brown Bear, What Do You See? by
    Bill Martin, Jr.
A Color of His Own by Leo Lionni
Grandpa Green by Lane Smith

Materials

green copy paper, one piece per child
green paper circles
green stuffed animals or beanbag toys
    (optional)
tape

Preparation

Tape a few of the paper circles on the floor around the classroom prior to this activity.

What to Do

1. Introduce the color green as you hand each child a green paper circle and a green piece of copy paper.
2. Begin the activity by hopping from one green circle to another. Hold the green circle high in the air as you move about.
3. As you move around the classroom, keep an eye out for green items. Once you spot an item that is green, set the green paper circle on or near the item and recite the sentence, "Green is the color of _____" (name the green item).
4. After finishing your demonstration, invite the children to get up and move around the room in the same manner by saying, "Go green!"

5. Allow some time for the children to find green items around the classroom. Once the room is relatively quiet, call out, "Go green!" again. Continue the activity until children have found three or more green items.

Assessment

1. Can the child hop from color to color?

2. Did the child find green items and correctly identify them?

Mary Murray, Mazomanie, WI

Mellow Yellow

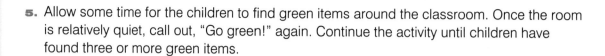

AGES **4+**

Learning Objectives

Children will:

1. Identify specific colors.

2. Improve gross motor skills.

Vocabulary

banana
crayon
lemon
marker
sort
yellow

Children's Books

Is it Red? Is it Yellow? Is it Blue? by Tana Hoban
Little Blue and Little Yellow by Leo Lionni
Red Leaf, Yellow Leaf by Lois Ehlert

Materials

children's slide (or create a ramp using blocks and a book)
collection of colored objects that are *not* yellow
pairs of yellow objects that go together, such as lemon and banana, yellow shirt and shorts, yellow baseball cap and hat, and so on

What to Do

1. Give each child a yellow object and ask her to line up near the ladder of the slide. When a child is positioned at the top of the slide, have the child complete this sentence frame before going down the slide: "I have a yellow____ in my hand."

2. After each child has gone down the slide, have the class sit in a circle. Recite the following: "Mellow yellow, mellow yellow, find a special friend."

3. Suggest to the children that they look for a partner—their partners should be holding objects that go together with their own, for example, banana and lemon, shirt and shorts, crayon and marker, and so on.)

4. Once all pairs are seated together, ask the pairs of children to tell how their yellow objects go together.

banana   lemon   sunflower

Assessment

1. Can the child identify yellow objects?
2. Can the child determine how objects go together?
3. Are the child's gross motor skills improving?

Mary Murray, Mazomanie, WI

Peekaboo

AGES 4+

Learning Objectives
Children will:
1. Identify various colors.
2. Follow directions.
3. Develop critical thinking skills.

Vocabulary
color
cover
group
peek
uncover

Children's Books
Color Dance by Ann Jonas
A Color of His Own by Leo Lionni
Color Zoo by Lois Ehlert

Materials
8 colors of 8" x 11" fabric
8 like-colored objects that are similar, such as toys, foods, or animals

Preparation
Place each item on the table. Cover each item with a piece of matching colored fabric.

What to Do
1. Invite individual children or small groups of children to play this peekaboo game.
2. Ask the children to come to the table, peek under each colored fabric, and then cover the object back up.
3. As the children peek at each item, help them to identify each object and its color.
4. After the children peek at all eight objects, encourage them to think of a name for the group of like objects (all toys, all animals, all foods).
5. Each day while the children are learning about colors, set a different category of objects beneath the colored fabric squares.

covering with a red cloth

apple

Assessment

1. Can the child name the objects and their colors?
2. Is the child developing the thinking skills necessary to classify the objects into one category?
3. Is the child able to understand and follow the directions?

Mary Murray, Mazomanie, WI

Pom-Pom Pass

AGES 4+

Learning Objectives

Children will:

1. Identify colors and color words.
2. Develop and improve oral language skills.

Vocabulary

cheer	pass	turn
colors	pom-pom	wait

Children's Books

Is it Red? Is it Yellow? Is it Blue? by Tana Hoban
One Fish, Two Fish, Red Fish, Blue Fish by Dr. Seuss
Purple, Green, and Yellow by Robert N. Munsch

Materials

color chart
music
scissors
tape
tissue paper

Preparation

Make a tissue paper pom-pom by stacking six colors of 12" x 12" tissue paper squares on top of each other. Make a 6" cut every inch or so, down the length of the stack of tissue paper, cutting all six pieces at one time. Roll up the stack, keeping the sheets together, and then tape the rolled portion into a handle. Gently fluff and separate the cut pieces to create a pom-pom effect.

What to Do

1. Have children sit in a circle, and display the color chart for them to see.
2. Play or sing a favorite color song as the children pass the pom-pom around the circle.
3. When the music stops, the child holding the pom-pom stands up and says his favorite color that is in the pom-pom.
4. Ask the child holding the pom-pom to point to another color on the color chart, and then point to the same color in the pom-pom. Identify the color that the child is pointing at.
5. Ask the child holding the pom-pom to pass it to a person across the circle, and repeat the activity.

Assessment

Can the child name the colors on the chart or in the pom-pom?

Mary Murray, Mazomanie, WI

Color Me Rainbow

AGES 5+

Learning Objectives

Children will:

1. Improve color recognition by using articles of clothing.
2. Improve oral language skills by describing the clothes that they are wearing.

Vocabulary

belt
boots
gloves
hat
shirt
shoes
socks

Children's Books

Animals Should Definitely Not Wear Clothing by Judi Barrett
Ella Sarah Gets Dressed by Margaret Chodos-Irvine
Naked Mole Rat Gets Dressed by Mo Willems

Materials

unbreakable, full-length mirror
various colors of clothing items

Preparation

Create a colorful dress-up corner activity by displaying the assorted clothing items on hooks or hangers, or by storing them in a basket near the full-length mirror.

What to Do

1. Invite the children to dress up in the colorful clothing. Suggest that they place a different color item on each part of their body.
2. Once the children have covered themselves with color, invite them to stand before the mirror. Encourage each child to look at himself in the mirror and tell about the colors of clothing he sees, as the child completes this sentence: "I'm wearing a _____ _____."
(Ask the children to name the color and the clothing item each time they recite a sentence, for example, red belt, blue hat, pink shirt, green shoes, and so on.)

Assessment

1. Does the child wear a different color on each part of her body?
2. Can the child name the articles of clothing and the colors of the clothing that she is wearing?

Mary Murray, Mazomanie, WI

Teacher-to-Teacher Tip

To expand the activity, invite three or more children to have a color fashion show for the class. Invite various children to name the colors and articles of clothing the three children are modeling.

Color Walk

AGES 5+

Learning Objectives
Children will:
1. Identify colors in nature.
2. Develop vocabulary and oral language skills.

Children's Books
The Deep Blue Sea: A Book of Colors by Audrey Wood
Red Leaf, Yellow Leaf by Lois Ehlert
What Color Is It? by Bobbie Kalman

Vocabulary

birds	nature	trees
flowers	sky	walk
insects	sun	

Materials
chart paper
digital camera
markers

What to Do
1. Take the class on an outdoor color adventure. Invite the children to follow you as you walk through an area near your school, looking for colors in nature.
2. Invite the children to comment on the colors they see. Help the children distinguish between colors in nature and man-made colors.
3. Take photographs of different colors in nature, such as a green tree, a patch of purple irises, a blue sky, and so on.
4. Make a list of the items that you see while walking or once you have returned to the classroom.
5. Print and display the photos on a special bulletin board in the classroom as a reminder of this colorful event.

Assessment
Can the child recall some of the items he saw while on the nature walk and the color of those items?

Mary Murray, Mazomanie, WI

> **Teacher-to-Teacher Tip**
> If you do not have a color printer, ask a parent volunteer to print the pictures and create the classroom photo display.

AGES 5+

Goo Pond

Learning Objectives
Children will:
1. Practice color identification skills.
2. Develop fine and gross motor skills.
3. Practice problem-solving skills.

Vocabulary

around	out
blue	pond
green	red
in	yellow

Children's Books
Color Dance by Ann Jonas
A Color of His Own by Leo Lionni
Color Zoo by Lois Ehlert
In the Small, Small Pond by Denise Fleming
Life in a Pond by Allan Fowler
Pond Circle by Stefano Vitale

Materials
beanbags (usually sold in sets of red, blue, yellow, and green)
colored tape (red, blue, yellow, green— available at stores and in catalogs)
masking tape

Preparation
- Use masking tape to outline a "pond" on one side of the room.
- Use the colored tape to outline colored squares on the opposite side of the room. Make one square for each color.

What to Do
1. Show the children the pond and tell them it is Goo Pond. Say, "Goo Pond is filled with yucky goo that we have to be very careful never to step in because if we do, we'll get stuck in the goo."
2. Show the children the beanbags. Talk about the shape and colors of the beanbags.
3. Show the children the squares marked by colored tape. Help the children recognize that the colors of the squares match the colors of the beanbags.
4. Spread the beanbags out into Goo Pond, making sure to keep them close enough to the edges so the children can reach the beanbags.
5. Say, "We have to work together to rescue the beanbags from Goo Pond before they get stuck and sink to the bottom. After we pull a beanbag from the pond, we will put it in the square that matches its color. We will place the red beanbags in the square that is red, and the yellow ones in the square that is yellow. Remember we must stay outside of Goo Pond, so do not ever let your feet go past the edge of Goo Pond."
6. Ask the children how they might get to the other side of Goo Pond if they cannot walk through it. One way to help the children reach beanbags is by holding their hands and letting them stretch to reach while you anchor them. What other ways do the children suggest?
7. Let the children rescue the beanbags.
8. If time allows, play this game again to reinforce the concepts. As the children are rescuing beanbags, have fun by helping the children pretend to be afraid of Goo Pond.

Assessment
1. What did the child learn about identifying colors?
2. Is the child developing greater control of her fine and gross motor skills by doing this activity?
3. Is the child developing problem-solving skills by doing this activity?

Melissa McKenzie, Cypress, TX

Teacher-to-Teacher Tip
Older children can help you count how many beanbags you have of each color. Compare the results: Which color had the most? the least? Were any the same? When talking about colors, remember to say, "This beanbag is red" as opposed to "This is a red beanbag" because children learn colors better if you say the object first and then the color.
(For an interesting look at this subject, see Dye, Melody. 2011. "Why Johnny Can't Name His Colors," *Scientific American Mind* May/June.)

Hop and Wave

Learning Objectives

Children will:

1. Improve gross motor skills.
2. Develop color recognition skills.
3. Take turns and cooperate with others.

Vocabulary

color	jump	streamer
hop	square	wave

Children's Books

Is it Red? Is it Yellow? Is it Blue? by Tana Hoban
Little Blue and Little Yellow by Leo Lionni
Of Colors and Things by Tana Hoban
White Rabbit's Color Book by Alan Baker

Materials

8 colors of 8" felt or paper squares (two of each color)
8 colors of 18" paper streamers or strips of fabric (two of each color)

Preparation

- Lay the colorful squares randomly about on the floor in a large open area.
- Set a streamer of the same color on top of each square.

What to Do

1. Ask the children to identify each color aloud as you lead them around the room, highlighting the various colors on the floor.
2. Demonstrate how to pick up a colorful streamer and wave it back and forth above your head. Say the color as you do so, elongating the word, like "*bblllluuuuuuuuuee*," or "*yellllooooooowwwww*."
3. Invite the children to jump or hop around the room from square to square. Each time a child comes to a square, he picks up the streamer and announces the color as directed above, waving the streamer back and forth.
4. Advise the children that only one child may be at a square at a time, so they may have to wait for a turn.
5. Encourage the children to listen to their classmates announce each elongated color word as they move around the room.
6. Allow the children to play for several minutes as they recite color words and get exercise at the same time.

Assessment

1. Can the child identify the colors correctly?
2. Is the activity helping the child develop her gross motor skills?
3. Is the child learning to take turns and cooperate with the other children?

Mary Murray, Mazomanie, WI

Teacher-to-Teacher Tip

Play the game with three or four colors if you are unable to get streamers or felt in eight different colors.

Sock Walk

Learning Objectives

Children will:

1. Develop and improve color recognition skills.
2. Match like colors.
3. Follow directions.
4. Improve gross motor skills.

Vocabulary

arms

counterclockwise

link

sock

walk

Children's Books

Animals Should Definitely Not Wear Clothing by Judi Barrett

Mouse Paint by Ellen Stoll Walsh

My Many Colored Days by Dr. Seuss

A Pair of Socks by Stuart J. Murphy

Materials

several pairs of colored socks in various colors, one pair per child

What to Do

1. If your center allows, ask the children to take off their shoes. If children are already wearing colored socks, have them display their feet and tell the colors of their socks. Hand each child a pair of socks to put on over his own.
2. Invite the children to stand up and form a very large circle. (Use a gymnasium, if possible.)
3. Define the word *counterclockwise* for the children. Ask them to walk counterclockwise and single file around the circle.
4. Invite the children to listen as you call out two colors, such as red and blue. Tell the children wearing socks with those colors to link arms together with two or three other children wearing red or blue socks and continue walking. The rest of the class continues walking alone.
5. Repeat the previous step until all the children are paired up. At any time, call out the word *rainbow*. At that time, the children will join together to form one long line by placing their hands on the shoulders or waist of the person in front of them, and will walk in unison until the next two colors are called. Play for several minutes.

Assessment

1. Can the child identify the color of his (and other children's) socks?
2. Can the child sort socks by color?
3. Can the child follow verbal directions?
4. Are the child's gross motor skills improving?

Mary Murray, Mazomanie, WI

Sounds like Fun

AGES
3+

Learning Objectives
Children will:
1. Identify objects based on sounds.
2. Learn about guessing.

Vocabulary

five senses	see	tattle
hear	smell	thud
loud	soft	touch
quiet	taste	

Children's Books
Hearing by Rebecca Rissman
Hearing by Maria Ruis, J. M. Parramon, and
    J. J. Puig
My Five Senses by Aliki
My Five Senses by Margaret Miller

Materials
basket
plastic Easter eggs
small objects to put in the plastic Easter eggs,
    such as pebbles, paper clips, cotton balls,
    keys, and other things that make distinct
    sounds

Preparation
Fill each egg with one or more of the objects,
and then place the eggs in a basket.

What to Do
1. Ask the children to sit in a circle, and then show them the eggs.
2. Tell the children that you have something very special inside the eggs but you don't quite remember what is in each egg. (Sometimes it helps if you say the items came from the classroom.) Ask, "Can you help me figure out what is in each egg just by using your ears? We can open the eggs after everyone has guessed what is in each one."
3. Pass one egg around the circle and ask the children to describe what they hear. This is a good time to introduce the concepts of *loud* and *soft* and other descriptive words.
4. After the children pass the eggs around the circle, open them. (The children might like it if you peek inside and gasp or include a little drama: "Oh, it was rocks! The rocks made a rattling noise.")
5. Pass all the eggs around so the children can see what was in each egg.
6. Close the eggs and repeat, if the children are interested. Can they remember what was in each egg and what it sounded like?

Assessment
1. Is the child able to use his sense of hearing to identify the objects in the eggs?
2. Did the child participate in the guessing part of the activity, and were her guesses correct?

Pamela Hagler, Dalton, OH

Teacher-to-Teacher Tip
If the children are very young and unable to resist opening the eggs, gently shake each egg in each child's ear.

Digging Deep

Learning Objectives
Children will:
1. Use their sense of touch.
2. Identify colors.

Vocabulary
colors	feel	touch
dig	guess	

Children's Books
Colors Everywhere by Tana Hoban
My Five Senses by Aliki
My Five Senses by Margaret Miller
Seeing by Rebecca Rissman
Sight by Maria Ruis, J. M. Parramon, and
   J. J. Puig
Touch by Maria Ruis, J. M. Parramon, and
   J. J. Puig
Touching by Rebecca Rissman
White on Black by Tana Hoban

Materials
10 objects of varying color, texture, and weight
large cardboard box, such as a copy
   paper box
shredded white paper

Preparation
Place heavy objects in the bottom of the empty box. Add shredded paper to cover the objects. Place lightweight objects on the shredded paper, and then cover with more shredded paper.

What to Do
1. Invite the children to take turns digging through the shredded paper to search for objects.
2. When a child finds each object, he removes it from the box, displays it on the table or floor, and names its color.
3. Encourage the child to talk about the texture, color, and weight of each item.
4. After the child finds all ten items, he places them back in the box so the next child can dig for colors.

Assessment
1. How well is the child able to use his sense of touch to find the objects in the box?
2. Is the child able to identify the colors of the objects?

Mary Murray, Mazomanie, WI

Teacher-to-Teacher Tip
Listen as individual children talk about the texture, weight, and color of the objects. Ask a child to dig for a red item, a blue item, and so on. Observe their ability to follow directions to find a specific color.

Finding Tiny Animals

AGES
4+

Learning Objectives
Children will:
1. Develop fine motor skills.
2. Learn language skills.

Vocabulary

empty	lid	twist
feel	open	
jar	touch	

Children's Books
Animals: A Visual Encyclopedia by
    DK Publishing
First Animal Encyclopedia by DK Publishing
Hearing by Rebecca Rissman
Hearing by Maria Ruis, J. M. Parramon, and
    J. J. Puig
My Five Senses by Aliki
My Five Senses by Margaret Miller
Seeing by Rebecca Rissman
Sight by Maria Ruis, J. M. Parramon, and
    J. J. Puig
Smell by Maria Ruis, J. M. Parramon, and
    J. J. Puig
Smelling by Rebecca Rissman
Touch by Maria Ruis, J. M. Parramon, and
    J. J. Puig
Touching by Rebecca Rissman

Materials
6 small toy animals (1"–2" in size)
6 empty, clean, plastic jars with lids
6 types of material to fill the jars, such as
    cotton balls, sand, shredded paper,
    crumpled newsprint or tissue paper, curling
    ribbon (curled), seashells, paper punches,
    confetti, grass seed, and so on

Preparation
Fill each jar half full with one type of
material. Place a small toy animal inside
each jar, and then fill the jars to the top with
the remaining material.

What to Do
1. Display the six jars at the sensory table. Invite the children to select a jar and remove its lid.
2. Ask the child to feel the material in each jar and to describe what the material feels like.
   Encourage the child to search for the animal in each jar.
3. Once the child discovers the animal, ask
   her to describe the animal and name it.
4. Help the children replace the filler and the
   animal into the jar.
5. Repeat with the rest of the jars.

cotton balls

Assessment

1. Are the child's fine motor skills improving?
2. What language skills is the child learning as she describes each material in the jar and the animal found in each jar?

Mary Murray, Mazomanie, WI

Guess a Pet

AGES 4+

Learning Objectives

Children will:
1. Use their sense of touch.
2. Develop their language skills.

Vocabulary

beak	fins	tail
ears	furry	whiskers
eyes	legs	wings
feathers	scales	
feet	soft	

Children's Books

Wanted: The Perfect Pet by Fiona Roberton
The World According to Humphrey by Betty G. Birney

Materials

5 or more beanbag pets or other toy pets
5 or more large, brown grocery bags
clothespins
scissors
tape

Preparation

- Cut two 6" holes in each bag near the bottom, so that a child can reach both hands into the bag and touch what's inside.
- Place a toy pet inside each bag; clip each bag shut with a clothespin.

What to Do

1. Invite one child or a small group of children to stand near a bag at the table.
2. Ask one child to place his hands in the holes of each bag and pick up the toy pet.
3. As the child feels the animal, encourage him to think about what he is feeling and specifically note the various body parts of the animal.
4. When the child thinks he knows the type of pet he is holding, he may unclip the top of the bag and look inside.
5. Ask the child not to show the animal to the other children or to say the name of the pet out loud.
6. Have children explore until they have touched and identified several of the pets at the table.

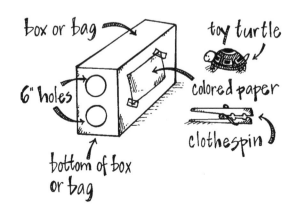

box or bag
toy turtle
6" holes
colored paper
clothespin
bottom of box or bag

7. Ask the children to describe how they figured out what they were touching. Did the animal feel furry, scaly, or feathery? Did the animal have wings or whiskers or fins?

Assessment
1. How accurate is the child's sense of touch?
2. Is this activity helping the child to develop his language skills?

Mary Murray, Mazomanie, WI

Pom-Pom Surprise

AGES 4+

Learning Objectives
Children will:
1. Use their senses.
2. Use descriptive language.

Vocabulary
big	medium-sized	small
color	pom-poms	soft
fuzzy	round	tiny

Children's Books
My Five Senses by Aliki
My Five Senses by Margaret Miller
Seeing by Rebecca Rissman
Sight by Maria Ruis, J. M. Parramon, and J. J. Puig
Touch by Maria Ruis, J. M. Parramon, and J. J. Puig
Touching by Rebecca Rissman

What to Do
1. Invite a small group of children to come to the table. Explain that they are going to use their senses to explore color and texture.
2. Tell the children to open one container at a time and peek inside.

Materials
100 or more craft pom-poms (available at craft, school supply, or department stores)
8 or more transparent containers with lids, between 2 ounces and 32 ounces in size

Preparation
Place an assortment of pom-poms inside each container. Vary the number in each container, placing only one pom-pom in one container and a large number in another and so on. Place the lid on top of each container and the containers on a table.

3. Invite the children to spill out the pom-poms in one container onto the table, and then help the children explore the pom-poms by counting and naming the colors, sorting pom-poms into color groups or by creating piles or lines of pom-poms.
   Note: If a child opens a container with just one pom-pom, she may describe it and then select a different container.
4. Encourage the children to feel the pom-poms and then to describe their texture.
5. Let the children explore all the different containers of pom-poms and put them away so they are ready for the next group of children.

Assessment
1. Is the child using her senses to note the color, shape, and textures of the pom-poms?
2. Is the child using descriptive language to describe the appearance of the pom-poms?

Mary Murray, Mazomanie, WI

> **Teacher-to-Teacher Tip**
> Use colored cotton balls, small plastic blocks, or other manipulatives instead of pom-poms.

Rockin' with Rocks

AGES 4+

Learning Objectives
Children will:
1. Use their five senses to explore rocks.
2. Compare and contrast an assortment of rocks.
3. Enhance oral language skills.

Vocabulary
big	rock
hard	small
heavy	soft
light	

Children's Books
I Am a Rock by Jean Marzollo
Rocks and Minerals by DK Publishing

Materials
assortment of rocks
decorative gift or photo box
marker
stickers

Preparation
● Hide several rocks around the classroom, one per child.
● Decorate a box and label it "Rock Box."

What to Do
1. Invite children to go on a rock hunt. Encourage them to look high and low until they find a rock to bring back to the circle.
2. Ask them to place their discoveries in your rock box.
3. Invite children to stand in a single-file line. Explain to the children that you will remove a rock from the rock box and hand a rock to the first child in line. That child will observe the rock, noting its texture, color, and any other details, and then pass it beneath his legs to the person behind him. After he passes it, give him another rock.

4. Continue the activity until all the rocks have been passed. Ask the children to help bring the rocks back to you. (Just place the "used" rocks to one side.)
5. Then invite the children to sit down. Allow time for children to share what they noticed about the rocks regarding texture, color, size, weight. How are the rocks alike? How are they different? How do they feel? hard or soft? heavy or light? What colors did they notice? How big were the rocks?

Assessment

1. Is the child able to tell you some characteristics of rocks?
2. Is the child able to use gross motor skills to pass the rocks behind him?

Mary Murray, Mazomanie, WI

Texture Obstacle Course

AGES
4+

Learning Objectives

Children will:
1. Improve their gross motor skills.
2. Describe different textures.

Vocabulary

crawl — run
jump — through
obstacle course — under
over

Children's Books

My Five Senses by Aliki
My Five Senses by Margaret Miller
Touch by Maria Ruis, J. M. Parramon, and J. J. Puig
Touching by Rebecca Rissman
What Is Texture? by Stephanie Fitzgerald

Materials

glue
materials with texture, such as sandpaper, bubble wrap, aluminum foil, fake fur, contact paper (sticky side up), bark from a tree, and so on
objects to jump over, crawl through, climb under, and so on, such as jump rope, plastic hoop, rubber tire, small table, balance beam, and so on
plastic cones
tape

Preparation

● Tape or glue textured materials to each object in the obstacle course.
● Create a simple obstacle course in the classroom or outdoors.

What to Do

1. Demonstrate how to move through the obstacle course as you show the class how to jump into the hoop, over the box, under the table, over the rope, and so on.
2. Tell the children that as they move through the obstacle course, they are to touch each texture and describe it.
3. Invite the children to move through the obstacle course, identifying each texture as they go.
4. Allow time for children to complete the course several times.

Assessment

1. Is the child improving her gross motor skills?
2. Is the child able to describe the different textures?

Mary Murray, Mazomanie, WI

Five Senses Chart

AGES 5+

Learning Objectives
Children will:
1. Identify how the senses are used.
2. Use sorting skills.

Vocabulary

hearing	smell	touch
senses	sort	
sight	taste	

Children's Books
Hearing by Rebecca Rissman
Hearing by Maria Ruis, J. M. Parramon, and J. J. Puig
My Five Senses by Aliki
My Five Senses by Margaret Miller
Seeing by Rebecca Rissman
Sight by Maria Ruis, J. M. Parramon, and J. J. Puig
Smell by Maria Ruis, J. M. Parramon, and J. J. Puig
Smelling by Rebecca Rissman
Taste by Maria Ruis, J. M. Parramon, and J. J. Puig
Tasting by Rebecca Rissman
Touch by Maria Ruis, J. M. Parramon, and J. J. Puig
Touching by Rebecca Rissman

Materials
large piece of bulletin board paper
larger images that represent each of the five senses (ear, hand, mouth, eye, nose)
markers
15–20 small pictures that can easily be associated with one or more of the five senses, such as a glass of milk, a rainbow, snow, a bell, a flower, and so on
tape

Preparation
Prepare the bulletin board paper by taping images that represent each of the five senses down the center of the page.

What to Do

1. Review information about the five senses.
2. Tell the children that the bulletin board chart they will be helping to create is about the five senses.
3. Point to each picture on the paper and ask the children which sense they think each picture represents.
4. Show the children a small picture. Describe what you are thinking as you place the small picture on the chart. For example, tape a picture of a bell to the paper, point to the large picture of an ear, and say, "Can I hear a bell? Yes, I can hear a bell." Draw a line from the bell to the ear. Repeat for each sense.
5. Give a child a picture to tape on the chart. Help the child connect the picture to the sense or senses that it can go with. Ask questions such as, "How does the kitten feel?"
6. Repeat until all pictures are on the chart.
7. Look at the chart and then ask questions such as, "Which sense did we use most often?"
8. Allow children to use the chart during center time, adding pictures from collage material.

Assessment

1. Is the child able to identify the sense associated with the object in each picture?
2. Is the child able to sort the pictures by which sense is used?

Rachael Partain, Mechanicsburg, PA

Teacher-to-Teacher Tip
Use this activity after the children have learned about each of the five senses.

Dairy Snacks

Learning Objectives
Children will:
1. Learn about milk and milk products.
2. Taste milk and milk products.

Vocabulary
butter   dairy
cheese   milk
cream   yogurt

Children's Books
Clarabelle: Making Milk and So Much More by Cris Peterson
Milk: From Cow to Carton by Aliki
Milk and Cheese by Nancy Dickman
The Milk Makers by Gail Gibbons

Materials
milk and milk products, such as yogurt, butter, cheese, cottage cheese, ice cream, and chocolate milk

What to Do
1. Before snack time, read a few books about milk and milk products (see suggestions). Talk about where these foods come from and how they are produced.
2. For snack, taste an assortment of milk products such as yogurt, butter, cheese, cottage cheese, ice cream, chocolate milk, and any other that are appropriate for the children in your class.
   Safety note: Check for allergies, food sensitivities, and cultural restrictions before serving food to children.

chocolate milk

crackers with cream cheese

cheese

spoons   yogurt

Assessment
1. What did the child learn about where milk and milk products come from?
2. Did the child like the milk and milk products served for snack?

Mary Murray, Mazomanie, WI

Teacher-to-Teacher Tip
Put plastic toys of farm animals and a toy barn in the block area for the children's play.

HEALTH and NUTRITION

Steps for Washing Hands

AGES 3+

Learning Objectives
Children will:
1. Learn the correct way to wash their hands.
2. Use a visual prop to help them follow directions.

Vocabulary

bubbles	fingers	soap
clean	germs	warm
drain	palms	waste can
dry	paper towel	water
faucet	rinse	wrists
fingernails	scrub	

Materials
card stock
pictures showing children washing their hands
computer and color printer
laminating materials or clear contact paper

Preparation
On card stock, make a poster showing children step-by-step pictures of the correct way to wash their hands. Take your own photos or use photos from the Internet. Laminate for durability.

What to Do
1. Display the poster.
2. Talk with the children about the importance of good hand washing. Point out that by doing a good job of hand washing, they will be less likely to catch colds and spread germs that cause sicknesses.
3. Demonstrate each step in the process and ask the children to follow your directions.
4. Place the poster near the sink for future reference.

Assessment
1. Is the child improving his hand-washing skills?
2. Is the child following the directions on the hand-washing poster?

Jackie Wright, Enid, OK

> **Teacher-to-Teacher Tip**
> Text and pictures for this activity can be found at www.dubuque.k12.ia.us /Prescott/Handwash/

Animal Stretch

AGES 4+

Learning Objectives
Children will:
1. Learn a new physical activity.
2. Follow verbal instructions.

Vocabulary

balance	reach
movement	stretch

Another Encyclopedia of Theme Activities

Children's Books
The ABCs of Yoga for Kids by Teresa Power
Animals in Motion by Pamela Hickman
Move! by Robin Page
The Yoga Zoo Adventure: Animal Poses and Games for Little Kids by Helen Purperhart

What to Do
1. Have the children face you in a well-spaced line.
2. Explain that moving helps us stay healthy and that stretching warms up our muscles. It makes us feel better. It is also important to do before we run and jump because it can keep us from getting hurt.
3. Ask the children if they have heard of yoga. Explain that yoga is a type of exercise that includes stretches. Some of them are named after animals because you stretch and move like that animal.
4. Ask the children how they think an eagle might stretch? a cat?
5. Have the children get on their hands and knees, toes turned under. Have them take a deep breath. As they exhale, have them raise their hips to the ceiling and straighten their knees. They will be in an upside down V. Kneel back down. What animal was this? What animal stretches its legs out, hikes up its tail, and yawns big? A dog!

Assessment
1. Is the child able to follow your instructions?
2. Is the child able to copy the posture?
3. Does the child join in the discussion about how various animals move?

Sue Bradford Edwards, Florissant, MO

Preparation
Do the stretch ahead of time so you can talk the children through it.

> **Teacher-to-Teacher Tip**
> You might need to demonstrate the posture while the children watch.

Classroom Garden: What Do Animals Eat?

AGES 4+

Learning Objectives
Children will:
1. Learn that some food is eaten by both animals and people.
2. Grow from seeds some foods that people eat.

Vocabulary
carrots	lettuce
compare	seeds
grass	sunflower
grow	

Children's Books
Growing Vegetable Soup by Lois Ehlert
Planting a Garden by Lois Ehlert
The Tiny Seed by Eric Carle

Materials
chart paper
cups
marker
potting soil
seeds, such as carrot, lettuce, and radish

Preparation
Set up a garden station with potting soil, seeds, and cups.

What to Do
1. Ask the children, "What plants do animals eat?" and "What plants do people eat?"
2. Draw a Venn diagram on chart paper and record the children's answers to show that some foods only animals eat, some only people eat, and some are eaten by both animals and people.
3. Help the children plant and care for seeds that will grow into foods that people eat.
4. Place the seeds in a sunny window and observe their growth. When the seeds yield food, serve it for snack.
5. To extend learning, have the children record and measure plant growth.

Assessment
1. Did the child participate in the discussion about the plants that animals eat and the plants that people eat?
2. Did the child participate in growing food from seeds?

MaryLouise Alu Curto, Mercerville, NJ

> **Teacher-to-Teacher Tip**
> Punch holes in cups before filling. Place lids under cups.

Clean and Healthy

AGES 4+

Learning Objectives
Children will:
1. Learn about the tools to use to be clean.
2. Sing a song about being clean and healthy.

Vocabulary
brush   nails
clean   soap
comb   toothpaste
cut   trim
healthy

Children's Books
Brushing Teeth by Mari C. Shuh
Go Wash Up: Keeping Clean by Amanda Doering Tourville
Keeping Your Body Clean by Mary Elizabeth Salzmann

Materials
personal care items, such as a toothbrush, toothpaste, hairbrush, bar of soap, comb, and towel

What to Do
1. Display the objects on the table, and ask the children how each item helps us stay clean.
2. Teach the children the following song:

"If You're Clean, You're Healthy"
by Shyamala Shanmugasundaram
(Tune: "London Bridge Is Falling Down")

Trim your nails, and keep them clean,
Keep them clean, keep them clean.
Trim your nails, and keep them clean.
Being clean is good.

Brush your teeth twice a day,
twice a day, twice a day.
Brush your teeth twice a day.
Being clean is good.

Take a bath to wash dirt away,
dirt away, dirt away.
Take a bath to wash dirt away.
Being clean is good.

Wash your hands after you sneeze,
after you sneeze, after you sneeze.
Wash your hands after you sneeze.
If you're clean, you're healthy.

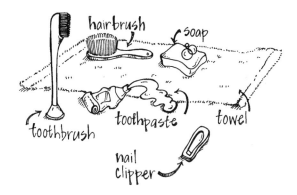

Assessment
1. Does the child understand how to use each item to stay clean?
2. Is the child able to sing the song about being clean and healthy?

Shyamala Shanmugasundaram, Annanagar East, Chennai, India

Sun Safety

AGES
4+

Learning Objectives
Children will:
1. Learn about sun safety.
2. Practice sorting skills.

Vocabulary
protect   sunburn   sunscreen

Children's Books
Have You Ever Seen a Hippo with Sunscreen?
    by Etta Kaner
OUCH! Sunburn by Donna Shepherd

Materials
bag to hold everything
protective gear for wearing in the sun
    (sunglasses, a hat, sunscreen, and
    umbrella)
silly dress-up items (a crown, a feather boa, a
    wand, and so on)

Preparation
Place the dress-up items and the protective
sun gear in the bag.

What to Do

1. Explain to the children that the sun's rays are strong enough to burn our skin, so it's important to wear the right protective gear when we play outside during the day.
2. Select one child to be your helper, and invite the rest of the class to help you dress him for a day out in the sun.
3. Pull the first item out of the bag, and ask the children if it's something that will protect skin on a sunny day. If the answer is yes, give it to your helper to put on. If the answer is no, put the item aside.
4. Continue pulling items out of the bag until it is empty and your helper is all set for a day of fun in the sun.

Assessment

1. What did the child learn about sun safety?
2. Was the child able to sort the items in the bag into those that protect against the sun and those that do not?

Erin Huffstetler, Maryville, TN

What's Healthy?

AGES
4+

Learning Objectives

Children will:

1. Learn the names of healthy vegetables.
2. Identify shapes and colors.

Vocabulary

colors
green
healthy
long
pink
red
round
shapes
vegetables
yellow

Children's Books

Good Enough to Eat by Lizzy Rockwell
Gregory, the Terrible Eater by Mitchell Sharmat
Growing Vegetable Soup by Lois Ehlert
The Vegetables We Eat by Gail Gibbons
You Are What You Eat by Sharon Gordon

Materials

baskets
real vegetables
vegetable chart (use a search engine to find one on the Internet

Preparation

- Ask the children to bring their favorite vegetable to class. Bring in some extra ones for any children who do not or cannot bring in a vegetable.
- Print out a vegetable chart in color.

What to Do

1. Ask the children to show and talk about their favorite vegetables.
2. Display all the vegetables in the basket.
3. Pass the basket around, and ask the children to touch and feel the vegetables. Discuss the color of each vegetable and how healthy it is.
4. Show the children a chart of vegetables. Ask, "What's green and healthy?" Encourage children to look at the chart and find the answer. Repeat with different colors and shapes. (What's orange, big, and healthy? Pumpkins. What's brown and healthy? Potatoes.)
5. Discuss other colorful healthy food.

Assessment

1. Is the child able to identify vegetables by name?
2. Is the child able to identify different vegetables by shape and color?

Shyamala Shanmugasundaram,
Annanagar East, Chennai, India

> **Teacher-to-Teacher Tip**
> The activity can be repeated with a fruit chart.

V Is for Vitamins

AGES 5+

Learning Objectives
Children will:
1. Learn about different kinds of vegetables.
2. Learn a rhyme about vegetables.

Vocabulary

brown	red
green	vegetables
healthy	vitamins
orange	yellow

Children's Books
Eating the Alphabet by Lois Ehlert
Food for Thought by Saxton Freyman and Joost Elffers
Good Enough to Eat by Lizzy Rockwell
The Monster Health Book: A Guide to Eating Healthy, Being Active, and Feeling Great for Monsters and Kids by Edward Miller
The Vegetables We Eat by Gail Gibbons
You Are What You Eat by Sharon Gordon

Materials
real vegetables or pictures of vegetables

What to Do

1. Talk with the children about the importance of eating healthy food.
2. Show the children the vegetables or the pictures of vegetables.
3. Teach the children the following rhyme:

HEALTH and NUTRITION

The Vitamin Rhyme
by Shyamala Shanmugasundaram

V is for vitamins
A, B, C, D, and E.
You'll find them in vegetables
Yellow, orange, brown, and green.
Asparagus, broccoli, peas, and string
*   beans,*
Pumpkins, potatoes, and all kinds of
*   greens.*

Assessment
1. What did the child learn about different kinds of vegetables?
2. Is the child able to say the rhyme about vegetables?

**Shyamala Shanmugasundaram,
Annanagar East, Chennai, India**

Create Caterpillars

Learning Objectives
Children will:
1. Practice fine motor skills.
2. Learn about caterpillars.

Vocabulary
butterfly
caterpillar
cocoon
moth
playdough

Children's Books
Caterpillars and Butterflies by Stephanie Turnbull
The Crunching Munching Caterpillar by Sheridan Cain
Ten Little Caterpillars by Bill Martin, Jr.

Materials
playdough in a variety of colors
playdough tools
small paintbrushes

What to Do
1. Ask the children what they know about caterpillars. Ask if they can guess what caterpillars grow into.
2. Read a book about caterpillars, such as *Caterpillars and Butterflies* by Stephanie Turnbull. Explain that caterpillars eventually make cocoons and turn into moths and butterflies.
3. Tell the children that they are going to make caterpillars out of playdough. Encourage them to roll the dough between their hands or use tools to make caterpillar shapes. They can use the back end of a paintbrush to make indentations for the eyes and mouths on their caterpillars.

leaf from outside
playdough

Assessment
1. Is the child improving her fine motor skills?
2. What did the child learn about caterpillars?

Laura D. Wynkoop,
San Dimas, CA

Teacher-to-Teacher Tip
For added fun, have the children make green leaves out of playdough and put their caterpillars on the leaves.

Ant Antics

Learning Objectives
Children will:
1. Learn about ants.
2. Sing a song.

Vocabulary
ant	jaw	sing
colony	legs	
eyes	march	

Children's Books
Ants by Cheryl Coughlan
Army Ant Parade by April Pulley Sayre
Busy Ants by Kristin L. Nelson
Thinking about Ants by Barbara Brenner
Those Amazing Ants by Patricia Demuth

Materials
3" x 5" index cards
markers
picnic basket
picnic blanket
plastic food items
plastic toy ants

Preparation
● Write one of the following ant facts on a 3" x 5" note card:
  ■ Ants are insects.
  ■ Ants can be many colors but are usually black or brown.
  ■ Ants have a hard body.
  ■ Ants have six legs and two eyes.
  ■ Ants have strong jaws to carry things.
  ■ Ants live and work in colonies.
  ■ Some ants have wings.
● Place the cards and plastic food in a picnic basket.

What to Do
1. Read a book about ants with the children.
2. Invite the children to gather around the picnic basket, on or near the blanket. Each time you remove a food item with an "ant facts" card, read the card aloud.
3. Invite the children to march around the circle as they sing "The Ants Go Marching."

"The Ants Go Marching"
(Traditional)
(Tune: "When Johnny Comes Marching Home Again")

The ants go marching one by one, hurrah, hurrah!
The ants go marching one by one, hurrah, hurrah!
The ants go marching one by one.
The little one stops to have some fun,
And they all go marching down into the ground
To get out of the rain. Boom! Boom! Boom!

Subsequent verses:
The ants go marching two by two...
The little one stops to tie his shoe...

The ants go marching three by three...
The little one stops to climb a tree...

The ants go marching four by four...
The little one stops to shut the door...

The ants go marching five by five...
The little one stops to go for a drive...

4. When the children move to learning centers, invite them to create anthills with the sand in the sand and water table, and then manipulate plastic toy ants climbing up, down, and into the anthills.

Assessment
1. What did the child learn about ants?
2. Is the child able to sing the song with the class?

Mary Murray, Mazomanie, WI

Teacher-to-Teacher Tip
Take a field trip outdoors and look for anthills. Invite small groups of children to gather around and observe the ants in action. Provide magnifying glasses so children can get an up-close view of the ants. Consider setting up an ant farm, available at your local educational or department store. Children will enjoy watching real ants at work.

AGES
4+

Beautiful Butterflies

Learning Objectives
Children will:
1. Develop fine motor skills.
2. Learn about butterflies.

Vocabulary
antennae   insect
fragile   scales

Children's Books
Are You a Butterfly? by Judy Allen and Tudor Humphries
Born to Be a Butterfly by Karen Wallace
Butterflies by Emily Neye
From Caterpillar to Butterfly by Deborah Heiligman

Materials

chenille craft stems (also called pipe cleaners)
clothespins
glue sticks
markers
round stickers in a variety of colors
scissors
tissue paper in a variety of colors

Preparation

Precut the chenille craft stems into sets of antennae (a 2" piece of craft stem, bent into a V).

What to Do

1. Ask the children what they know about butterflies. Let them share some of their knowledge and experience with these insects.
2. Read a book about butterflies with the children. If possible, read one that contains a diagram of the butterfly body including the antennae. Encourage the children to talk about the butterfly's colorful wings, how it moves, and what it eats.
3. Explain that one remarkable fact about butterflies is that they smell using their antennae. Each butterfly has two antennae that are attached to their heads. Look at a diagram of a butterfly, pointing out the antennae.
4. Ask the children to select and decorate pieces of tissue paper using stickers and markers. Explain that they will use the paper to make their own butterflies. Explain that butterfly wings are fragile and covered in tiny scales. The children can add scales (stickers) to the wings of their butterflies if they wish.
5. Assist the children as they pinch the pieces of colored tissue paper in the middle to make wings. They will use the clothespin to clasp the center of the tissue paper and spread out the paper to make wings. The clothespin will form the body of the butterfly.
6. They can decorate the butterfly body with stickers if they wish. Each child should attach their antennae to the body with one of the round stickers, which will also serve as a head.

Assessment

1. Is the child improving his fine motor skills as he creates a butterfly?

2. What did the child learn about butterflies?

Sue Bradford Edwards, Florissant, MO

Buckets of Worms

Learning Objectives

Children will:

1. Learn a poem about worms.
2. Compare the lengths of two yarn "worms."

Vocabulary

equal	shorter	thin
fat	skinny	worms
longer	thick	

Children's Books

Earthworms by Claire Llewellyn
Wiggling Worms at Work by Wendy Pfeffer
Wonderful Worms by Linda Glaser
Yucky Worms by Vivian French

Another Encyclopedia of Theme Activities

Materials

12" x 18" brown construction paper
2 plastic sand pails
20 strands of yarn in a variety of colors and
    thicknesses, cut into 1"–15" lengths

Preparation

Place 10 different strands of yarn in each
plastic pail.

What to Do

1. Invite two children at a time to work with the buckets of "worms." Each child selects a bucket.
2. Teach the children this poem:

Worms, Worms, Worms
    by Mary Murray

Worms, worms, worms,
Short or long, fat or thin,
Worms, worms, worms.
One, two, three, put your hand in.

On the word *in*, each child places his hand in the bucket, pulls out a worm, and places the worms next to each other on the brown construction paper (the dirt).

3. Help the children compare the lengths of the two worms and determine which worm is longer, which is shorter, which is fatter, and which is thinner.
4. Children then push the worms off the paper and repeat the activity. The game continues until all the worms have been drawn from the buckets and compared.
5. After all the children have had a turn comparing the yarn worms, place the buckets, yarn worms, and construction paper in a center for the children to use independently.

Assessment

1. Is the child able to recite the poem about worms?
2. Is the child improving her ability to compare lengths?

Mary Murray, Mazomanie, WI

Teacher-to-Teacher Tip

If possible, bring in a bucket containing two or more real earthworms. Lay them on a large sheet of paper. Invite the children to observe the worms, compare their attributes, and watch them wiggle as an introduction to this activity.

Honeycomb Hopping

AGES
4+

Learning Objectives

Children will:
1. Learn about bees.
2. Follow directions.
3. Practice gross motor skills.

Vocabulary

arrow
bees
hexagon
honeycomb
hop

INSECTS and BUGS

Children's Books

Are You a Bee? by Judy Allen
The Honey Makers by Gail Gibbons
The Life and Times of the Honeybee by Charles
   Micucci

Materials

construction paper, poster board, or tagboard
markers
scissors

Preparation

- Cut 20 hexagon shapes approximately 15" in diameter out of construction paper, poster board, or tagboard.
- Draw a large arrow on each hexagon.
- Tape the hexagons on the floor, connecting one to another in a honeycomb fashion, so that the arrows follow each other in a path.

What to Do

1. Read a book about bees, such as *The Life and Times of the Honeybee* by Charles Micucci. In particular, talk with the children about the honeycombs that bees make. Discuss the hexagon shape of the cells, the use of the honeycomb in the hive, and what the honeycomb is made of.
2. Show the children how to hop from one hexagon in the "honeycomb" to another by following the arrows until they get to the end.
3. Let each child have a turn hopping in the honeycomb.

Assessment

1. What did the child learn about bees?
2. Was the child able to follow directions?
3. Are the child's gross motor skills improving when jumping in the honeycomb?

Fingerplays, Songs, and Poems

I'm Bringing Home a Baby Bumblebee

I'm bringing home a baby bumblebee.
  (Hold hands together as if trapping a bee inside.)
Won't my mommy be so proud of me?
I'm bringing home a baby bumblebee.
Ouch! It stung me! (Pull hands apart when the bee "stings.")

Here Is the Beehive

Here is the beehive.
Where are the bees? (Hold hands together.)
Hiding inside where nobody sees.
Soon they come creeping out of the hive,
  (Pull hands apart.)
1, 2, 3, 4, 5! (Hold up each finger as you count to 5.)

Sandra Ryan, Buffalo, NY

Another Encyclopedia of Theme Activities

Insect Art

AGES 4+

Learning Objectives
Children will:
1. Learn about insects.
2. Work cooperatively to create a class mural.

Vocabulary
antennae	creep	legs
body	fly	shape
color	head	size
crawl	jump	wing

Children's Books
The Best Book of Bugs by Claire Llewellyn
Bugs A to Z by Caroline Lawton
Bugs Are Insects by Anne Rockwell
Ed Emberley's Fingerprint Drawing Book by Ed Emberley
Insects by Robin Bernard
It's a Good Thing There Are Insects by Allan Fowler

Materials
art materials such as markers, crayons, paint and paintbrushes, and stickers
construction paper shapes
glue sticks
large sheet of mural paper
stamp pad
tape

Preparation
Hang a large sheet of mural paper on the wall within the children's reach.

What to Do
1. Review what the children know about bugs or insects. Consider reading one or two books about insects.
2. Show the children the mural paper, the art materials, construction paper shapes, and glue sticks.
3. Ask the children to use the materials to draw insects on the mural paper. For example, the children can use the glue sticks and precut paper shapes as insect body parts—head, legs, antennae, wings, and so on.
4. When each child has finished his insect, write that child's name next to the insect.

Assessment
1. What did the child learn about insects?
2. Was the child able to work cooperatively to create a class mural?

Mary Murray, Mazomanie, WI

Teacher-to-Teacher Tips
- Display photographs of various insects.
- Hand one child a butterfly net. Invite the child to "catch" one of the insects on the mural and then describe that insect.

INSECTS and BUGS

Insect Parts

Learning Objectives

Children will:

1. Match puzzle pieces of insects divided into the three main body parts.
2. Learn about the body parts of insects.

Vocabulary

ant	fly	wasp
beetle	grasshopper	
bug	insect	

Children's Books

The Best Book of Bugs by Claire Llewellyn
Bugs A to Z by Caroline Lawton
Bugs Are Insects by Anne Rockwell
Insects by Robin Bernard
It's a Good Thing There Are Insects by Allan Fowler
Miss Spider's Tea Party by David Kirk

Materials

construction paper in assorted colors
felt
flannel board
glue stick
laminating materials or clear contact paper
pictures of insects
scissors

Preparation

- Glue each insect picture on a different color construction paper.
- Cut each insect picture into its three main body parts—head, thorax, and abdomen.
- Laminate or cover with clear contact paper.
- Glue felt on the backs of each puzzle piece.

What to Do

1. Read the children one or more books about insects.
2. Talk with the children about the different body parts of insects—head, thorax, and abdomen.
3. Let the children use the insect puzzle pieces and flannel board to put the puzzle pieces for one insect together or to create a mix-and-match insect using puzzle pieces from different insects.

Assessment

1. Is the child able to find and match the puzzle pieces for one or more insects?
2. What did the child learn about the body parts of insects?

Jackie Wright, Enid, OK

Teacher-to-Teacher Tips

- Using a different color background for each insect makes these puzzles self-correcting so the children can complete the puzzles independently.
- If desired, add a chart with pictures of the bugs and their names for the children to reference as they put the puzzle pieces together.

Insect Zoo

AGES 4+

Learning Objectives
Children will:
1. Learn about insects.
2. Use observation skills.

Vocabulary
butterfly	insect	magnify
crawl	katydid	study
fly	ladybug	wings
head	legs	

Children's Books
The Best Book of Bugs by Claire Llewellyn
Bugs A to Z by Caroline Lawton
Bugs Are Insects by Anne Rockwell
Earthworms by Claire Llewellyn
Insects by Robin Bernard
It's a Good Thing There Are Insects by Allan
    Fowler

Materials
clear plastic containers with lids
magnifying glasses
photographs of various insects (use a search
    engine to find photos on the Internet)
sign that reads "Insect Zoo"

Preparation
- Place a picture of a different type of insect inside each container and replace the lid.
- Display the jars along the length of a wall or table with a sign that reads "Insect Zoo."
- Place several magnifying glasses near the containers.

What to Do
1. Invite several children to go the insect zoo. Encourage each child to use a magnifying glass to observe, describe, and identify one of the insects on display.
2. Ask the children questions to develop their observation skills. "Does the insect have wings? How many?" "How many legs do you count?" "What do the eyes look like?"
3. Read one or two books to the children and then suggest that the children look at the insect zoo again.
4. Repeat the activity until all children have had an opportunity to study the insects in the insect zoo.

Assessment
1. What did the child learn about insects?
2. Are the child's observation skills improving?

Mary Murray, Mazomanie, WI

Teacher-to-Teacher Tips
Bring in live insects for a short-term time of observation, and then invite the class to set the insects free outdoors together.

INSECTS and BUGS

Make Your Own Bug

AGES
4+

Learning Objectives

Children will:

1. Learn about the body parts of insects.
2. Develop their creativity as they create insects.

Vocabulary

antennae
body
eyes
head
insect
legs
thorax
wings

Children's Books

The Best Book of Bugs by Claire Llewellyn
Bugs Are Insects by Anne Rockwell
I Like Bugs by Margaret Wise Brown
Insects by Robin Bernard
It's a Good Thing There Are Insects by Allan Fowler

Materials

collection of materials such as different lengths of chenille craft stems (also called pipe cleaners), colored toothpicks, buttons, colorful beads, and so on
photographs or pictures of various insects
playdough or modeling dough

What to Do

1. Remind the children that insects come in many different sizes and shapes but they all have this in common: three body parts (head, abdomen, thorax), six jointed legs, antennae, and an exoskeleton (outer skeleton).
2. Display several pictures of insects for children to observe.
3. Invite the children to roll a lump of modeling dough into an insect body shape (or three shapes put together).
4. Encourage the children to insert a selection of other items into the body to add legs, antennae, eyes, wings, and other features to their insect. Encourage the children's creativity.
5. Display the completed insects in a prominent place along the length of a classroom wall or in the art center.
6. Suggest that the children name their insects. Write the name of the insect and the child's name on separate index cards.
7. Take the class on a walking tour of the "insect art" on display.

toothpick
modeling dough
beads
chenille sticks

Assessment

1. What did the child learn about the body part of insects?
2. Is the child developing her creativity as she creates an insect?

Mary Murray, Mazomanie, WI

Teacher-to-Teacher Tips

- Consider displaying the colorful insects among a collection of real twigs, leaves, plants, and rocks.
- If you have a set of building materials such as Tinkertoys, LEGO® bricks, or K'Nex, invite the children to use these materials to create various insects.
- Give each child a chance to tell the class about his insect. Invite the child to point out the various parts of the insect's body, identify what the insect is, and describe what it eats.

Spiderwebs

AGES
4+

Learning Objectives

Children will:
1. Develop fine motor skills.
2. Learn about spiders and spiderwebs.

Vocabulary

spider   spiderweb   weave

Children's Books

Aaaarrgghh! Spider! by Lydia Monks
Are You a Spider? by Judy Allen
Spinning Spiders by Melvin Berger
The Very Busy Spider by Eric Carle

Materials

black construction paper
black yarn
hole punch
masking tape
sturdy paper plates, one for each child

Preparation

- Punch holes around the edge of each plate about 2" apart and about 2" from the edge of the plate.
- Cut pieces of yarn about 2' long. Thread one end through a hole on each plate, knot it, and then wrap the other end in masking tape.
- Cut small spider shapes out of the black construction paper and punch a hole in each.

What to Do

1. Read a book about spiders, such as *Aaaarrgghh! Spider!* by Lydia Monks.
2. Give each child a paper plate, and show them how to lace the yarn in and out of the holes. Encourage the children to go in and out in any order so that the yarn crosses over the plate repeatedly to look like a web.

3. After the children have finished lacing, tie the construction paper spiders to the end of their yarn pieces, and let the spiders hang from the plates.

Assessment

1. Does the child have the fine motor skills to lace the yarn in and out of the holes in the paper plate?
2. What did the child learn about spiders and spiderwebs?

Fingerplays, Songs, and Poems

The Itsy Bitsy Spider

*The itsy bitsy spider crawled up the
waterspout.
Down came the rain and washed the
spider out.
Out came the sun and dried up all the rain.
And the itsy bitsy spider crawled up the
spout again.*

Note: If you are unfamiliar with the hand motions for this fingerplay, see http://www .thingamababy.com/baby/2005/08/how_to_ perform_.html for some helpful photos.

Sandra Ryan, Buffalo, NY

hole
yarn
paper spider

Bug Corner

AGES 5+

Learning Objectives

Children will:

1. Identify insects and insect names.
2. Learn about insects by looking at books.

Vocabulary

antennae	legs
bench	quiet
book	read
bugs	rest
insects	sit

Children's Books

The Best Book of Bugs by Claire Llewellyn
Bugs A to Z by Caroline Lawton
Bugs Are Insects by Anne Rockwell
Earthworms by Claire Llewellyn
Insects by Robin Bernard
It's a Good Thing There Are Insects
    by Allan Fowler

Materials

basket
books about insects
marker
pictures of insects (use a search engine to find these on the Internet)
strips of paper
tape

Preparation

● Hang pictures of insects in the reading area. Label each picture with the name of the insect.
● Place the books about insects in the basket and place the basket in the reading area.

What to Do

1. Read a few books about bugs and insects. Point out the body parts of an insect: the head, antennae, legs, wings, and so on.
2. Show the children the pictures of insects hanging in the reading area.
3. Encourage the children to look at the books about insects and the insect pictures.

Assessment

1. Is the child able to identify insects and insect names?
2. What is the child learning about insects by looking at the books and pictures?

Mary Murray, Mazomanie, WI

Pizza Box Butterfly

AGES 5+

Learning Objectives

Children will:
1. Learn about butterflies and symmetry.
2. Develop their creativity.

Vocabulary

antennae	butterfly	wings
body	fly	

Children's Books

Bugs Are Insects by Anne Rockwell
I Wish I Were a Butterfly by James Howe
Insects by Robin Bernard
It's a Good Thing There Are Insects by Allan Fowler

Materials

chenille craft stems (also called pipe cleaners)
hole punch or pointed scissors
markers
materials to decorate the butterflies, such as glue, cotton balls, construction paper, yarn pieces, tissue paper, and paint and paintbrushes
small, unused pizza boxes, one for each child
yarn or string

Preparation

Precut a butterfly out of each pizza box. When you open the box, the middle becomes the stem of the butterfly with the top and bottom of the box being each wing (this creates the natural fold of the wings on the sides of the body).

What to Do

1. Have the children decorate their butterflies with the materials provided. You can suggest that they try to make each wing look the same because butterflies are symmetrical (explain what this means). Use chenille stems to create antennae.
2. Punch two holes along the butterfly's "back" and lace string or yarn through the holes, tying the ends tightly together to make a handle on the butterfly.
3. Show children how to use the handles to hold their butterflies and make them "fly."

Assessment

1. What did the child learn about butterflies and about symmetry?
2. Is the child using his creative skills to make a butterfly?

Sandy L. Scott, Meridian, ID

H–E–A–R–T

AGES 3+

Learning Objectives
Children will:
1. Express their feelings to others.
2. Sing a song.

Vocabulary
friend
heart
kindness
love
song
spell

Children's Books
Little Blue and Little Yellow by Leo Lionni
The Rainbow Fish by Marcus Pfister
The Velveteen Rabbit by Margery Williams

Materials
chart paper
construction paper
markers and crayons
scissors

Preparation
- Cut heart shapes from the construction paper.
- Draw a large heart on the chart paper and in the middle write the word *heart*.

What to Do
1. Teach the children the following song:

   "H–E–A–R–T" by Jackie Wright
   (Tune: "Bingo")

   To show your friends you love them so
   Just give them each your heart.
   H-E-A-R-T, H-E-A-R-T, H-E-A-R-T,
   That spells the word heart.
2. Point to each letter in the word as you sing the song.
3. Give the children the heart shapes to decorate.
4. Let them choose whether to give the shapes to a classmate or to bring them home to their families.

Assessment
1. What did the child learn about expressing his feelings?
2. Did the child learn and then sing the song?

Jackie Wright, Enid, OK

KINDNESS

Card Compliments

Learning objectives

Children will:

1. Learn about the meaning of the word *compliment*.
2. Learn how to give a compliment.

Vocabulary

compliment	kind
friend	smile

Children's Books

Being a Pig Is Nice: A Child's View of Manners by Sally Lloyd-Jones

It's Nice to Be Nice by Debra K. Isakson

The Nice Book by David Ezra Stein

What to Do

1. Write the word *compliment* on chart paper. Ask the class if anyone knows what this word means. Provide examples of compliments, such as "Johnny, I like your shirt," or "Kate, you have a beautiful smile," or "Curt, you are great at drawing."
2. Ask one child in the class to pick a name from the paper bag. Read the name on the paper or stick.
3. Tell the class to say a compliment to that child.

Assessment

1. Is the child learning the meaning of the word *compliment*?
2. Is the child learning how to give a compliment?

Fingerplays, Songs, and Poems

"Make New Friends"

(Traditional)

Make new friends,
But keep the old.
One is silver,
The other is gold.

Materials

chart paper
markers
paper
paper bag
wooden craft sticks

Preparation

Write each child's name on a slip of paper or a wooden craft stick. Place all the slips of paper or sticks in a paper bag.

A circle is round,
It has no end.
That's how long,
I will be your friend.

"The More We Get Together" (Traditional)

The more we get together,
Together, together,
The more we get together,
The happier we'll be.

For your friends are my friends,
And my friends are your friends.
Oh, the more we get together,
The happier we'll be!

Tina Cho, Newton, IA

Friendship Bracelets

Learning Objectives

Children will:
1. Practice fine motor skills.
2. Learn about the value of sharing.

Vocabulary
bracelet   kindness
friends   share

Children's Books
Friends by Helme Heine
Friends at School by Rochelle Bunnett

Materials
box
hole punch
objects to string, such as straws, large beads,
    paper flowers (or shapes)
scissors
tape
yarn or string

Preparation
- Cut yarn in lengths that are about 4" longer than the children's wrists. Wrap one end with a piece of tape.
- Cut straws into ½" pieces.
- Punch holes in paper shapes.

What to Do
1. Provide the objects to string and the lengths of yarn.
2. Ask each child to make a bracelet by stringing different objects on a length of yarn.
3. Help the children tie each beaded length of yarn.
4. Place all the bracelets into a box.
5. At group or circle time, each child takes one bracelet out of the box and puts it on.
6. Engage the children in a discussion about sharing with others, and about how they each have a bracelet from one of their friends in the classroom.
7. Let the children wear the bracelets during group or circle time, and then put the bracelets back in the box at the end of group or circle time.
8. Repeat on another day.

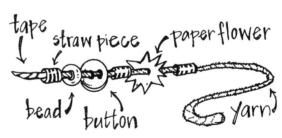

Assessment
1. Are the child's fine motor skills improving as she creates one or more bracelets?
2. What is the child learning about the value of sharing?

Kay Shogren

Teacher-to-Teacher Tip
Let the children make as many bracelets as they want, but tell them that the first one has to go in the box. This helps with children who want to make a bracelet to take home.

Good Classroom Behavior

AGES 4+

Learning Objectives
Children will:
1. Learn manners.
2. Be kind to one another.

Vocabulary
agree
disagree
friend
kindness
play
please
share
thank you

Children's Books
Being a Pig Is Nice: A Child's View of Manners by Sally Lloyd-Jones
It's Nice to Be Nice by Debra K. Isakson
The Nice Book by David Ezra Stein

Materials
chart paper
marker

Preparation
Write "Good Classroom Behavior" at the top of a piece of chart paper. Draw two columns under the title. Label one "Yes" and the other "No."

What to Do
1. Explain the chart to the children. Tell them that you are going to describe certain behavior and they should decide if the behavior is good classroom behavior or not. If it is, you will write the words under "Yes," and if it is not, you will write the words under "No."
2. Begin by describing behavior you see in the classroom, such as the following:
   - say *please* and *thank you*
   - take a toy away from your friend
   - ask a classmate to play with you
   - make fun of a friend's painting
   - leave trash on the table when you finish eating
   - use your words when you are angry
   - share with your classmates
   - tell a classmate you won't be her friend
3. After you have described a few things that might happen in the classroom, ask the children for their ideas. Write their ideas in the appropriate column.

Assessment
1. What did the child learn about good behavior in the classroom?
2. What did the child learn about being kind and considerate to one another?

Jackie Wright, Enid, OK

It's Fun! It's Cool! Lend a Hand!

AGES 4+

Learning Objectives
Children will:
1. Learn how to work together to clean up the classroom.
2. Understand that pictures and symbols have meaning and that print carries a message.

Vocabulary
clean up
friends
good
hand
helping
write

Children's Books
Chicken and Cat Clean Up by Sara Varon
Clean Your Room, Harvey Moon! by Pat Cummings

Materials
Clean Your Room, Harvey Moon! by Pat Cummings
many copies of the outline of a hand
marker
paper bag
scissors

Preparation
Copy and cut out hands or help the children cut out hands.

What to Do
1. Write on the bulletin board, "Helping Hands Are Cool."
2. At group or circle time, talk with the children about how they can help at clean-up time. Write each answer on one of the hands. Put all the hands in a paper bag.
3. Read *Clean Your Room, Harvey Moon!* Ask the children to describe page 13. Ask them if they want their classroom to look like that! Explain that all of them will need to help clean up the classroom so we can find things when we need them.
4. When it is clean-up time, let each child pick one of the hands from the paper bag. Tell each child what his hand says, which is what the child will do to help clean up.

Assessment
1. Is the child learning that his contribution to cleaning up the classroom is important?
2. Is the child beginning to understand that pictures and symbols have meaning and that print carries a message?

Fingerplays, Songs, and Poems
In the back of *Clean Your Room, Harvey Moon!* is a poem, "Pick Up Your Room," by Mary Ann Hoberman.

Carol Hupp, Farmersville, IL

KINDNESS

Kindness Cards

Learning Objectives
Children will:
1. Recognize and label basic feelings.
2. Become aware of the feelings of others.

Vocabulary
card
congratulations
empathy
envelope
feelings
happy
kindness
sad
smile
thanks

Children's Books
Kindness Counts! by Debby Anderson
Kindness Is Cooler, Mrs. Ruler by Margery Cuyler
Ordinary Mary's Extraordinary Deed by Emily Pearson

Materials
art materials, such as crayons, markers, glue, and collage materials
box with a slot cut into it
large, blank index cards
markers
scissors

Preparation
Decorate a box with a slot cut into the top or side, and label it as "The Kindness Box."

What to Do
1. Read one or more of the suggested books to the children.
2. Talk with the children about feelings and then discuss the meaning of kindness.
3. Ask the children to brainstorm ways they can be kind to others. Write their responses on large index cards.
4. Introduce "The Kindness Box," and invite the children to use art materials to decorate the index cards and then put them into the box.
5. Explain that the cards they made will be given to people who need an extra smile. Explain that by helping someone smile, they are being kind.
6. Let the children know that anytime one of the children in the class needs an extra smile, the children can give that child one of the cards.

Assessment
1. Is the child able to participate in the class discussion about feelings?
2. Is the child becoming aware of the feelings of others?

Donna Austin-Ahner, Lehighton, PA

Teacher-to-Teacher Tip
Let the children's families know that if they are aware of someone who could use an extra smile, you'd be happy to send them a handmade card if they can provide you with a name and address!

My Friends Are Kind

Learning Objectives
Children will:
1. Understand the meaning of the word *kindness*.
2. Notice when they or their friends are being kind.

Vocabulary
friends
kindness

Children's Books
Kindness Is Cooler, Mrs. Ruler by Margery Cuyler
Ordinary Mary's Extraordinary Deed by Emily Pearson

Materials
camera
duct tape
markers
paper
stapler

What to Do
1. Engage the children in a discussion about the meaning of the word *kindness* and how people show kindness.
2. Take a picture of each child.
3. Tell the children that you are going to be watching them during the next day or so to see how they show kindness to their friends, that you will write down what they do and then make a book about the children in the class being kind to each other.
4. Print out photos of the children. On each photo write one or more ways that child is kind. For example, write, "Alexa is kind by sharing the clothes in the dramatic play center."
5. Create a class book about kindness by stapling the pages together and covering the staples with duct tape.
6. Read the book to the class by talking about each picture. Let the children talk about the ways that they see their friends being kind.

Assessment
1. Does the child understand the meaning of the word *kindness*?
2. Is the child noticing when she or her friends are being kind?

Holly Dzierzanowski, Bastrop, TX

Teacher-to-Teacher Tip
If you do this with older children, they can help you look for ways that they are being kind or their friends are being kind and dictate that information to you for the book.

Helping Hands

AGES 5+

Learning Objectives
Children will:
1. Practice fine motor skills.
2. Learn that print has meaning.

Vocabulary
friend   kindness

Children's Books
Help! A Story of Friendship by Holly Keller
If Everybody Did by Jo Ann Stover

Materials
fingerpaints
large butcher paper
marker
sticky notes
tray or lids for paint

Preparation
- Place a large piece of butcher paper on a table.
- Put paint in tray or lids.
- Write "Helping Hands of (your class or group name)" in the center of butcher paper. Write each child's name on the paper, leaving room around each name for that child's handprint.

What to Do
1. Work with one or two children at a time during choice time.
2. Ask each child to paint his hands or put his hands in the paint in the tray or lids.
3. Help each child find his name and press his hand onto the paper by his name.
4. After the child has added his handprints to the paper, ask the child to name one or more kind things that he does.
5. Write what the child says on a sticky note and ask him to place it on the butcher paper poster. The note does not have to be by his name.
6. Read what you wrote, thanking the child and saying, "That was really kind when you _____."
7. Continue doing this anytime you notice someone being kind, and soon the children will come to you with things they or others have done, asking you to post the good deeds.

Assessment
1. Is the child developing better fine motor skills?
2. Is the child beginning to understand that print has meaning?

Tracey Neumarke, Chicago, IL

Teacher-to-Teacher Tip
Once the children have added their handprints to the butcher paper poster, have another large paper for them to do any fingerpainting they want. Hang this in the room as a class painting.

It's My Good Fortune to Have Friends!

AGES 5+

Learning Objectives

Children will:

1. Learn to appreciate others.
2. Learn how to express themselves and show kindness.

Vocabulary

fortunate   special
fortune   talent

Children's Books

Elmer's Special Day by David McKee
Fortune Cookie Fortunes by Grace Lin
The Good Luck Cat by Paul Lee

Materials

art materials, such as markers, crayons, stickers, strips and dots of colored paper, glue, and any other decorations you may want to use
fortune cookies
small boxes such as the kind take-out Chinese food comes in

Preparation

Write one child's name on each take-out box.

What to Do

1. Discuss with the children that each one is special. One way we show kindness is by identifying what is special about each person. Every person has talents! We are so lucky (and fortunate) to have such good friends! Tell the children that *fortunate* is a word that is very similar to "fortune." Ask the children if they know what a fortune is. Several children may say that they have eaten fortune cookies. Open a fortune cookie and read the fortune.
2. Discuss how fortunes are hidden in the cookies and how it is fun to find the fortunes.
3. Tell the children that they are going to make their own fortunes for each other. Give each child a take-out box. Let them decorate it any way they want.
4. Tape the lids so there is room to insert the fortunes.
5. Give each child a strip of paper. Ask the child to tell you one kind thing to describe someone else in the class so you can write the word or words on the paper. The words could be things such as *shares toys*, *climbs high*, *likes to read*, and so on.
6. Help the child put this fortune in the other child's box.
7. Over a week's time or more, have the children make one fortune for everyone in the group.
8. Later in the day or a few days later, let the children open their own boxes and read all of the kind words their friends wrote about them. Then discuss how this made them feel. Say, "Isn't it nice to know what your friends appreciate about you? How

tape
nice

K I N D N E S S

can we show our appreciation if we don't write it down? Showing kindness is wonderful for the person who receives the kindness and for the person who gives it!"

9. After reading the children's fortunes, let the children take their fortune boxes home.

Assessment

1. Is the child learning to appreciate others?

2. Is the child learning how to express himself and to show kindness to others?

Susan Bahner Lancaster, Knoxville, TN

Have You Ever Been to a Zoo?

AGES 3+

Learning Objectives
Children will:
1. Develop math skills.
2. Develop oral language skills.

Vocabulary
animal names
cage
zookeeper

Children's Books
1, 2, 3 to the Zoo by Eric Carle
Dear Zoo by Rod Campbell
From Head to Toe by Eric Carle
Good Night, Gorilla by Peggy Rathmann
Sam Who Never Forgets by Eve Rice

Materials
chart paper
marker

Preparation
Write "Have You Ever Been to a Zoo?" at the top of the chart paper. Create two columns, writing "Yes" at the top of one column and "No" at the top of the second column.

What to Do
1. Read one or two books about zoos (see list of suggestions) to the children, and then talk with them about the animals that typically may be seen in a zoo.
2. Ask each child, "Have you ever been to a zoo?"
3. Make a mark in the appropriate column.
4. After every child has answered the question, count the number of responses by pointing to each mark as you count. Write the total for each column.
5. Have more children or fewer children been to a zoo?

Assessment
1. Is the child beginning to develop math skills?
2. Does the child participate in this group activity?

Fingerplays, Songs, and Poems
"Going to the Zoo" (Available on *Singable Songs for the Very Young* by Raffi, and also on CDs by other artists.)

Jackie Wright, Enid, OK

MATH

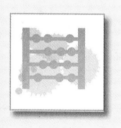

Sorting Seashells

AGES 3+

Learning Objectives
Children will:
1. Use fine motor skills.
2. Learn about shells.

Vocabulary
beach
ocean
sand
shells

Children's Books
Seashells by Ann O. Squire
Seashells by the Seashore by Marianne Berkes
Seashells, Crabs and Sea Stars by Christiane Kump Tibbitts
Shells! Shells! Shells! by Nancy Elizabeth Wallace

Materials
Per child:
1 empty plastic baby food jar with lid (other jars will also work)
assortment of seashells
basket

What to Do
1. Read one of the books about seashells.
2. Show the children the basket of seashells.
3. Encourage the children to explore the characteristics of the seashells and then to sort them by one characteristic. For example, sort the seashells into groups that are pointy and not pointy, round and not round, or white and not white.
4. When the children are finished exploring and sorting the seashells, ask them to place all the shells in the basket so the shells are ready for the next child or group of children.

Assessment
1. How well did the child use his fine motor skills?
2. What did the child learn about shells?

Donna Alice Patton, Hillsboro, OH

Clap the Syllables in Our Names

AGES 4+

Learning Objectives
Children will:
1. Learn about phonemic awareness.
2. Learn to discriminate the sounds in their own and others' names.
3. Recognize printed names.

Vocabulary
clap
name
number
syllable

Another Encyclopedia of Theme Activities

Children's Books

Andy, That's My Name by Tomie dePaola
Chrysanthemum by Kevin Henkes
My Name Is Yoon by Helen Recorvits
The Name Jar by Yangsook Choi

Materials

chart paper
marker

What to Do

1. Explain to the children that all words have parts called *syllables* and that today they are going to learn the number of syllables in the children's names by clapping each syllable in the names.
2. Show the children how to hold their hands under their chins as they say the names to feel how many times their jaw drops. Explain that each time their jaw drops is one syllable.
3. Write one child's name on the chart paper. Say the name and then ask the group to say the name. How many times did their jaws drop? Write that number next to the child's name.
4. Repeat for the rest of the children.
5. How many names have one syllable? two syllables? three syllables? four syllables? Do any names have five syllables?
6. Ask each child to point to her name on the chart paper, say how many syllables are in her name, and then move to the next activity or time of day.

Assessment

1. What did the child learn about phonemic awareness?
2. Is the child able to discriminate the sounds and syllables in his own name and other children's names?
3. Is the child able to recognize his printed name?

Jackie Wright, Enid, OK

> **Teacher-to-Teacher Tip**
> Depending on the ages and abilities of the children in your class, work with a small group of children or the entire class.

The Counting Construction Worker

AGES 4+

Learning Objectives

Children will:
1. Improve their counting skills
2. Improve their fine motor skills.

Vocabulary

belt   measure
match   tool

Children's Books

Construction Workers by Tami Deedrick
Tools We Use: Builders by Dana Meachen Rau

Materials

collection of nuts, bolts, and screws in a box
tape measure
tool belt

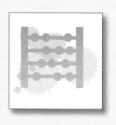

What to Do

1. Invite the children to spill out the collection of nut, bolts, and screws.
2. Suggest that the children sort and count the objects, then lay them out in graph formation on the table (each material in a separate vertical or horizontal line).
3. Let the children walk around the room and use a tape measure to measure different objects in the classroom.
4. Invite the children to wear the tool belt and pretend to fix various broken things in the classroom.

Assessment

1. Is the child improving her counting skills?
2. Does the child have the fine motor skills to do this activity?

Mary Murray, Mazomanie, WI

tool belt

Teacher-to-Teacher Tip
This activity will require close supervision of the children while they are examining, sorting, and using the nuts, bolts, and screws.

Dinosaur Egg Hunt and Hatch

AGES 4+

Learning Objectives
Children will:
1. Search for eggs in the grass.
2. Learn counting skills.
3. Learn about dinosaurs.

Vocabulary

count	find	open
crack	grass	reptile
dinosaur	hatch	shell
eggs	hidden	

Children's Books
The Big Book of Dinosaurs by Angela Wilkes
The Last Dinosaur Egg by Andrew Hegeman
Why, Why, Why Did Dinosaurs Lay Eggs? by Camilla de la Bédoyère

Materials
basket
plastic eggs that open (like Easter eggs), at least three for each child in the class
small plastic toy dinosaurs or small pictures of dinosaurs (ones that will fit inside the eggs), enough to put one in each plastic egg

Preparation

- Place one dinosaur picture or toy inside each egg.
- Before the children go outside to play, hide the eggs in the grass outside your school building.

Another Encyclopedia of Theme Activities

What to Do

1. Tell the children that you are taking them on a dinosaur egg hunt. Remind the children that dinosaurs were reptiles. The name *dinosaur* means "terrible lizard." Explain that reptiles lay eggs, and that each young dinosaur hatched from an egg.
2. Gather the children outdoors and explain that each child is to find three (or more) hidden dinosaur eggs in the grass and the area around your school.
3. Call out, "Dinosaur Egg Hunt!" On that announcement, the children may race around and find their three dinosaur eggs.
4. Gather the children together and sit in a circle in the grass. Help each child count her eggs and then open them while the class observes.
5. Help the children name each type of dinosaur that "hatches" from her eggs.
6. After all of the eggs have been "hatched," ask children to place their dinosaurs back inside the eggs and place the eggs in your basket. Invite the children to cover their eyes while you hide the eggs again. Repeat the activity several times.

Assessment

1. Is the child able to find the eggs hidden in the grass?
2. Is the child able to count the eggs he found?
3. What did the child learn about dinosaurs?

Mary Murray, Mazomanie, WI

Teacher-to-Teacher Tips
- Attach small dinosaur stickers to small pieces of card stock for an inexpensive way to fill the eggs.
- Allow a few children to help you hide the eggs each time you play the game.

Ducks in a Pond

AGES
4+

Learning Objectives

Children will:

1. Practice counting skills.
2. Develop an understanding of numbers and relationships.

Vocabulary

count   inside   pond
duck   outside

Children's Books

How Do You Count a Dozen Ducklings?
    by In Seon Chae
Little Quack by Lauren Thompson
Quack and Count by Keith Baker

Materials

5–10 rubber ducks
blue paper circle (for the "pond")

What to Do

1. Teach the children the song "Five Little Ducks."

"Five Little Ducks"
(Traditional)

Five little ducks went out one day
Over the hills and far away,
Mommy duck called, "Quack, quack,
    quack,"
But only four little ducks came back.

Four little ducks went out one day
Over the hills and far away,
Mommy duck called, "Quack, quack,
    quack,"
But only three little ducks came back.

Three little ducks went out one day
Over the hills and far away,
Mommy duck called, "Quack, quack,
    quack,"
But only two little ducks came back.

Two little ducks went out one day
Over the hills and far away,
Mommy duck called, "Quack, quack,
    quack,"
But only one little duck came back.

One little duck went out one day
Over the hills and far away,
Mommy duck called, "Quack, quack,
    quack,"
But no little ducks came wandering back.

No little ducks went out one day
Over the hills and far away,
Mommy duck called, "Quack, quack,
    quack,"
And five little ducks came wandering back.

2. Suggest that the children use the blue paper "pond" and the rubber ducks to act out the song as you sing it again.

3. Expand this activity, if appropriate, by placing some of the ducks in the pond and some of the ducks outside the pond. Ask the children how many ducks are in the pond. Ask the children how many ducks are outside the pond. How many ducks are there in all?

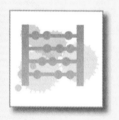

Assessment

1. Is the child developing counting skills?
2. Does the child understand how to use numbers in counting?

Laura D. Wynkoop, San Dimas, CA

Fishbowl Fun

AGES
4+

Learning Objectives
Children will:

1. Learn about numbers.
2. Put numbers in order.
3. Practice counting.

Vocabulary
breath
bubbles
fins
fish
swim
tail
water

Children's Books

Fish Eyes: A Book You Can Count On
    by Lois Ehlert
Rainbow Fish by Marcus Pfister
Rainbow Fish 1, 2, 3 by Marcus Pfister
Swimmy by Leo Lionni

Materials

construction paper in many colors (other
    than blue)
large piece of blue construction paper
marker
scissors

What to Do

1. Work with one child or a small group of children.
2. Invite one child to turn over one of the fish.
3. Help the child count the number of dots on the fish and to say the number written on the fish.
4. Repeat with the other fish. If you are working with a group of children, give each child a chance to turn over a fish, count the dots, and say the number.
5. After all the fish have been turned over, help the children put the fish in order from 1 to 5 (or the number of fish in the paper fishbowl) and then count the fish aloud.

Assessment

1. What did the child learn about numbers?
2. Is the child able to put the fish in numerical order?
3. Is the child improving her counting skills?

Mary Murray, Mazomanie, WI

Preparation

● Cut the large piece of blue construction paper into a lake or fishbowl shape.
● Cut up to 10 paper fish shapes or other underwater creatures, such as crab, sea horse, or lobster, out of other colors of construction paper.
● Write one number from 1 to 5 and the corresponding number of dots on each fish.
● Place the fish facedown on the construction paper fishbowl.

Food Shape Sorting

AGES
4+

Learning Objectives

Children will:
1. Sort based on shape.
2. Practice counting.

Vocabulary

bake	cookie	oven
bread	muffin	scone
cake		

Children's Books

Mr. Cookie Baker by Monica Wellington
Out and About at the Bakery by Jennifer A. Ericsson
What Happens at a Bakery? by Kathleen Pohl

Materials

felt
flannel board
scissors

Preparation

Cut the felt into shapes that represent cookies, bread loaves, scones, and muffins.

What to Do

1. Place the felt and the flannel board in one of the learning centers, such as home living or math.
2. Invite the children to sort the felt bakery shapes and then count them.
3. If appropriate, suggest that the children group the like baked goods together on the flannel board and then form a bar graph using the felt shapes.
4. Help the children use one-to-one correspondence to count the shapes and then compare the loaves of bread, number of cookies, and so on.

Assessment

1. Is the child able to sort the bakery shapes?
2. What did the child learn about counting?
3. Is the child able to create a bar graph with the bakery shapes?

Mary Murray, Mazomanie, WI

Hide the Bugs Counting Game

AGES 4+

Learning Objectives

Children will:
1. Practice counting.
2. Learn about one-to-one correspondence.
3. Practice number recognition.

Vocabulary

bird   hide   leaf
bug   insect

Children's Books

Bugs Rule! by Kathryn Stevens
Chirp, Chirp! Crickets in Your Backyard by
    Nancy Leowen

Materials

green construction paper
permanent marker
plastic zip-top bag
scissors
small bug stickers

Preparation

- Cut green construction paper into 10 simple leaf shapes, about the size of a half sheet of paper. Use the scraps to cut smaller leaf shapes large enough to cover the bug stickers.
- Print one number from 1 to 10 on each of the large leaf shapes, and add the corresponding number of bug stickers to each leaf.
- Place the large and small leaf shapes into the plastic bag for ease in storage.

What to Do

1. Explain that many insects hide under leaves for shade and to avoid getting eaten by birds.
2. Select a large leaf shape with more than one bug on it. Invite the children to count with you as you demonstrate "hiding" the bugs by placing a small leaf shape over each bug.
3. Count again as you remove each leaf shape to reveal the bugs underneath.
4. Play this game individually with children, letting them hide and uncover the bugs with the small leaf shapes as you count together.

number
large leaf shapes
bug sticker
small leaf shapes

Assessment

1. Is the child developing counting skills?
2. Does the child understand the one-to-one correspondence of the bugs to the leaves covering them?
3. Does the child recognize any of the numbers on the leaves?

Kay Flowers, Summerfield, OH

> **Teacher-to-Teacher Tip**
> Introduce addition by counting the bugs on two of the large leaf shapes, as in "one bug plus two bugs is one-two-three bugs."

Learning to Measure

AGES 4+

Learning Objectives

Children will:

1. Develop fine motor skills.
2. Begin to understand the concept of measuring.

Vocabulary

between	measurement	size
compare	object	understand
measure	relative	

Children's Books

Inch by Inch by Leo Lionni
Inchworm and a Half by Elinor J. Pinczes
Me and the Measure of Things by Joan Sweeney
Measuring Penny by Loreen Leedy

Materials

markers
paper
scissors

What to Do

1. Help the children trace a part of themselves—hand, arm, leg, finger, or any other part of the body—on paper.
2. Help the children cut out the body part and use it to measure items around the classroom.
3. Ask the children, "How many arms long is the table?" or "How many hands does it take to measure the chair?" or "How can we measure the circle area?"
4. This method gives children a concrete understanding of the concept of measuring. You can explain that horses are measured with hands.

M A T H

Assessment

1. Is the child developing the fine motor skills necessary to trace objects on paper and cut out shapes?
2. Is the child beginning to understand the concept of measuring?

Sandy L. Scott, Meridian, ID

My Number Book

AGES
4+

Learning Objectives
Children will:
1. Learn about numbers.
2. Learn one-to-one correspondence.

Vocabulary

book	match	numeral
collage	number	one-to-one

Children's Books
Numbers by Henry Arthur Pluckrose
The Right Number of Elephants
   by Jeff Sheppard

Materials
collage materials, such as feathers, flower
   petals, stickers, pieces of colored straw,
   pennies, buttons, wooden craft sticks, and
   pom-poms
marker
paper
stapler
tape

Preparation
Create one of the following books for each child in the class: Staple six pages together and cover the staples with tape. On the cover, write "[Child's name]'s Number Book." Write one numeral from 1 to 5 and the corresponding number of dots in the center of each page.

What to Do
1. Give each child a book containing the numbers 1 through 5.
2. Print the child's name on the cover of the book.
3. Give the children a variety of collage materials that they can glue into their books.
4. Have the children look at the numeral, count the dots on the page, and then count the correct number of items to glue on each page. For example, on the page labeled with the numeral 1, the child would count the one dot, and then could glue one colored straw or one button on the page. On the page labeled with the numeral 4, the child would count the four dots, and then might glue four flower petals or feathers on the page.

Assessment
1. Is the child learning about numbers?
2. Is the child beginning to understand one-to-one correspondence?

Natural Numerals

AGES 4+

Learning Objectives

Children will:

1. Use natural materials for counting practice.
2. Use natural materials to create written numbers.
3. Recognize numerals.

Vocabulary

dirt	number	pebble
natural	numeral	stone

Children's Books

Mother Goose Numbers on the Loose by Leo and Diane Dillon
Numbers by Henry Arthur Pluckrose

Materials

small sticks
small stones or pebbles

What to Do

1. Using your finger or a twig, draw a numeral in the dirt about 1' in size. Demonstrate how to arrange broken sticks or pebbles in the drawn line to make a natural numeral.

2. Draw more numerals in the dirt, and let the children find their own sticks and pebbles. Help the children recognize the written numerals and place the materials in the drawn lines. Ask the children if it still looks like the numeral they named before. If not, help them move their materials to better match the lines.

3. Add a challenge by placing stones or pebbles beside the numerals in the correct amount. Let the children count aloud with you as you place the pebbles.

4. This activity is best done outdoors but can also be done indoors with a sand table or in a jelly roll pan filled with sand. Let children pick up natural materials outdoors first, and then bring them inside to use in this activity.

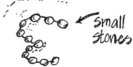

small stones

Assessment

1. Is the child able to place the natural materials inside the numeral?
2. Is the child able to use natural materials to create written numbers?
3. Is the child able to recognize numerals?

Kay Flowers, Summerfield, OH

Teacher-to-Teacher Tip

For even more practice, draw numerals in the dirt and invite the children to make matching side-by-side numerals with their materials so that now instead of one 3, for example, there will be two. This is a much more difficult activity, so try this only if you feel the children are ready. You want this to be a positive experience.

Picture Patterns

AGES 4+

Learning Objectives

Children will:
1. Learn about patterns.
2. Create patterns.

Vocabulary

copy   pattern
different   same

Children's Books

A-B-A-B-A a Book of Pattern Play by Brian P. Cleary
Pattern by Henry Arthur Pluckrose
Pattern Fish by Trudy Harris

Materials

cat and dog stickers
paper

What to Do

1. Do this activity with one child or a small group of children.
2. Show the children how to make a simple AB, AB, AB pattern with the cat and dog stickers by placing first a cat sticker, then a dog sticker, then a cat sticker, then a dog sticker, then a cat sticker, then a dog sticker on a piece of paper.
3. Ask one child to continue the pattern.
4. Repeat for the other children.
5. Once the children understand this pattern, add another sticker to create an ABC, ABC, ABC pattern, or use two or more stickers to create a more complicated pattern, such as ABBA, ABBA, ABBA or AABBCC, AABBCC, AABBCC.

Assessment

1. What did the child learn about patterns?
2. Is the child able to re-create existing patterns or create his own patterns?

Mary Murray, Mazomanie, WI

Sets of Pets

AGES 4+

Learning Objectives
Children will:
1. Practice counting.
2. Learn about one-to-one correspondence.
3. Practice fine motor skills.

Vocabulary
bird	dog	mouse
cat	fish	numbers

Children's Books
Guinea Pigs Add Up by Margery Cuyler
So Many Cats! by Beatrice Schenk de Regniers
Ten Dogs in the Window by Claire Masurel

Materials
plastic toy dogs, cats, birds, fish, and mice
boxes or plastic containers in a variety of sizes such as margarine containers, checkbook boxes, and so on
numeral cards, 1–10

Preparation
- Place a select number of toy pets (from 1 to 10) inside each container.
- Place the containers of toy animals at a table.

What to Do
1. Do this activity with one child or a small group of children.
2. Invite one child to spill out one container, count the number of pets inside, and then say the number aloud.
3. Help the child display the matching number card near the set of pets.
4. After the child has counted a group of pets, ask him to name each type of animal.
5. The child returns the toy animals to the first container before repeating the above with another container.

Assessment
1. What is the child learning about counting?
2. What is the child learning about one-to-one correspondence?
3. Is the child developing her fine motor skills by doing this activity?

Teacher-to-Teacher Tip
For older children, include a larger number of pets inside each container. For younger children, limit the number of pets to between 1 and 5.

Fingerplays, Songs, and Poems

One, Two, Three, Four, Five (Traditional)
One, two, three, four, five.
I caught a fish alive.
Six seven eight nine ten.
I let it go again.

Mary Murray, Mazomanie, WI

MATH

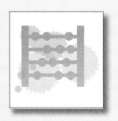

Which One Doesn't Belong?

AGES 4+

Learning Objectives
Children will:
1. Learn nursery rhymes.
2. Use thinking skills.

Vocabulary
words from nursery rhymes, for example, *lamb, fleece, white, school, tuffet, spider, curds, whey, sheep, cow, chicken, fiddle, cat, moon, dog, dish,* and *spoon*

Materials
card stock
contact paper or laminating materials
felt
flannel board
glue stick
pictures of characters and items from various nursery rhymes

Preparation
- For each nursery rhyme, make five cards with four pictures of characters and items from familiar nursery rhymes and one picture of a character or item that is not part of the nursery rhyme. For example, for the following rhymes, glue the following pictures on the pieces of card stock:
  - "Mary Had a Little Lamb"—Mary, lamb with white fleece, a school, children, and a cat
  - "Little Boy Blue"—a boy, a horn, sheep, cow, and a chicken
  - "Little Miss Muffet"—Miss Muffet, a spoon, a bowl, a spider, and a dog
  - "Hey, Diddle Diddle"—cat playing a fiddle, cow, moon, little dog laughing, and a mouse
- Laminate the cards for durability. Use glue to attach the cards to felt for flannel board use.

- Before presenting the activity, make sure the children know the following nursery rhymes: "Mary Had a Little Lamb," "Little Boy Blue," "Little Miss Muffet," and "Hey, Diddle Diddle."

Hey Diddle Diddle
Hey diddle diddle,
The cat and the fiddle,
The cow jumped over the moon,
The little dog laughed to see such sport,
And the dish ran away with the spoon.

Little Boy Blue
Little Boy Blue, come blow your horn,
The sheep's in the meadow; the cow's
*   in the corn.*
Where's the little boy who looks after
*   the sheep?*
He's under the haystack, fast asleep.

Little Miss Muffet
Little Miss Muffet sat on her tuffet,
Eating her curds and whey.
Along came a spider
And sat down beside her,
And frightened Miss Muffet away.

Mary Had a Little Lamb
Mary had a little lamb, little lamb, little lamb.
Mary had a little lamb,
Its fleece was white as snow.

Everywhere that Mary went, Mary went,
*   Mary went,*
Everywhere that Mary went,
The lamb was sure to go.

It followed her to school one day,
*   school one day, school one day.*
It followed her to school one day,
Which was against the rules.

It made the children laugh and play,
  laugh and play, laugh and play.
It made the children laugh and play,
To see a lamb at school.

What to Do

1. At group or circle time, use a flannel board to present one card at a time to the class.
2. Let the children discover that one picture does not belong, and then ask them to look carefully at the pictures and name the rhyme they think the pictures represent.
3. After they give the correct name of the rhyme, ask one child to point to the one picture that does not belong, and then say the rhyme together.
4. Continue with the cards for the other rhymes.
5. Tell the children that you are going to place these cards in the literacy center, where they can do this activity independently.

Assessment

1. Is the child improving his ability to recite nursery rhymes from memory?
2. Can the child identify the one item that does not belong with the nursery rhyme?

Jackie Wright, Enid, OK

Will They Balance?

AGES
4+

Learning Objectives

Children will:
1. Learn how to weigh things.
2. Learn the meaning of *balance*.
3. Work on comparing and contrasting skills.

Vocabulary

balance	contrast	scales
compare	rocks	weight

What to Do

1. Place a balance scale and a collection of rocks at the math center.
2. Invite the children to use the rocks and the balance scale to explore the concept of balance.

Children's Books

If You Find a Rock by Peggy Christian
You Can Use a Balance by Linda Bullock

Materials

balance scale
different types of rocks

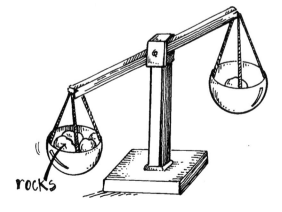

rocks

3. If the ages and abilities of the children in the class support it, suggest that the children estimate weight and then compare and contrast the weights of various rocks. Encourage the children to verbalize their findings: "The black rock is heavier than the white rock" or "The bumpy rock weighs more than the smooth rock."

Assessment
1. Is the child learning how to weigh things?
2. Is the child learning the meaning of *balance*?
3. Is the child developing comparing and contrasting skills?

Mary Murray, Mazomanie, WI

Carpet Numbers

AGES
5+

Learning Objectives
Children will:
1. Learn counting skills.
2. Explore one-to-one correspondence.

Vocabulary
count   numeral   same
number   object

Children's Books
Best Counting Book Ever by Richard Scarry
The Coin Counting Book by Rozanne Lanczak Williams
Counting Crocodiles by Judy Sierra

What to Do
1. Show the children the numeral carpets. Explain how the number of circles or squares on each carpet is the same as the numeral on the carpet.
2. Show the children how to place small toys in each circle or square and then to count each object.
3. Find other fun items to count and cover spaces with.
4. At circle or group time, let the children sit on the number carpets. Ask the each child to identify her number.

Materials
10 or more plain carpet pieces (For younger children, begin with 5 carpet pieces.)
classroom objects to count, such as teddy bear counters, small cars, and small blocks
paint or permanent markers

Preparation
Use paint or markers to write numerals on each carpet piece. Draw the corresponding number of circles or boxes for the number on each carpet piece.

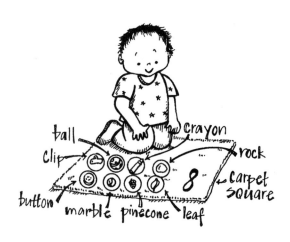
ball
crayon
clip
rock
button
marble
pinecone
leaf
8"
carpet square

Another Encyclopedia of Theme Activities

5. At the end of group time, ask the children to stack the carpet squares in numerical order as they leave the circle.
6. Place the number carpets out for obstacle course challenges, such as clap this many times at this place, jump this many times at this square, and so on.

Assessment

1. Is the child using this hands-on experience to learn counting skills?
2. Is the child exploring and beginning to understand one-to-one correspondence?

Bev Schumacher, Racine, WI

Flower Counter

Learning Objectives
Children will:
1. Improve counting skills.
2. Improve fine motor skills.

Vocabulary

count　　　number　　　sunflower

Children's Books
The Sunflower Parable by Liz Curtis Higgs
Sunflowers by Mary Ann McDonald

What to Do
1. Show the children the sunflowers and the sunflower seeds.
2. Suggest that the children count out the designated number of seeds and set them on each flower center.
3. If appropriate, write a simple math addition equation on each flower. Ask the children to display the two sets of seeds and then add them together.

Materials
black sunflower seeds
marker
scissors
yellow paper

Preparation
● Cut 10 sunflowers from the yellow paper.
● Number each yellow flower shape from 1 to 5 or 1 to 10, depending on the ages and abilities of the children in your class.

Assessment

1. Are the child's counting skills improving by doing this activity?
2. Is the child developing improved fine motor skills by doing this activity?

Mary Murray, Mazomanie, WI

Race to the Finish

AGES 5+

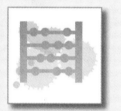

Learning Objectives
Children will:
1. Develop counting skills.
2. Learn number recognition.

Vocabulary
count   move   roll
die   number

Children's Books
Numbers by Henry Arthur Pluckrose
The Racecar Alphabet by Brian Floca
The Wheels on the Race Car by Alex Zane

Materials
cube-shaped block to make your own die
number stickers
permanent marker
small toy car
yardstick

Preparation
- Place the number stickers in order on the yardstick spaced apart at least the length of the toy car.
- Write the word *Start* by the number 1 and *Finish* by the last number. This is your racetrack.
- Make a die using the cube-shaped block. Write the numbers on it that you want the children to learn.

What to Do
1. Do this activity with one child or a small group of children.
2. One child rolls the die, identifies the number, and then moves the car that number of spaces.
3. The child continues until the car has reached the finish line.

Assessment
1. Is the child developing improved counting skills by doing this activity?
2. Is the child learning number recognition?

Tracey Neumarke, Chicago, IL

Size 'Em Up!

AGES 5+

Learning Objectives

Children will:
1. Understand size relationships.
2. Practice estimating size.
3. Use critical thinking skills.

Vocabulary

big	medium	smallest
bigger	small	
biggest	smaller	

Children's Books

Actual Size by Steve Jenkins
Size by Henry Arthur Pluckrose
Ten Dogs in the Window by Claire Masurel

Materials

large box containing an assortment of stuffed toy pets of varying sizes

What to Do

1. Invite the children to remove the pets from the box.
2. Ask the children to determine which animal is smallest and which is largest, and then to line up the pets in order from smallest to largest.
3. Encourage the children to verbalize what they are doing as they work.
4. Tell the children to return the pets to the box when they are finished.

Assessment

1. Is the child able to put the animals in size order?
2. Is the child estimating size as she does the activity?
3. Is the child improving his use of critical thinking skills as he does the activity?

Mary Murray, Mazomanie, WI

Teacher-to-Teacher Tips

- For older children, incorporate a larger number of animals.
- Create a smaller version of this activity by filling a lunch bag with paper animal shapes of varying size.

M A T H

Spill 'Em Out!

AGES 5+

Learning Objectives
Children will:
1. Learn about counting.
2. Learn about numbers.

Vocabulary
bag   pet
count   spill

Children's Books
My Pet by Debbie Bailey
Pets by Tony Ross
Rats and Mice by Honor Head

Materials
brown paper bags or decorative gift bags
music
objects related to the plastic or beanbag pets, such as craft feathers for birds, dog biscuits for dogs, toy mice for cats, rocks for snakes, and seashells for fish
toy plastic or beanbag pets, such as birds, dogs, cats, snakes, and fish

Preparation
- Make one bag for each child in the group.
- Considering the children's ages and abilities, place the appropriate number of objects in each bag along with the related pet.

What to Do
1. Invite a small group of children to sit in a circle. Hand one bag to each child in the circle.
2. Play some music as you instruct the children to pass the bags around the circle.
3. When the music stops, each child empties her bag, names the pet inside, and counts the related items.
4. After each child has counted the number of items in her bag, ask the children to place the items back in their bags.
5. Start the music again and repeat the activity until everyone has had several opportunities to name a pet and count the objects in the bag.

Assessment
1. Does the child improve his counting skills as he does this activity?
2. What is the child learning about numbers?

Mary Murray, Mazomanie, WI

The Little Red Hen Song

Learning Objectives
Children will:
1. Learn a new song.
2. Develop language and singing skills.

Vocabulary

bake	eat	plant	thresh
bread	hen	seed	tune
cut	oven	sing	wheat
dough			

Children's Books
The Little Red Hen by Paul Galdone
The Little Red Hen by Diane Muldrow
The Little Red Hen by Jerry Pinkney

Materials
none needed

What to Do
1. Teach the children the song "The Little Red Hen."

"The Little Red Hen"
by Jackie Wright
(Tune: "Here We Go 'Round the Mulberry Bush")

This is the way I plant the seed,
Plant the seed, plant the seed.
This is the way I plant the seed,
Early in the morning.

This is the way I cut the wheat,
Cut the wheat, cut the wheat.
This is the way I cut the wheat,
Early in the morning.

This is the way I thresh the wheat,
Thresh the wheat, thresh the wheat.
This is the way I thresh the wheat,
Early in the morning.

This is the way I make the dough,
Make the dough, make the dough.
This is the way I make the dough,
Early in the morning.

This is the way I bake the bread,
Bake the bread, bake the bread.
This is the way I bake the bread,
Early in the morning.

This is the way I eat the bread,
Eat the bread, eat the bread.
This is the way I eat the bread,
Early in the morning.

2. Read one of the suggested books, then talk with the children about the song and the story.

Assessment
1. Is the child able to learn and sing the new song?
2. What language and singing skills is the child developing?

Jackie Wright, Enid, OK

MUSIC and MOVEMENT

One Elephant Went Out to Play

AGES 3+

Learning Objectives
Children will:
1. Learn the words and tune to a new song.
2. Act out the song.

Vocabulary
elephant   play

fun   spiderweb

Children's Books
One Elephant Went Out to Play by Sanja Rescek
The Right Number of Elephants by Jeff
    Sheppard

Materials
none needed

What to Do
1. Teach the children the following traditional song:

   One elephant went out to play,
   Upon a spider's web one day.
   He had such enormous fun
   That he called for another elephant to come.

2. Show the children how to hold one arm like an elephant's trunk and reach between their legs to grab the arm of another child.
3. Select one child to be the lead elephant. Sing the song again as this child walks around the circle.
4. As you sing the next verse, select another child to be an elephant. The first child reaches through his legs to grab the "trunk" of the elephant joining him.

   Two elephants went out to play
   Upon a spider's web one day.
   They had such enormous fun
   That they called for another elephant to come.

5. Select another child until the entire class is a group of connected elephants singing the song and walking around the circle.

Assessment
1. Is the child able to learn the words and the tune to the song?
2. Is the child able to act like an elephant as the class acts out the song?

Jackie Wright, Enid, OK

Animal Parade

Learning Objectives

Children will:

1. Express themselves in creative movements.
2. Understand different types of movement.

Vocabulary

gallop	swim
hop	tiptoe
jump	waddle
prance	

Children's Books

Biggest, Strongest, Fastest by Steve Jenkins
Move! by Robin Page
Playground Day by Jennifer Merz
Swing, Slither, or Swim: A Book About Animal Movements by Patricia M. Stockland

Materials

pictures of animals in motion or books about how animals move (see suggestions)

Preparation

Find a spacious area for the parade.

What to Do

1. Show the children pictures of animals in motion or read one of the books about how animals move. Brainstorm ways to represent animal movements. For example, a penguin can waddle: with arms at your side and hands out. An elephant can stretch its trunk: outstretched arms with hands clasped can represent an elephant's trunk. Rabbits can hop, horses can gallop, and mice can walk softly on tiptoe.

2. After the class has practiced animal movements, they are ready for a parade. Each child can move like a different animal or the whole class can demonstrate how one animal moves.

3. Use different types of music and encourage the children to move to the rhythm.

a penguin

Assessment

1. Is the child able to express how animals move using creative movements?

2. Does the child understand different types of movement (hop, gallop, waddle, and so on) and attempt different types of movement?

MaryLouise Alu Curto, Mercerville, NJ

Teacher-to-Teacher Tip

You can play Simon Says with animal movements.

MUSIC and MOVEMENT

Books with a Beat

AGES 4+

Learning Objectives
Children will:
1. Learn to anticipate parts of a book.
2. Learn about beat and rhythm.

Vocabulary
beat	gently
books	rhythm
bounce	words
freeze	

Children's Books
Bear Snores On by Karma Wilson
Bear Wants More by Karma Wilson
Bear's New Friend by Karma Wilson

Materials
beanbag or stuffed animals, one for each child

Preparation
Read *Bear Snores On* ahead of time to know when to speak loudly, softly, quickly, and slowly.

What to Do
1. Gather the children in a circle.
2. Tell the children that you are going to hand them something very special and they are to place it quietly in their laps until you tell them to "wake it up." Pass out the beanbags (or small stuffed animals) one at a time.
3. Ask the preschoolers to "wake up" the animal by gently bouncing it on their laps. Instruct them to slowly and gently bounce their beanbag animal while you read them a book but to listen for a surprise!
4. As the children bounce their beanbags, read *Bear Snores On* using loud, soft, fast, and slow speech patterns.
5. Before you get to the part about the bear snoring on, say, "Freeze." Ask the children to stop gently bouncing their beanbag animals while you read the next part of the book about the bear snoring in a slow whisper voice.
6. Continue this pattern as you read the book. Suggest that the children whisper with you the part of the book about the bear snoring. Children love the anticipation and the repetition.
7. Collect the beanbag animals quietly because they are tired and need to rest, just like the bear in the story.

Assessment
1. Is the child able to anticipate the repeating part of the book?
2. Is the child able to bounce the beanbag animal to a beat?
3. Is the child able to follow the directions?

Kara Stokke, Maumelle, AR

Teacher-to-Teacher Tip
Use this technique with other books to highlight the dramatic parts of the stories and to keep the children actively engaged.

Circle Fun

AGES 4+

Learning Objectives
Children will:
1. Learn gross motor skills.
2. Learn new vocabulary.
3. Follow directions.

Vocabulary
around	inside	outside
in	out	

Children's Books
Circles by Sarah L. Schuette
Round and Square by Miriam Schlein
So Many Circles, So Many Squares
   by Tana Hoban

Materials
circle poly spots (from school supply stores or catalogs) or small hoops, one per child
"The Circle" by Hap Palmer (*Getting to Know Myself* CD) or "The Circle Song" by KidzUp Production Inc. (*The Top 30 Preschool Songs* CD; also available on iTunes)

Preparation
- Use circle poly spots to mark each child's personal space, but arrange the spots in a big circle on the floor. Leave enough room between the spots for the children to walk around their spots.
- Listen to both songs a few times so that you are familiar with them before trying to lead the children.

What to Do
1. Ask the children to sit on their spots and then talk about the shape that they've formed. (It's a circle!)
2. Tell the children that the class is going to sing "The Circle" together.
3. Teach the children the movements in "The Circle" (clap four times, tap knees three times, tap shoes two times, shout hurray one time) before you start playing the song.
4. Play the song and do the movements.
5. After singing this song, introduce another circle song and have the children stand up and prepare to move all around their big circle.
6. Follow the prompts in the song to know what to do: walk around the circle, stand inside the circle, and so on.

Assessment
1. What gross motor skills did the child learn?
2. Which new words did the child learn?
3. Is the child able to follow the directions?

Melissa McKenzie, Cypress, TX

Teacher-to-Teacher Tip
If you have time, play "The Circle" by Hap Palmer a second time if you had children who were really challenged with the concepts of inside and outside. Observe whether these children are more successful the second time.

MUSIC and MOVEMENT

Fascinating Fish

AGES
4+

Learning Objectives

Children will:

1. Learn basic facts about fish.
2. Improve fine motor skills.
3. Develop oral language skills.

Vocabulary

count   fish
fingers   numbers

What to Do

1. Teach the children the following fingerplay.

Five Little Fishies

Five little fishies, swimming in a pool
  (Wiggle five fingers)
The first one said, "The pool is cool."
  (Show one finger)
The second one said, "The pool is deep."
  (Show two fingers)
The third one said, "I want to sleep."
  (Show three fingers)

The fourth one said, "Let's take a dip."
  (Show four fingers)
The fifth one said, "I spy a ship." (Show
  five fingers)
Fisher boat comes,
Line goes kersplash, (Pretend to throw
  fishing line)
Away the five little fishies dash. (Wiggle five
  fingers away)

2. Repeat the fingerplay and then teach the children some of the following fish facts:
   - Fish have scales, fins, and gills.
   - Fish swim in water.
   - Fish lay eggs.
   - Fish eat plant life, algae, and other fish.
   - There are many kinds of fish.

Assessment

1. What did the child learn about fish?
2. Is the child able to do the fingerplay?
3. Is the child able to learn the words to the fingerplay?

Mary Murray, Mazomanie, WI

Children's Books

Fish Eyes: A Book You Can Count On
  by Lois Ehlert
Fish Wish by Bob Barner
The Rainbow Fish by Marcus Pfister
Swimmy by Leo Lionni

Materials

none needed

From Egg to Duck

Learning Objectives
Children will:
1. Learn about ducks.
2. Learn about life cycles.

Vocabulary
duck
duckling
egg
hatch

Children's Books
Duck by Louise Spilsbury
I'm a Duck by Teri Sloat
Mallard Duck at Meadow View Pond
    by Wendy Pfeffer
*A New Duck: My First Look at the Life Cycle of a
    Bird* by Pamela Hickman

Materials
books about ducks (see suggestions) or
    photos of a duck egg, a hatching egg, a
    duckling, and a duck

What to Do
1. Teach the children the song "Two Fuzzy Ducklings."

"Two Fuzzy Ducklings"
    by Laura Wynkoop
(Tune: "Two Little Blackbirds")

*Two fuzzy ducklings sitting near a lake.
    (Start with your hands behind your back.)
One named Jane. (Bring one hand to the
    front with your index finger extended.)
One named Jake. (Bring your other hand to
    the front with your index finger extended.)
Swim away, Jane! (Move the hand
    representing Jane behind your back.)
Swim away, Jake! (Do the same with your "Jake" hand.)
Come back, Jane! (Bring "Jane" back to the front.)
Come back, Jake! (Bring "Jake" back to the front.)*

2. Read one of the books about ducks or show the children photos of a duck egg, a hatching egg, a duckling, and a duck.
3. Discuss the life cycle of a duck. Explain that an egg hatches into a duckling, which begins the life cycle of a duck.

Assessment
1. What did the child learn about ducks?
2. What did the child learn about the life cycle of ducks?
3. Is the child able to learn the song and sing it with the class?

Laura D. Wynkoop, San Dimas, CA

MUSIC and MOVEMENT

Hush, Little Baby

AGES 4+

Learning Objectives
Children will:
1. Practice rhyming skills.
2. Learn the words to a traditional lullaby.

Vocabulary
billy goat	diamond ring	mockingbird
bull	horse	Rover
cart	looking glass	

Children's Books
Lala Salama: A Tanzanian Lullaby by Patricia MacLachan
Time for Bed by Mem Fox

Materials
none needed

What to Do
1. Read the children one of the lullaby books (see suggestions).
2. Teach the children "Hush, Little Baby," a traditional lullaby.

"Hush, Little Baby"

Hush, little baby, don't say a word.
Mama's going to buy you a mockingbird.
If that mockingbird won't sing,
Mama's going to buy you a diamond ring.
If that diamond ring turns brass,
Mama's going to buy you a looking glass.
If that looking glass gets broke,
Mama's going to buy you a billy goat.
If that billy goat won't pull,
Mama's going to buy you a cart and bull.
If that cart and bull turn over,
Mama's going to buy you a dog named Rover
If that dog named Rover won't bark,
Mama's going to buy you a horse and cart.
If that horse and cart fall down,
You'll still be the sweetest little baby in town.

3. Talk with the children about the vocabulary in the song. Explain terms that the children might not understand.
4. Sing the song again, emphasizing the rhyming words: *word/mockingbird, sing/ring, brass/glass, pull/bull, over/Rover,* and *down/town.*
5. Suggest that the children sing this lullaby to the babies in the home living area.

Assessment
1. Is the child able to recognize the rhyming words?
2. Is the child able to learn the words to this song?

Jackie Wright, Enid, OK

I'm Looking for a Heart

AGES 4+

Learning Objectives
Children will:
1. Learn a new song.
2. Practice visual discrimination skills.
3. Recognize sight words.

Vocabulary
basket
heart
words that are printed on the hearts

Children's Books
Best Little Word Book Ever by Richard Scarry
My Heart Is Like a Zoo by Michael Hall
There's a Wocket in My Pocket! by Dr. Seuss

Materials
basket
construction paper
marker
scissors

Preparation
● Cut the construction paper into hearts. Create pairs of hearts that match by writing the same word on two hearts.
● Print sight words that the children are learning, or print words that relate to the monthly theme.

What to Do
1. Place one set of hearts in a basket, and bring the basket to group or circle time.
2. Stack the other set of hearts near you.
3. Sing the following song as you hold up a heart from the stack:

"I'm Looking for a Heart"
   by Jackie Wright
(Tune: "Camptown Races")

I am looking for a heart
With a word I'll show you.
Search inside the basket
And then we will have two!

4. Take one heart from the stack near you. Then invite a volunteer to look inside the basket and find the heart with the same word as the one you are holding (from the stack).
5. When the child finds the match, tell the children what the word is.
6. Set this pair aside and repeat the song until all the words are matched.

Assessment
1. Is the child able to learn the new song?
2. Does the child have the visual discrimination skills to recognize when the two words match?
3. Is the child able to recognize the sight words?

Jackie Wright, Enid, OK

MUSIC and MOVEMENT

Musical "Tree-Struments"

Learning Objectives
Children will:
1. Explore the sounds that natural objects can make.
2. Develop listening skills.

Vocabulary

acorn	sounds
drums	stick
instruments	wood
pinecone	

What to Do
1. Display a variety of wooden sticks from tree branches.
2. Invite the children to tap them together to hear what they sound like.
3. Suggest that the children tap a stick on a slice of tree trunk and use it like a drum.
4. Place five acorns in one container and five pinecones in another.
5. The children can cover the containers, give them a shake, and compare their sounds.

Assessment
1. Did the child explore the sounds that natural objects make?
2. Did the child develop her listening skills?

Mary Murray, Mazomanie, WI

Children's Books
Different Sounds by Charlotte Guillain
Making Sounds by Charlotte Guillain
Sound by Melissa Gish
What Is Sound? by Charlotte Guillain

Materials

acorns and pinecones, if available
plastic containers
slice of tree trunk
sticks from trees (no longer than 12")

Stories with Sound

Learning Objectives
Children will:
1. Be introduced to classic stories.
2. Learn storytelling.
3. Follow directions.

Vocabulary

sounds
stories

Another Encyclopedia of Theme Activities

Children's Books
Cat Goes Fiddle-I-Fee by Paul Galdone
The Elves and the Shoemaker by Paul Galdone
The Gingerbread Boy by Paul Galdone
Henny Penny by Paul Galdone
The Little Red Hen by Paul Galdone
The Three Bears by Paul Galdone
The Three Billy Goats Gruff by Paul Galdone
The Three Little Kittens by Paul Galdone
The Three Little Pigs by Paul Galdone

Materials
any classic tale by Paul Galdone
box labeled "sounds"
classroom items that make sounds (or instruments if you have some), one for each child

Preparation
- Before doing the activity with the children, read the classic tale you have chosen. Decide where the children will add their sounds in the story.
- Prepare the sound box by placing the classroom items or classroom musical instruments in the box.

What to Do
1. Have the children sit in a circle.
2. Place the sound box in the middle of the circle.
3. Pick one child at a time to choose from the box until every child has a sound maker.
4. Tell the children that they should listen as you read the story. You will ask them for sound at different times, but until then, they need to keep their sounds silent and in their laps.
5. Read the story with great enthusiasm! (One suggestion when reading *The Three Little Kittens* is for the children to play their sounds during the part of the story when the kittens say "meow, meow, meow" and "purr, purr.")

Assessment
1. Does the child enjoy the classic stories?
2. What did the child learn about storytelling?
3. Is the child able to follow directions about when to play his instrument?

Kara Stokke, Maumelle, AR

Teacher-to-Teacher Tip
Use this technique to engage the children's participation and anticipation as you read any book.

I Like Animals

AGES 5+

Learning Objectives
Children will:
1. Learn a song and rhythm skills.
2. Develop gross motor skills.
3. Improve their oral language skills.

Vocabulary
arrow	dog	snake
beat	fish	sticks
bird	march	turtle
cat	sing	

MUSIC and MOVEMENT

Children's Books

The Furry Animal Alphabet Book by Jerry Pallotta

Zoopa: An Animal Alphabet by Gianna Marino

Materials

rhythm sticks, one pair per child (or other percussion rhythm instruments)

What to Do

1. Invite the children to form a large circle.
2. Teach the children how to march in a circle and then teach the children the following song:

"I Like Animals"
by Mary Murray
(Tune: "Mary Had a Little Lamb")

I like animals, yes I do.
Yes I do. Yes I do.
I like animals, oh, yes I do.
How about you?

3. At the end of the song, select one child and ask him to name his favorite animal.
4. Give each child a pair of rhythm sticks.
5. Sing the song again and suggest that each child play the rhythm sticks to the beat of the song.
6. Continue singing until all the children have had a turn to name their favorite animals.

Assessment

1. Is the child able to learn the song and march around the circle?
2. Is the child able to tap her rhythm sticks to the beat of the song?
3. Is the child able to learn the words to the song?

Mary Murray, Mazomanie, WI

Teacher-to-Teacher Tip

To make simple rhythm instruments for this activity, place a small handful of unpopped corn kernels inside a plastic egg or yogurt container with a lid, and tape it shut. These shakers are great for small hands to make music. For younger children, omit the rhythm instruments, and simply have the children march and sing.

At the Grocery Store

AGES
3+

Learning Objectives

Children will:

1. Learn that grocery stores are where you buy food.
2. Learn about the many jobs at the grocery store.

Vocabulary

bag	grocery	shop
cart	shelf	store
food		

Children's Books

At the Supermarket by Anne Rockwell
Grandpa's Corner Store by Dyanne DiSalvo
Max Goes to the Grocery Store by Adria F. Klein
Our Corner Grocery Store by Joanne Schwartz
Working at a Grocery Store by Katie Marsico

Materials

brown grocery bags
collection of grocery items

Preparation

Place the grocery store materials in the dramatic play area.

What to Do

1. Read one of the books about grocery stores.
2. Talk with the children about what a grocery store is and the jobs that people need to do in a grocery store. Explain that in big grocery stores, each job is done by a separate person, but in small stores like corner grocery stores, many jobs may be done by one person.
3. Ask the children what they like about the grocery store and the food they like from grocery stores.
4. Tell the children that there are grocery store materials in the dramatic play area for them to use in their play.

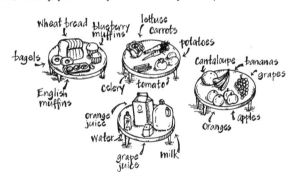

Assessment

1. Does the child understand that grocery stores are where you buy food?
2. Can the child describe the jobs at a grocery store?

Mary Murray, Mazomanie, WI

At the Library

AGES 3+

Learning Objectives

Children will:

1. Learn about the library.
2. Learn that reading books is helpful and enjoyable.

Vocabulary

books   library
librarian   read

What to Do

1. Display the books standing up on a table.
2. Ask the children to form a line behind you.
3. Lead the children around the classroom as you sing "At the Library."

> **"At the Library"**
> by Mary Murray
> *(Tune: "The More We Get Together")*
>
> *We're going to the library, library, library.*
> *We're going to the library to check out*
> *   some books.*
> *There's this book and that book, there's*
> *   this book and that book.*
> *We're going to the library to check out*
> *   some books.*
>
> *We're going to the library, library, library.*
> *We're going to the library to take back our*
> *   books.*
> *There's this book and that book, there's*
> *   this book and that book.*
> *We're going to the library to take back our*
> *   books.*

Children's Books

Homer, the Library Cat by Reeve Lindbergh
The Library by Sarah Stewart
The Library Doors by Toni Buzzeo
A Visit to the Library by Blake A. Hoena

Materials

bell
fiction and nonfiction books, at least one per
   child

4. Invite the children to sit and listen quietly as you read one of the suggested books.
5. Talk with the children about the library or the many jobs a library worker may have.

Assessment

1. What did the child learn about the library?
2. Is the child beginning to understand that reading books is helpful and enjoyable?

Mary Murray, Mazomanie, WI

Town Puzzles

AGES
3+

Learning Objectives
Children will:
1. Learn about the buildings in their community.
2. Develop observation skills.

Vocabulary
(There may be more, depending on your area.)

airport	hospital
apartments	houses
bakery	library
bank	park
church	police department
department store	school
doctor's office	street
fire department	train station

Children's Books
Busy, Busy Town by Richard Scarry
The City Kid & the Suburb Kid by Deb Pilutti
A Day in a City by Nicholas Harris
I Live in the Desert by Gini Holland
I Live in the Mountains by Gini Holland
I Live Near the Ocean by Gini Holland
Living in Urban Communities by Kristin Sterling
Places in My Community by Bobbie Kalman
Where Do I Live? by Neil Chesanow

Materials
clear contact paper
photos of important buildings in your community
poster board of any color
scissors
white card stock

Preparation
- Download photos. Print two copies of each community building on white card stock. Trim off excess edges around the photos. Attach one photo to a piece of poster board cut slightly larger than the photo. Laminate both the photo on card stock and the poster board photo.
- Cut the card stock photo into several pieces to make a puzzle.

What to Do
1. Show the children the photos during group time.
2. Talk with the children about the buildings in the pictures, their names, and what happens in each building.
3. Place the puzzles in various learning centers throughout the room.
4. Allow each child to choose a puzzle to work. Discuss the building and whether the child or someone they know has ever been to the building.
5. Suggest that the children examine the details of the buildings.

Assessment
1. What did the child learn about the buildings in his community?
2. What observation skills did the child use to notice the details of the buildings in the photos?

Tina R. Durham-Woehler, Lebanon, TN

At the Bakery

AGES **4+**

Learning Objectives
Children will:
1. Learn about bakeries and bakers.
2. Develop fine motor skills.

Vocabulary

bake	icing	rolling pin
baker	milk	spatula
bowl	mix	spoon
eggs	oven	sugar
flour	pan	

Children's Books
Jalapeño Bagels by Natasha Wing
The Little Red Hen traditional story
    by many authors
Sun Bread by Elisa Kleven
Tony's Bread by Tomi dePaola
What Happens in a Bakery? by Kathleen Pohl

Materials
brown cardboard box to use as an oven
equipment found in a bakery, such as mixing
    bowls and spoons; clean, empty food
    containers of milk, butter, sugar, vanilla,
    flour, baking powder; pot holders; cookie
    sheets; spatulas; flour sifter; rolling pin;
    and cookie cutters
plates
sign that reads "Bakery"

What to Do
1. Tell the children they will be learning about a very special place in the community called the bakery.
2. Talk with the children about bakeries and what bakers do. Read one of the suggested books.
3. Show and describe the baking equipment to the children and then invite various children to use the equipment and pretend to perform the following tasks:
   - measure and add ingredients to a bowl and mix cookie dough
   - put cookie shapes on cookie sheet
   - sift flour
   - roll out cookie dough
   - cut out cookie shapes
   - carry cookie sheet to oven
   - remove hot cookie sheet from oven
   - remove cookies from cookie sheet and put them on a plate
4. Ask the children what they think they might find at a bakery.
5. Sing "It's Fun to Be a Baker" with the children.

box ↓ ←details drawn on

"It's Fun to Be a Baker"
  by Mary Murray
(Tune: "Did You Ever See a Lassie?")

It's fun to be a baker, a baker, a baker.
Oh, it's fun to be a baker and bake all day long.
You mix and you measure ingredients together.
Oh, it's fun to be a baker and bake all day long!

6. Place the baking equipment in the dramatic play area for the children's use.

Assessment
1. What did the child learn about bakeries and bakers?
2. Does the child have the fine motor skills to act out what bakers do?

Mary Murray, Mazomanie, WI

Construction Worker Puzzle

AGES 4+

Learning Objectives
Children will:
1. Develop fine motor skills.
2. Interact cooperatively with other children.
3. Develop language skills.

Vocabulary
above	hard hat	tool belt
construction worker	next to	under
	pliers	wrench
hammer	screwdriver	

Children's Books
A Day in the Life of a Construction Worker
  by Heather Adamson
Monkey with a Tool Belt by Chris Monroe
Toolbox Twins by Lola M. Schaefer

Materials
card stock
clear contact paper
computer and color printer
felt
flannel board
picture of a construction worker wearing a tool belt and hard hat (Use a search engine, such as Google Images, to find a picture.)
rubber cement (for adult use only)
scissors

Preparation
● Print on card stock a large picture of a construction worker wearing a tool belt and hard hat, then reduce the size of the image and print the smaller image on card stock.
● Laminate both pictures or cover them with clear contact paper.
● Cut the large picture into puzzle pieces (enough for each child in your class). Use rubber cement to attach the puzzle pieces to felt. Cut around the puzzle pieces again, trimming away the excess felt.

What to Do

1. Display the small picture of a construction worker wearing a tool belt and hard hat where the children can see and use it as a guide.
2. Distribute one puzzle piece to each child.
3. Ask one child to put his piece on the flannel board.
4. Encourage the other children to figure out how their pieces fit to complete the puzzle.
5. Ask them to talk about their pieces and help one another decide which piece belongs where.
6. Let one child at a time place her puzzle piece on the flannel board.
7. Once the puzzle is complete, put the puzzle pieces, small picture, and flannel board in a center.

Assessment

1. Is the child able to work cooperatively with the other children to complete the puzzle?
2. Is the child developing the fine motor skills necessary to work on a puzzle?
3. Is the child developing the language skills he needs to make himself understood by others?

Jackie Wright, Enid, OK

The Cook

AGES
4+

Learning Objectives

Children will:

1. Learn about the job of a cook or chef in a restaurant.
2. Develop language skills.

Vocabulary

chef	food	restaurant
cook	menu	table

Children's Books

Food for Thought by Saxton Freymann and Joost Eifferes
I Want to Be a Chef by Dan Liebman

Materials

chart paper
cooking equipment, such as a large plastic bowl, measuring spoons, empty spice bottles, empty food containers, pot, wooden spoon
marker

What to Do

1. At group or circle time, talk with the children about cooks and making food to eat. Explain that in our homes, families make food to eat, and in our community restaurants, cooks make food to eat.
2. Place the cooking equipment in the middle of the circle. Ask the children to describe how each piece of equipment is used.

3. Invite the children to talk about what foods they like to eat at their favorite restaurants. Record some of their favorite foods on a word list and display it at the writing center.

4. Tell the children that the equipment will be in the home living center for them to use to pretend to be cooks in a restaurant.

Assessment

1. What did the child learn about the job of a cook or chef in a restaurant?

2. Does the child have the language skills to participate in the class discussions?

Mary Murray, Mazomanie, WI

wooden spoon — soup pot — bowl — spice bottle — sauce pan — frying pan

Doorbells

AGES **4+**

Learning Objectives
Children will:
1. Learn about sound.
2. Develop language skills.

Vocabulary

bell	ding-dong	ring
buzzer	house	sound

Children's Book
The Doorbell Rang by Pat Hutchins

Materials
handbells or xylophone

What to Do

1. Talk with the children about why houses and homes have doorbells. Explain that a ringing doorbell tells us when someone is at the door.

2. Ask the children to describe the sounds of their doorbells. Is it a sound like a buzzer? Does it have a ding-dong sound? Or is it a different sound?

3. Ask one child at a time to use the xylophone to make a doorbell sound.

4. Tell the children that the xylophone will be in the home living area for visitors to use to announce their arrival.

Assessment

1. Is the child able to understand why houses and homes have doorbells?

2. Is the child able to describe the sound of his doorbell at home?

Mary Murray, Mazomanie, WI

Matching Houses

AGES 4+

Learning Objectives
Children will:
1. Match like patterns.
2. Use thinking skills.

Vocabulary

color	house	pattern
design	match	same

Children's Books
Homes in Many Cultures by Heather Adamson
Houses and Homes by Ann Morris
Let's Go Home: The Wonderful Things About a House by Cynthia Rylant
A Pair of Socks by Stuart J. Murphy

Materials
glue or tape
poster board or tagboard
scissors
wallpaper/upholstery sample book

Preparation
- Cut two house shapes from each different pattern of wallpaper. (For young children, start with five different patterns. Use 20 or more different patterns with older children.)
- Attach each shape to tagboard for durability.
- Divide the house shapes into two piles with one house shape of each pattern in each pile.

What to Do
1. Ask a small group of children to form a circle on the carpeted area of the classroom.
2. Place one pile of house shapes facedown in front of you. Give the other shapes to five (or more if you are using more house shapes) children.
3. Explain that they will be playing a house-matching game. Ask the children to play the game without talking.
4. Turn over the first house shape in your stack and place it in the center of the circle.
5. Ask the five children to look at their house shapes. If they hold the matching house, they are to place it next to your house card.
6. Continue playing this silent matching game until all the cards have been matched.
7. Collect all the cards and repeat the activity. This time describe the pattern or color of material on your card and invite each child to repeat your description as he matches his card with yours.

Assessment
1. Is the child able to match like patterns?
2. Is the child able to describe the patterns and understand when the two patterns match?

Mary Murray, Mazomanie, WI

Taking Care of Buildings

AGES
4+

Learning Objectives
Children will:
1. Learn about the many jobs of a building maintenance person.
2. Develop oral language skills.

Vocabulary
broom   mop   wrench
bucket   pliers
ladder   tools

Children's Books
The A+ Custodian by Louise Borden
That's Our Custodian! by Ann Morris

Materials
brown grocery bags
marker
scissors
tools and objects that a building maintenance person would use, such as a hand broom, dustpan, wrench, hammer, duct tape, washcloth, small pail, small waste basket, trash bag, key ring of keys, and so on
Safety note: Select only items that are safe for the children to handle.

Preparation
Select a few items and place each one in a separate bag. Close each bag.

What to Do
1. At group or circle time, ask the children if they know who takes care of their building. (The building maintenance person/custodian.) Tell the children his name.
2. Talk with the children about the many jobs that person does. If possible, read one of the suggested books.
3. Give one of the bags to one child. Ask that child to reach into the bag and describe what is in the bag without looking at the object.
4. The rest of the children guess what the object is. After the children have guessed, ask the child to take the object out of the bag. Talk with the children about the object and how it is used by the custodian.
5. Repeat with another object.

Assessment
1. What did the child learn about the many jobs of a building maintenance person?
2. Is the child able to describe the tool and to discuss how a custodian uses different tools?

Mary Murray, Mazomanie, WI

MY COMMUNITY / NEIGHBORHOOD

Tools of the Trade

AGES 4+

Learning Objectives
Children will:
1. Learn that a community is made up of people with different interests doing different jobs.
2. Learn that workers use tools to do their jobs.

Vocabulary

career	doctor	mail carrier
community	fire helmet	police officer
dentist	firefighter	stethoscope
dentist's chair	mailbox	teacher

Children's Books
Career Day by Anne Rockwell
Guess Who? by Margaret Miller
Whose Hat Is This? A Look at Hats Workers Wear by Sharon Katz Cooper

Materials
card stock
clear contact paper
marker
pictures of community helpers
pictures of tools workers need for their jobs

Preparation
● On card stock, make two sets of cards for a matching activity. One set should be pictures of workers in the community, such as a firefighter, doctor, mail carrier, teacher, dentist, and police officer. Label the pictures. The second set should be objects the workers might use to perform their jobs, such as a fire helmet, stethoscope, mailbox, book, dentist's chair, and police car.
● Laminate both sets of cards, or cover them with clear contact paper.

What to Do
1. Distribute all the cards to the children.
2. Ask each child to describe the card he has and tell what the person does or how an object is used.
3. Challenge the children to match each object with the correct community worker.

Assessment
1. What did the child learn about the workers in her community?
2. What did the child learn about the tools workers use to do their jobs?

Jackie Wright, Enid, OK

Miniature Neighborhood

AGES 5+

Learning Objectives
Children will:
1. Build with connecting blocks.
2. Improve oral language skills.

Vocabulary
buildings   people
families   shops
houses   workers
neighborhood

Children's Book
Places in My Community by Bobbie Kalman

Materials
5" x 7" note cards
fine-line permanent marker
large connecting blocks
small connecting blocks such as LEGOs,
    including several flat base pieces
small toy plastic people

What to Do
1. As you teach the class about people in the neighborhood, introduce this fun building and role-playing activity.
2. Use the set of large blocks and toy people to create a neighborhood. Design a village with various shops, a school, library, homes, and more.
3. Manipulate the toy plastic people within the neighborhood as you teach about places such as the barber shop, bank, post office, gas station, and more.
4. Give each child a base block from the LEGO set or a 5" x 7" note card. Invite the children to attach or display blocks to this base, creating a smaller version of a neighborhood that includes various buildings and homes.
5. Allow each child time to talk about his neighborhood and identify the various buildings, shops, and houses. Ask each child to tell the class about the people in his neighborhood, perhaps explaining where they work or where they live. Allow time for each child to tell the class about the people in his mini neighborhood.

Assessment
1. Is the child able to use the blocks to create a mini neighborhood?
2. Is the child able to describe the mini neighborhood she created?

Mary Murray, Mazomanie, WI

My Town

AGES
5+

Learning Objectives
Children will:
1. Learn about the buildings in their community.
2. Develop eye-hand coordination.

Vocabulary
(Modify this list so it reflects your specific area.)

airport	hospital
apartment	houses
bakery	library
bank	park
church	police department
department store	school
doctor's office	street
fire department	train station

Children's Books
The City Kid & the Suburb Kid by Deb Pilutti
A Day in a City by Nicholas Harris
I Live in the Desert by Gini Holland
I Live in the Mountains by Gini Holland
I Live Near the Ocean by Gini Holland
Living in Urban Communities by Kristin Sterling
Places in My Community by Bobbie Kalman
Where Do I Live? by Neil Chesanow

Materials
clear packing tape
paint cups
paintbrushes
pictures of important buildings in your immediate community
smocks
tablecloth
tempera paint
various sized cardboard boxes

Preparation
● Collect boxes that resemble the shape of the community buildings in your area. Tape the boxes shut with the packing tape.
● Add a small amount of paint in each cup that coordinates with the colors of the buildings in your photos.
● Cover the painting space with a tablecloth.
● Laminate community photos.

What to Do
1. Show the children the photos during group time. Discuss the buildings in the pictures, their names, and what happens in each building.
2. Place the boxes on the table along with the pictures.
3. Allow each child to choose a building to create using the box. Two children can work on the same box if the building is larger.
4. Encourage the children to examine details of the buildings. Place the boxes in a protected area to dry.
5. When the boxes are dry, add them to the block center for community play.

Assessment

1. What has the child learned about the buildings in her community?
2. What has the child learned about the people who work in those buildings?
3. Does the child have the eye-hand coordination necessary to re-create community buildings by painting the boxes?

Tina R. Durham-Woehler, Lebanon, TN

Teacher-to-Teacher Tips

● Schedule classroom visitors from some of the community places in your area. Ask them to discuss what their jobs are and what they do to help the community. Take pictures during the visit to use for later reference by the children and for future activities.

● Schedule a field trip to a larger community business or space that the children can relate to or have interests in. Take photos and allow the children to come back to the classroom and draw and talk about what they saw and remembered about their trip. Use the photos and drawings to make a book about where the children live. Display it on the shelf for the children's use. Read it with the children in both small and large groups.

Neighborhood Wall Mural

AGES 5+

Learning Objectives

Children will:

1. Express themselves creatively.
2. Use paints and paintbrushes.
3. Learn about colors.
4. Work cooperatively with others.

Vocabulary

buildings	neighborhood
colors	paint
cooperate	paintbrush
houses	people

Children's Books

Busy, Busy Town by Richard Scarry
The City Kid & the Suburb Kid by Deb Pilutti
A Day in a City by Nicholas Harris
Places in My Community by Bobbie Kalman
Where Do I Live? by Neil Chesanow

Materials

art paper (20" x 30" or larger)
marker
paintbrushes
paints
tape

Preparation

Use the marker to draw a different place in the neighborhood, such as a home, apartment building, doctor's office, post office, library, grocery store, salon, or flower shop, on each sheet of art paper.

What to Do

1. Provide a small group of children with a set of paints and one neighborhood picture. Invite them to work together to paint the building.
2. Ask the children to add extra details to the picture, including people, bushes, trees, flowers, vehicles, animals, insects, and signs.
3. When all the neighborhood pictures are complete, let them dry and then hang them down the length of a wall at the children's level to create a neighborhood. Invite groups of children to tell about their specific work of art.

Assessment

1. Is the child able to use his creativity to draw or paint on the classroom murals?
2. Is the child able to manipulate the paints and paintbrushes effectively?
3. What did the child learn about colors?
4. Is the child able to work cooperatively with other children?

Mary Murray, Mazomanie, WI

Teacher-to-Teacher Tips

- Use the display for a classroom transition activity. Invite children to "walk through the neighborhood" and admire the artwork as they move from one activity to another.
- Take a walk in the neighborhood before doing this activity. As you walk, help the children notice the details in their neighborhood.

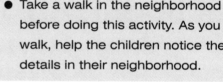

New Neighbors

AGES 5+

Learning Objectives

Children will:
1. Improve social skills.
2. Learn to follow directions.
3. Show kindness to others.

Vocabulary

greet   neighbor
introduce   new
meet

Children's Book
Be My Neighbor by Maya Ajmera and
John Ivanko, with words of wisdom by
Fred Rogers

Materials
bell
carpet squares (one per child)
music

Preparation
Place the carpet squares randomly about
the group area, keeping two carpet squares
together.

What to Do
1. Talk with the children about how one of the ways that a community works together is to welcome new neighbors. If appropriate, ask the children to talk about a time when they moved into a new neighborhood or when a new neighbor moved into the area.
2. Ask the children for suggestions about how to make a new neighbor feel welcome. Explain that the classroom is a lot like a neighborhood. Ask the children how to make a new member of the class feel welcome. One way is to greet their classmates.
3. Invite the children to join hands to form a large circle and then let go of hands for this group game.
4. Begin the music and have the children walk in a clockwise direction as the music plays.
5. When the music stops, each child finds a carpet square to sit on to then waits quietly for the bell to ring. When the bell rings, each pair of children stands up to greet their "new neighbor." Encourage the children to shake hands, introduce themselves, and say, "How are you? I'm glad we're neighbors."
6. Repeat the activity several times, having children greet a "new neighbor" each time the music stops.

Assessment
1. Does the child have the necessary social skills to do this activity?
2. Is the child able to follow the directions?
3. What did the child learn about showing kindness to others?

Mary Murray, Mazomanie, WI

Teacher-to-Teacher Tips
- Use sheets of colored card stock in place of carpet squares.
- Play this game in a large open area where a circle is already marked off on the floor.

Sidewalk Art

AGES 5+

Learning Objectives
Children will:
1. Learn to identify various people and places in the neighborhood.
2. Cooperate with others.

Vocabulary
building   house
chalk   neighborhood
color   people
draw   sidewalk

Children's Books
Busy, Busy Town by Richard Scarry
A Day in a City by Nicholas Harris
Places in My Community by Bobbie Kalman
Where Do I Live? by Neil Chesanow

Materials
colored sidewalk chalk

What to Do

1. Take the children outdoors and find a section of sidewalk or paved area for this class art project.
2. Provide each child with an assortment of colored chalk and a 2' x 2' space of sidewalk or pavement on which to work.
3. Have the children work side by side facing the same direction so when the artwork is complete, you will have a neighborhood of homes and buildings to admire.
4. Assign each child part of a community to draw, such as a home, school, library, barber shop, dry cleaners, restaurant, town hall, soccer field, hardware store, and so on. Remind children to use their whole space when making the initial outline of their drawing.
5. Suggest that the children add color and detail including people, trees, bushes, vehicles, and signs.
6. When all the children have finished their artwork, have each child stand near her drawing. Give each child a chance to tell the class about her part of the community.
7. Have the whole class line up at one end of the artwork, and then walk slowly through the "neighborhood" admiring one another's works of art.

Assessment

1. What did the child learn about the people and places in the neighborhood?
2. Is the child able to create a community building or place?
3. Is the child able to name the colors of chalk she used?

Mary Murray, Mazomanie, WI

Who Am I?

AGES
5+

Learning Objectives
Children will:
1. Learn what neighborhood helpers do.
2. Learn about their neighborhood and community.

Vocabulary

baker	forester	nurse
clerk	grocer	office worker
doctor	helpers	police officer
farmer	letter carrier	teacher
firefighter	neighborhood	

Another Encyclopedia of Theme Activities

Children's Books

Career Day by Anne Rockwell
Community Helpers from A to Z by Bobbie
   Kalman, Niki Walker
Hands by Lois Ehlert
Helpers in My Community by Bobbie Kalman
Whose Vehicle Is This? by Sharon Katz Cooper

Materials

paper
pictures of neighborhood helpers
tape

What to Do

1. Show the children the pictures of neighborhood helpers.
2. Tape each picture on a bulletin board.
3. Ask the children to describe what each neighborhood helper does. Write their answers under each picture.
4. Ask the children to guess the name of the occupation of each helper. If children are unsure about the name, tell them the name and then write the name under each picture.

Assessment

1. What did the child learn about his neighborhood helpers?
2. What did the child learn about the responsibilities of his neighborhood helpers?

MaryLouise Alu Curto, Mercerville, NJ

Teacher-to-Teacher Tip

Introduce two or three neighborhood helpers at a time.

Families Float in Boats

AGES 3+

Learning Objectives
Children will:
1. Explore at the water table.
2. Identify family members.

Vocabulary

boat	float	swim
family	people	water

Children's Books
The Boat in the Tree by John Shelley
Grandpa's Boat by Michael Catchpool

Materials
colorful plastic plates or bowls
plastic toy people

What to Do
1. Invite the children to place one or more boats (plate or bowl) on the water.
2. Suggest that the children add a "family" in each boat. Have the children set a group of toy people in each boat and call it a family.
3. Invite the children to imagine a story about the family members in the boat as they float around the water.
4. When the children are finished playing, they remove the people from the boats for the next set of children to work with.

Assessment
1. Is the child able to explore using the "boats" at the water table?
2. Is the child able to name the "family members" in her boat?
3. Is the child able to tell a story about where her boat family is going or what they are doing as they travel in their boat?

Mary Murray, Mazomanie, WI

Family Portrait

AGES 3+

Learning Objectives
Children will:
1. Learn about families.
2. Improve their fine motor skills.

Vocabulary

aunt	father	love
brother	grandfather	mother
cousin	grandmother	sister
family	home	uncle

Children's Books
Families by Ann Morris
Me and My Family Tree by Joan Sweeney

Materials
art supplies
brown construction paper, 9" x 11"
glue
white construction paper, 8" x 10"

What to Do
1. Help the children glue the white paper inside the larger brown paper to create a framed border.
2. Suggest that the children use art supplies and collage materials to create pictures of their own families.
3. Display the family artwork around the classroom.

Assessment
1. What did the child learn about the families of other children in the class?
2. Did you see improvement in the child's fine motor skills as he created the artwork?

Mary Murray, Mazomanie, WI

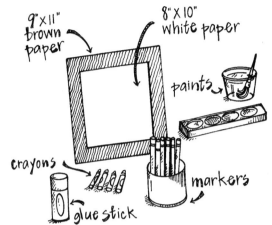

Family Time in the Car

AGES 3+

Learning Objectives
Children will:
1. Improve gross motor skills.
2. Improve oral language skills.

Vocabulary
car	families	push
drive	people	ride

Children's Books
A Chair for My Mother by Vera B. Williams
Just Me and My Little Brother by Mercer Mayer
My Father's Hands by Joanne Ryder
My Sister, Alicia May by Nancy Tupper Ling

Materials
4 large sturdy boxes
assorted dolls or stuffed toy animals
construction paper
glue
scissors

Preparation
- Create a car from each large box by adding construction paper wheels, headlights, taillights, license plates, and more.
- Display the four cars along with the collection of dolls and animals.

What to Do
1. Invite four children to select a car to push around the room.
2. Have the children create a family to sit inside the car by placing dolls or stuffed animals in the car, assigning each family member a role as mother, father, children, and so on.

3. Encourage the children to push the car around the room as the family goes for a drive.
4. When the car stops, the children can have the family members talk among themselves about what a nice time they had on the drive.

Assessment

1. Is the child able to push the box "car" around the classroom?
2. Is the child able to describe the family in the box "car" and tell a story about what the family was doing in the car?

Mary Murray, Mazomanie, WI

Friends Class Book

AGES
3+

Learning Objectives
Children will:
1. Identify classmates by name.
2. Improve oral language skills.

Vocabulary
book	page	turn
friends	read	

Children's Books
Just My Friend and Me by Mercer Mayer
Learning to Be a Good Friend: A Guidebook for Kids by Christine A. Adams

Materials
basket
beanbag chair
digital camera
photo album
photo paper
sign that reads "Friendship Book"

Preparation
- Take pictures of pairs of children using a digital camera. Be sure to include each child at least once in the set of photos. Print the photos and then place the photos in a photo album.
- Display the *Friendship Book* in a special basket. Attach the Friendship Book sign to the basket and display it in the book corner along with a beanbag chair or other soft chair for two.

What to Do
1. Invite a pair of children to sit together in the beanbag chair and read the class *Friendship Book*.
2. Encourage children to identify the friends on each page of the book and to read the book through from beginning to end.
3. When the children are finished looking at the book, they place it back in the basket so another pair of friends may read the book.

Assessment

1. Is the child able to identify his classmates by name?
2. Is the child able to describe what is happening in each photo?

Mary Murray, Mazomanie, WI

Share a Sack Lunch

AGES 3+

Learning Objectives

Children will:

1. Share a snack with another child.
2. Divide the snacks in half.
3. Develop social skills.

Vocabulary

drink	half	share
eat	lunch	whole

Children's Books

Teddy Bear's Picnic by Jimmy Kennedy
Should I Share My Ice Cream? by Mo Willems

Materials

black marker
sack lunches, one per pair of children

Preparation

- Invite parent volunteers to put sack lunches together. Make one for each pair of children.
- Print the words *Friends share!* on the front of each bag.
- Fill the bags with two juice boxes, two paper plates, two napkins, one sandwich cut in half, one small bag of snack crackers, one cookie, or other items to share.

What to Do

1. Remind children that friends share with one another.
2. Assign each child a partner for this activity.
3. Hand each pair of friends a sack lunch and read the words on the bag to them.
4. Have the children find a place in the classroom or outdoors to enjoy the snack.
5. Tell the children to share the lunch with each other. Instruct children to divide, or split in half, all the foods in the bag so the items are shared equally.
6. Remind the children to share the task of cleaning up as well.

Assessment

1. Is the child able to share a snack with another child?
2. Does the child understand the concept of dividing a snack in half?
3. Is the child developing the social skill of sharing?

Mary Murray, Mazomanie, WI

Teacher-to-Teacher Tip
Print the two children's names on each bag.

Families Count

AGES 4+

Learning Objectives
Children will:
1. Count the people in family groups.
2. Compare the sizes of families.

Vocabulary

count	large	small
family	people	

Children's Books

1-2-3: A Child's First Counting Book by Alison Jay
All Families Are Special by Norma Simon
Families by Ann Morris
Who's in a Family? by Robert Skutch

Materials
black marker
colored card stock
envelope
pictures of a small, a medium-sized, and a large family
small dry-erase board, marker, and eraser

Preparation
Draw a set of "smiley faces" on each piece of card stock to represent a family. Make a few cards that have families of different sizes. Place the cards in an envelope.

What to Do

1. Remind the children that families come in all different sizes. Display a picture of a small, a medium-sized, and a large family.
2. Talk with the children about how the three families are different, how they are the same, and how each family is special.
3. Describe how to play the Family Counts game. Invite two (or four) children to play the game at one time. Have children remove the family picture cards from the envelope and lay them out, facedown on the floor.
4. The first player turns over a card, counts the faces, and says how many people are in the family. Write the number on the dry-erase board.
5. Invite the next player to do the same. The game continues until all the family picture cards are facing up and the numbers are on the dry-erase board.
6. Talk with the children about the various sizes of family groups, helping the children understand which family pictures have more, less, or equal numbers of people.
7. When they are finished, the children wipe the numbers off the dry-erase board and play again or put the cards away for the next pair of players.

Assessment

1. Is the child able to count the people in the family groups?
2. Is the child able to compare the sizes of families?

Mary Murray, Mazomanie, WI

Teacher-to-Teacher Tip
Use family pictures cut from magazines in place of drawing smiley face family groups.

Find a Friend

AGES 4+

Learning Objectives
Children will:
1. Match like objects.
2. Follow directions.

Vocabulary
friend   hands   shake
glove   mitten

Children's Books
Arthur and the True Francine by Marc Tolon Brown
The Rainbow Fish by Marcus Pfister

Materials
laundry basket
pairs of matching gloves and mittens (one glove or mitten for each child)

Preparation
Place the pairs of mittens and gloves in a laundry basket. Include the exact amount of mittens and gloves so that each child gets one and none are left in the basket.

What to Do

1. Invite each child to select one mitten or glove from the basket and put it on. If there is one left over, choose it for yourself.
2. Help the children identify their right hands. Half the class will have a glove or mitten on the right hand, and half the class will have a bare right hand.
3. Tell the children to walk around the room and shake hands (using their right hands) with all the friends in their class. When a child comes to the friend with the matching glove or mitten, have them give one another a high five and then sit down together on the floor.
4. The last two children to remain standing are to tell the class one way they can be a good friend to others.
5. The last pair picks up the laundry basket and carries it around the room together, as they collect the mittens and gloves from their classmates. That same pair of children walks around a second time with the basket, inviting children to select a new glove or mitten.
6. Repeat the activity several times.

Assessment

1. Is the child able to find the match to her mitten or glove?
2. Is the child able to follow the directions for this activity?

Mary Murray, Mazomanie, WI

Fingerprint Family

AGES 4+

Learning Objectives
Children will:
1. Develop fine motor skills.
2. Learn about shapes and sizes.

Vocabulary
family	fingerprint	related
finger (index,	ink	skin
middle,	line	unique
ring, pinkie)	pattern	

Children's Book
Ed Emberley's Complete Funprint Drawing Book by Ed Emberley

Materials
paper
pens and pencils
water-based ink pads

Preparation
Make sure everyone's hands are clean and dry before you start—sticky or greasy fingers will mean prints are spoiled or uneven. Hands will also need to be washed during and after the activity to remove ink.

What to Do

1. Show the children how to tap their index fingers lightly over the surface of the ink pad until their index fingers are covered with a thin layer of ink. Then press the finger down flat onto the paper. Don't move it about, or the print will smudge. Suggest that the children try a few test prints on scrap paper to get used to making a good print.
2. Try making prints with different fingers. Thumbs make the biggest prints and pinkies the smallest ones. Experiment with using just the tips of fingers for smaller, rounder prints, or pressing sideways to make horizontal prints instead of vertical ones. (These are especially good for creating animal characters.)
3. Let the children use a pencil or fine marker pen to add details to turn each fingerprint into a tiny person or character. Draw on eyes, a nose, and a mouth to make faces, then add some hair or a hat above. Draw simple stick arms and legs, as long or short as you like, and maybe some clothing—skirts, ties, and buttons—or even simple spotted and striped details are easy but effective.
4. Suggest that the children create a fingerprint family or group of fingerprint friends.

Assessment

1. Is the child developing fine motor control as she creates fingerprint people or creatures?
2. Is the child able to make different sizes of fingerprint people?

Kirsty Neale, Orpington, Kent, UK

Teacher-to-Teacher Tip

The natural inclination of many children will be to squash their finger right down into the ink pad and then press it just as hard on the paper surface. Try to discourage this, as their prints will look more like blobs. Show them how, when you press lightly, the whorls and details in your fingerprint show up far more clearly and make each picture unique. A good starting place for fingerprint pictures is to create your family. The larger prints can be parents or grandparents, and smaller ones siblings, cousins, or self-portraits, with a few added sideways versions as family pets.

Friends Help Each Other

AGES 4+

Learning Objectives

Children will:
1. Improve their balance.
2. Learn to care about others.

Vocabulary

balance	friend	spot
beam	help	walk

Children's Books

Night Monkey, Day Monkey by Julia Donaldson
Peef and His Best Friend by Tom Hegg

Materials

wide masking tape or balance beam

Preparation

Display the balance beam in the center of the circle or place a line of wide masking tape on the floor to create a masking tape "balance beam."

What to Do

1. Invite one child to come forward and prepare to walk across the balance beam (or strip of masking tape). Have the child invite a friend to help "spot" him as he crosses the balance beam.
2. When both children are ready, the first child steps onto the beam and carefully walks across. The helper walks along next to the child, with her hand held up, ready to help balance the classmate.
3. When the first child steps off the balance beam, he says, "Thank you for being my friend." The spotter says, "You're welcome," in response.

4. The child who crossed the balance beam sits down, and the spotter invites a child to be her helper as she now takes a turn crossing the balance beam.
5. Continue until several or all children have had a turn.

Assessment

1. How well was the child able to balance on the beam or strip of masking tape?
2. How courteous and helpful is the child?

Mary Murray, Mazomanie, WI

Puddle Fun

AGES 4+

Learning Objectives
Children will:
1. Learn about working together.
2. Improve gross motor skills.

Vocabulary
puddle
rain
umbrella
walk
wet

Children's Books
My Red Umbrella by Robert Bright
Umbrella Parade by Kathy Feczke
Why Does It Rain? by Chris Arvetis

Materials
children's umbrella (one or more)
puddle shapes cut from blue felt

Preparation
Use the felt puddle shapes to create a trail of blue puddle shapes throughout the classroom.

What to Do

1. Invite a pair of children to work together at this activity. Remind the pair to share, take turns, and be considerate of their friend and others in the class as they walk along the puddles.
2. Invite the pair of friends to hold hands and walk around the room together, following the trail of rain puddles.
3. Encourage the children to cooperate together as they walk and to pretend that it is raining.
4. Suggest that the children talk about the rainy day walk as they move about the room together.

Assessment

1. Is the child able to cooperate with another child and walk along the path together?
2. Does the child have the coordination necessary to walk with another child along the path?

Mary Murray, Mazomanie, WI

Building Houses

Learning Objectives

Children will:

1. Build with blocks.
2. Develop oral language skills.

Vocabulary

apartment	duplex	house
blocks	family	
build	home	

Children's Books

Mi Casa = My House by George Ancona

Mi Familia = My Family by George Ancona

What to Do

1. Invite the children to use the blocks to build a house for a family.
2. Suggest that the children display a family picture near the completed home and then tell about the family and where they live.
3. Encourage the children to build several different homes for various families.
4. When the children are finished, they place the pictures back in the basket and put the blocks away.

Assessment

1. How well did the child build with blocks?
2. What language skills is the child developing as she talks about the family living in the block house or the apartment house?

Mary Murray, Mazomanie, WI

Materials

basket
building blocks
card stock
family pictures
glue

Preparation

- Cut several family pictures from magazines or use copies of the class family pictures. Place them in a basket.
- Glue each picture to a piece of card stock then place them in a basket in the block area.

Teacher-to-Teacher Tip

Encourage each child to draw a family who will live inside an apartment house. Create a large apartment building as the whole class works together, placing block upon block to build the structure. Invite each child to set one family picture near the apartment building and tell about one family that will live there.

MY FAMILY and FRIENDS

Friend of the Day

AGES 5+

Learning Objectives

Children will:

1. Learn the value of a friend.
2. Develop oral language and listening skills.

Vocabulary

day   important   person
friend   listen   special

Children's Books

Friends by Helme Heine
A Rainbow of Friends by P. K. Hallinan
A Splendid Friend, Indeed by Suzanne Bloom

Materials

chair
chart paper or colored copy paper
marker
sign that reads "Friend of the Day"
sticker or ribbon that says "I'm a Good Friend!"

Preparation

- Place a chair in the group area.
- Send home a letter similar to the following, designating a specific date for each child to be honored as the Friend of the Day:

Dear Parents,

We will soon be learning about the topic of friendship. Each day we will honor one child in the class as the Friend of the Day. Your child will be honored on _____. Your child is invited to bring in a favorite book to share with the class. Also, your child may bring in a snack to share, if desired. We hope to read the book and enjoy the snack together. There are ___ children in the class.

Thank you very much. We look forward to celebrating your child as a very special friend in our class.

Sincerely,

What to Do

1. Invite the Friend of the Day to sit in the chair.
2. Provide this child with a ribbon or sticker to wear throughout the day.
3. Invite the members of the class to raise their hands and tell something about the honored child and how he has been a good friend to others. Children might say that he shared his toys, said please, waited his turn, or helped clean up.
4. Record the children's comments on chart paper or a sheet of colored copy paper with the title "You're a Good Friend." Send the completed page home with the child to share with his family.
5. Invite the honored child to display the book he would like to share with the class, and then read the book aloud.
6. If the family sends a snack, enjoy the special snack that the child's family has provided. If the family cannot provide a snack, be sure to have a one ready that the child can help serve.
7. Optional: Have all the children in the class draw a picture of themselves, along with the Friend of the Day. Ask each child to tell about the picture of the two friends together. Let the Friend of the Day take the collection of pictures home to share with his family.

Assessment

1. What did the child learn about being a friend?
2. Is the child able to express what she thinks makes the Friend of the Day a good friend?

Mary Murray, Mazomanie, WI

Friendship Bench

AGES 5+

Learning Objectives

Children will:

1. Enjoy sharing a bench with a friend.
2. Learn to rest or play quietly.

Vocabulary

bench	names	quiet
friends	pictures	rest

Children's Books

Best Friends by Anna Michaels
Otto Goes to School by Todd Parr

Materials

comfy chair or bench large enough for two pillows

Preparation

Create a Friendship Bench. Place a comfy chair or bench (large enough for two children to sit on) in a quiet place in the classroom. Add pillows to make this a cozy place to sit quietly and rest or read.

What to Do

1. Place the Friendship Bench in the classroom.
2. Each day invite one pair of children to sit and rest, read, or play quietly on the bench during rest time.
3. When rest time comes to an end, invite the pair on the bench to shake hands, say, "I'm glad you're my friend," and then walk around the room together and tell each resting child that he may get up.

Assessment

1. How well does the child share the Friendship Bench with another child?
2. Is the child able to rest or play quietly on the Friendship Bench?

Mary Murray, Mazomanie, WI

Friendship Glasses

Learning Objectives
Children will:
1. Listen and follow directions.
2. Identify classmates as friends.

Vocabulary
eyes	glasses	see
friend	listen	

Children's Books
Brown Bear, Brown Bear, What Do You See? by Bill Martin, Jr.
Just the Way You Are by Marcus Pfister
A Splendid Friend, Indeed by Suzanne Bloom

Materials
large plastic toy eyeglasses

What to Do
1. Ask one child to put on the eyeglasses for this transition time activity.
2. Teach the class this call-and-response chant:
   Class chants: "_____, _____ who do you see?"
   Selected child responds: "I see a good friend looking at me."
3. The child looks through the eyeglasses and names a classmate, who moves on to the next activity or time of day.
4. The child wearing the glasses and the class continue until every child has been called on and is ready to move on to the next activity or time of day.

Assessment
1. Is the child able to listen to and follow the directions of this transition activity?
2. Is the child able to identify and name his classmates?

Mary Murray, Mazomanie, WI

Teacher-to-Teacher Tips
- Ring a soft bell or play a certain tune on the xylophone when it's time to transition from one activity to another. When the children hear the sound, they will be quick to listen and see who gets to wear the Friendship Glasses.
- Ask a different child to put on the Friendship Glasses each time you use this activity to transition from one activity to another.

It's All in the Family

AGES
5+

Learning Objectives
Children will:
1. Learn about families.
2. Learn new vocabulary.

Vocabulary
(Adapt this list to fit your children's interests.)

eat	read	travel
play	share	

Children's Books
The Family Book by Todd Parr
Families by Ann Morris
Me and My Family Tree by Joan Sweeney
Who's in a Family? by Robert Skutch

Materials
5 plastic hoops
chart paper
marker
pictures of 15 different families (magazine, catalogs, and the Internet are possible sources for pictures of families)

What to Do
1. Display the five hoops in a row down the center of the circle time area. Display three pictures inside each hoop.
2. Invite the children to join hands and stand around the pictures. Have the children chant this family song to the tune of "Ring around the Rosy."

    "Look at All the Families"
    Look at all the families,
    Lots and lots of families.
    Each one is special.
    We all sit down.

3. At the end of the chant, the children sit down, let go of hands, and then gather at the hoop nearest them.
4. Ask each small group to look at one of the family pictures and talk about some things that family might enjoy doing together. Repeat with another family picture.
5. Afterward or on another day, ask the larger group to list activities that families often do together. Write their ideas on chart paper. Title the list "Family Activities" and then display the list at the writing center.

Assessment
1. What did the child learn about families?
2. Did the child learn new vocabulary words as she discussed what families like to do?

Mary Murray, Mazomanie, WI

Teacher-to-Teacher Tip
Help the children understand and respect that families are diverse: some families have two people, some have lots more, some have a grandparent and one child, some have two parents and many children.

Reading Buddies

AGES 5+

Learning Objectives
Children will:
1. Learn to appreciate books.
2. Enjoy time with a friend.

Vocabulary

book	page	together
friend	read	turn

Children's Book
Reading Makes You Feel Good by Todd Parr

Materials
beach towels or carpet squares
books from the class library
large pillows

Preparation
Place beach towels or carpet squares and large pillows in different areas around the room.

What to Do
1. Explain to the children that one activity friends may enjoy is reading together. Demonstrate how two children can sit together on a beach towel or on two carpet squares and read a book together. Show the class how two children can lie on their backs against a large pillow or lie on their tummies and share a book together.
2. Assign each child a friend for this activity, and call the pairs of children "Reading Buddies."
3. Invite the Reading Buddies to select a book together from the book corner and then read the special book in a special place in the classroom. Encourage children to continue reading until center time is over or the children want to play at another center.
4. On another day, allow the children to select a new Reading Buddy and a new book and then repeat the activity.
5. Optional: Invite pairs of children to take turns telling the class what their book was about or invite one pair of Reading Buddies to tell another pair of children what their book was about.

Assessment
1. Is the child learning to enjoy and appreciate books?
2. Does the child enjoy reading with a friend?

Mary Murray, Mazomanie, WI

> **Teacher-to-Teacher Tip**
> Have Reading Buddies read together after rest time on a daily basis. Assign each child a Reading Buddy each day so that no child feels left out if she is not chosen by a friend.

Animal School

AGES 3+

Learning Objectives
Children will:
1. Improve oral language skills.
2. Learn about school.

Vocabulary

animal	school
hand	sit
learn	talk
listen	teacher

Children's Books
I Love School! by Philemon Sturges
If You Take a Mouse to School by Laura
Numeroff

Materials
10 beanbag toy animals
10 wooden blocks (to represent school desks)
basket

Preparation
Place the materials in a box or basket.

What to Do
1. Sit in a circle with the basket in front of you. Gather the children around the basket as you talk about school, teachers, and learning.
2. Remove the items from the basket and invite children to help you set up a small classroom using the blocks as furniture and the animals as children.
3. Use this as an opportunity to familiarize the children with what happens in the classroom, including the daily routine.
4. Invite the class to come up with a list of school rules for the animals to follow. Allow time for children to share something they have learned from a teacher.
5. When you and the children are finished talking, return the materials to the basket and allow time for small groups of children to use the materials independently to role-play about school.

Assessment
1. Is the child asking questions about school or discussing the topic with the rest of the class?
2. What did the child learn about school?

Mary Murray, Mazomanie, WI

Going to School Memory Game

AGES 4+

Learning Objectives
Children will:
1. Use thinking skills.
2. Practice listening skills.
3. Learn new vocabulary words.
4. Develop memory skills.

Vocabulary
chart   game
clue   remember

Children's Books
I Love School! by Philemon Sturges
Maisy Goes to Preschool by Lucy Cousins

Materials
chart paper
If You Take a Mouse to School by Laura Numeroff
index cards or sentence strips
marker
tape

What to Do
1. Gather the children for group or circle time. Read *If You Take a Mouse to School*.
2. Tell the children you are going to play a game. Ask them to think about what they would like to take to school with them; it can be anything they want.
3. Go around the circle and let each child share his response. Write the responses on the chart paper.
4. Ask the class if there is anyone who can go around the circle and name each child's response. Allow the children to help each other by giving clues if necessary.
5. Later that day or the next, write the objects that the children named on index cards or sentence strips.
6. Make a large *yes* and *no* graph on chart paper.
7. Add pictures of the objects that the children want to take to class or ask the children to draw the objects.
8. Gather the children in group or circle time. Hold up one card at a time and ask the children if they think that object should be taken to school and why. Tape the card in the appropriate column on the chart.

Assessment
1. How well was the child able to use her thinking skills to determine if an object should be brought to school?
2. How well did the child listen to the other children?
3. What new words did the child learn?
4. Was the child able to remember the other children's objects?

Shelley Hoster, Norcross, GA

Teacher-to-Teacher Tip
This is a great game to play at the end of the year during a "Going to Kindergarten" theme. You'd be surprised at how well children can do this, even in a class of 20 children. They can remember each other's objects throughout the day and at closing circle!

Meet New Friends

AGES 4+

Learning Objectives
Children will:
1. Match shapes or colors.
2. Follow directions.

Vocabulary
circle
square
triangle (other shapes appropriate for your group)

Children's Books
Making Friends by Fred Rogers
Will I Have a Friend? by Miriam Cohen

Materials
construction paper
music
scissors

Preparation
- Make two large cutouts of each shape (two squares, two circles, two hearts, and so on). The total number of shapes needs to match the number of children in the class. The shapes can be the same color or different colors, depending on the abilities of your group.
- Place the shapes on the floor in the group time areas.

What to Do
1. Explain to the children that when the music starts they will walk around the classroom, and when the music stops they will stop and pick up a shape.
2. Play music, and after a short while, stop the music.
3. When you are sure that all the children have a shape, ask the children to find a friend with the same shape.
4. Ask each pair of children to say each other's names. If they don't know their friend's name, tell them to ask their friend what his name is.
5. Tell the children to place their shapes back on the floor. Start the music again. Continue playing until the children have paired up with a variety of friends.

Assessment
1. Is the child able to match shapes and/or colors?
2. Is the child able to follow directions to stop and start with music cues?

Sandra Ryan, Buffalo, NY

MY SCHOOL

2+2

Playing with Others Outside

AGES

4+

Learning Objectives

Children will:

1. Learn the value of friends.
2. Describe what they like to play outside.

Vocabulary

climbing a tree   playing hide-and-seek
digging in the sand   playmate
flying a kite   riding bikes
friend   somersaulting
playing catch

Children's Books

Are You Ready to Play Outside? by Mo Willems
Rainbow Fish to the Rescue! by Marcus Pfister
Will I Have a Friend? by Miriam Cohen

Materials

crayons, markers, colored pencils
paper

What to Do

1. Talk about making new friends at school and the activities the children like to do when they go outside to play. Brainstorm what the children enjoy about playing with a friend and the things they like to do outside with their friends.
2. Encourage the children to use paper and crayons or markers to create drawings of what they like to do outside with their friends.
3. Use the children's drawings to make a class book about playing outside.

Assessment

1. What does the child say is the value of friends?
2. Is the child able to describe what he likes to do outside?

Jackie Wright, Enid, OK

Same and Different

Learning Objectives

Children will:

1. Differentiate between home and school.
2. Learn about the objects found only at school and home.

Vocabulary

bell	different	pencil
books	eraser	pens
chairs	home	pets
chalk	less	playground
classroom	more	same
clock	paper	sandbox

school	teacher	whiteboard
school bus	toys	
table	vehicles	

Materials

photographs of school, outdoors, classrooms, and home

Preparation

Ask the children to bring to school a picture of them at home or at school (indoors or outdoors).

What to Do

1. Talk with the children about objects that are found at school and at home. Encourage children to talk about objects found only at school, objects found only at home, and objects found both at home and at school.
2. Ask the children, "How is school the same as home?" Are there rooms at school and at home? Do both have people in them? Do you play, learn, sleep, or eat at home and at school? Are there chairs and tables at both places?
3. Then ask, "How is school different from home?" Does the bell ring at home for recess? Is there a teacher at home? Can you park the school bus at home? Is there a whiteboard at home? Do you have pets at school?
4. Ask the children to look at the pictures that the children brought from home and guess where they were taken—at home or at school.

Assessment

1. Is the child able to see the differences and similarities between home and school?
2. Was the child able to identify objects that are found only at school and at home?

Shyamala Shanmugasundaram,
Annanagar East, Chennai, India

School Is Cool

AGES 4+

Learning Objectives
Children will:
1. Understand that there are things that are found in school and things that are not found in school.
2. Practice sorting.

Vocabulary
(Adapt this list to fit the items you will discuss.)

book	food	tiger
bus	friend	toy
car	paper	truck
elephant	pencil	
family	teacher	

Children's Books
A Fine, Fine School by Sharon Creech
My First Day of School by P. K. Hallinan
A Rainbow of Friends by P. K. Hallinan
What to Expect at Preschool by Heidi Murkoff

Materials
10 plastic hoops
backpack
objects related to school and common objects not found in school

Preparation
Place the items inside the backpack.

What to Do
1. Read one of the suggested books.
2. Explain that school is a place to learn new things and a place to make new friends.
3. Pass the backpack around. Ask each child to remove one item from the backpack.
4. Then go around the circle and invite each child to say whether or not her item is something that pertains to school.
5. Sort the objects into two baskets or hoops, one for objects that are found in school and the other for objects that are not found in school.

Assessment
1. Is the child able to understand that some things are found in school and other things are not found in school?
2. Is the child able to participate in the sorting aspect of the activity?

Mary Murray, Mazomanie, WI

What I Like to Play

Learning Objectives
Children will:
1. Develop listening skills.
2. Develop oral language skills.

Vocabulary

baseball	hula-hoop	tag
basketball	jump rope	yo-yo
hopscotch	soccer ball	

Materials
crayons, markers
paper
tape

What to Do
1. Talk with the children about what they enjoy playing outside.
2. Brainstorm lots of ideas.
3. Ask the children to draw a picture that answers the question "What am I playing?"
4. When the children are finished drawing their pictures, write "What Am I Playing?" at the top of their pictures and the answer (as dictated by the child) on the bottom of the picture.

Assessment
1. Did the child participate in the brainstorming about things the children enjoy playing outside?
2. Did the child develop his listening and communication skills during the brainstorming session?

Jackie Wright, Enid, OK

riddle card

Who Is Here Today?

AGES
4+

Learning Objectives
Children will:
1. Learn to recognize the names of their classmates.
2. Learn a song.

Vocabulary

class	school
here	sing
name	

MY SCHOOL

Children's Books
Froggy Goes to School by Jonathan London
The Kissing Hand by Audrey Penn
Look Out Kindergarten, Here I Come!
   by Nancy Carlson

Materials
card stock, cut into 7½" x 3" cards, one for
   each child
computer and printer (optional)
marker

Preparation
Write (or use a computer to print) each child's
name on a piece of card stock.

What to Do
1. At group or circle time, sing the following song with the class. As you sing each child's
name, show the class that child's name card.

"Who Is Here Today?"
   by Jackie Wright
(Tune: "The Farmer in the Dell")

Who is here today?
Who is here today?
Hi-ho, the derry-o
Who is here today?

_____*'s here today.*
_____*'s here today.*
Hi-ho, the derry-o
_____*'s here today.*

2. Repeat the second verse for each child present, inserting his name in the blank.

Assessment
1. Does she enjoy singing the song?
2. Can the child recognize the names of
her classmates?
3. Does the child participate in singing the
song with the class?

Jackie Wright, Enid, OK

Class Photo Album

Learning Objectives
Children will:
1. Learn about numbers and number words.
2. Develop oral language skills.

Vocabulary
children   count   read
class   number

Children's Books
One Happy Classroom by Charnan Simon
Ten, Nine, Eight by Molly Bang

Materials
digital camera
large number cards
photo album

What to Do

1. Take photographs of groups of children from the classroom, beginning with a photo of one child to a photo of 10 or 20 children.
2. In each photo, have one child hold the number card according to the number of children in the photo.
3. Place the photographs in a small photo album.
4. Invite children to "read" the photo album and practice their counting and number recognition skills. The children can turn the pages of the book, say the numbers aloud, and count the groups of classmates.
5. Children enjoy finding themselves in the pictures and will want to "read" this book over and over.

Assessment

1. Is the child able to recognize the numbers on each page?
2. Is the child able to name the other children in the photos?

Mary Murray, Mazomanie, WI

Teacher-to-Teacher Tips

- Invite a parent volunteer to come in and take the photographs and print the pictures for this class project. Be sure to leave this fun photo album out for parents to look through during an open house event.
- In some schools, it is necessary to obtain permission from parents before taking photographs of their children.

A Map of My School

AGES 5+

Learning Objectives

Children will:

1. Learn about different areas of their school.
2. Begin to learn about maps.
3. Determine fire escape routes.

Vocabulary

classroom
exit signs
fire extinguishers
hallway

kitchen
office
playground
teacher

Children's Books

No Dragons for Tea: Fire Safety for Kids
  by Jean E. Pendziwol
Stop, Drop, and Roll: A Book About Fire Safety
  by Margery Cuyler

Materials

markers
paper

What to Do

1. Take the children on a walk around the school, starting in their classroom; count all the classrooms. Point out the exit signs and the fire extinguishers, and talk about what they are used for. Show the children where they would go in a fire, and perhaps practice what to do in a fire drill.

2. When you get back to the classroom, ask the children to describe what they noticed about the building, including the locations of all the classrooms and the locations of the fire extinguishers in the building. Use the information the children tell you to draw a map of the school. Draw arrows to show the route for the fire escape. Post this on the wall in the art center.

3. Give the children paper and markers let them draw a map of their school to take home and show their parents.

Assessment

1. What did the child learn about different areas of the school?
2. What does the child know about maps?
3. Does the child know what route to use in a fire?

Holly Dzierzanowski, Bastrop, TX

Teacher-to-Teacher Tip

This is a great activity to do at the beginning of the year, or when the class receives a new classmate, to help children familiarize themselves with the school and know the route to use in case of a fire.

My School

AGES 5+

Learning Objectives

Children will:

1. Learn about their school.
2. Use problem-solving skills.

Vocabulary

find   surprise
search   treasure hunt

Children's Books

The Art Treasure Hunt: I Spy with My Little Eye by Doris Kutschbach

Skippyjon Jones and the Treasure Hunt by Judy Schachner

Treasure by Suzanne Bloom

Preparation

- Leave clues in different places throughout the school. Example of clues include the following:
  - Go to where you would eat lunch. (cafeteria)
  - Where do you find different colors of paints? (art area)
  - Where do you find lots of books? (library)
  - Go to the place where you can swing really high. (playground)
  - Go to the place where the person who takes care of our room is. (janitor)
  - Where is the person who takes care of sick children? (nurse's office)
- Write each clue on an index card. Decide which places you want to visit and the order in which you want to visit each place. Keep the index cards in this order.

- Prior to the treasure-hunt tour of the school, meet with each person the child will meet. For example:
  - Set up a visit with the school custodian. Visit her room and tell her that when you visit with the children, you want her to talk to the children about her job in the school. She can explain how she uses the tools.
  - Set up a visit with the school nurse. Tell the nurse that you are going to ask the children to brainstorm a list of questions for him, and that you will be asking him these questions when the class visits his office.
  - Set up a visit with the cafeteria workers. Tell them that when you visit, you will want them to show the children the ovens, refrigerators, and other kitchen equipment.

What to Do

1. Go on a treasure-hunt tour of your school. Give the first clue to the children and then go to that place.
2. As you visit each part of the school, take photographs of each place in the school with one child in each photograph. Print the photos to create a class book.
3. When the treasure-hunt tour of the school is complete, brainstorm with the children a list of things they have learned about the school.

Assessment

1. What did the child learn about his school?
2. Was the child able to use problem-solving skills to figure out where to go in the school based on each clue?

Ann Scalley, Orleans, MA

Teacher-to-Teacher Tips

- This is a great activity to do at the beginning of the school year.
- Visit all the areas of the school on one day or spread this out over a few days.

Fuzzy Number Jump

Learning Objectives

Children will:

1. Improve their sensory skills.
2. Improve their gross motor skills.
3. Identify numerals.

Vocabulary

feel   soft
fuzzy   touch

Children's Books

Numbers by Henry Arthur Pluckrose
The Right Number of Elephants
   by Jeff Sheppard
Touch by Maria Rius

Materials

1 yard of imitation fur (can be purchased at
   local fabric store)
classroom objects, such as small cars and
   small plastic blocks
fabric scissors

Preparation

Cut numerals 1 through 5 (or 1 through 10,
depending on the ages and abilities of the
children in the class) from the fake fur. Make
each numeral 8" or more in height.

What to Do

1. Display the fuzzy numbers randomly about on the floor of the classroom. Place the corresponding number of classroom objects on top of each number.
2. Have small groups of children play this game together.
3. Invite one child to jump from number to number, landing next to, not on top of, each number.
4. Each time a child lands near a number, she feels the fuzzy number with her hands, counts the number of objects, and says the name of the numeral aloud.
5. After each child has jumped to several numbers, she gives a high five to a classmate, and then that child takes a turn.
6. Children play until everyone has had at least one turn to jump and feel the numbers.

Assessment

1. Does the child notice the texture of each number?
2. Is the child able to jump from number to number?
3. Is the child able to count the number of objects and then identify each numeral?

Mary Murray, Mazomanie, WI

Goodnight, Numbers

AGES 4+

Learning Objectives
Children will:
1. Develop oral language skills.
2. Improve their number recognition skills.

Vocabulary
good night   rest
quiet   whisper

Children's Books
Goodnight Moon by Margaret Wise Brown
One Was Johnny: A Counting Book
    by Maurice Sendak

Materials
black mural paper
chalk
flashlight

Preparation
- Use chalk to draw block numerals 1 through 5 (or 1 through 10, depending on the ages and abilities or the children in the class) on the black mural paper.
- Add a simple drawing of a face and closed eyes next to each number character.

What to Do
1. Turn the lights down low, making the room as dark as possible. Then have fun making the transition to rest time as follows.
2. Display the number chart.
3. Shine the light on the face next to numeral one. Invite the children to use a whisper voice as they chant "Goodnight, Mr. One." Shine the light on the face next to numeral two and repeat.
4. After the children have whispered good night to each numeral, invite them to quietly walk to their resting places to lie down.
5. For the next few minutes, continue shining the light on various number characters, allowing children to watch the light as they rest. Then turn off the flashlight for rest time.

Assessment
1. Does the child say goodnight to each number?
2. Is the child developing number recognition skills?

Mary Murray, Mazomanie, WI

Teacher-to-Teacher Tip
Walk around the room with a mini flashlight and smaller number chart. Sit with individual children and listen as they say good night to each number on the chart as you shine the light on various numbers.

How Big Were Dinosaurs?

AGES
4+

Learning Objectives
Children will:
1. Learn about numbers and size.
2. Learn about dinosaurs.

Vocabulary

carnivores	extinct	meters
distance	height	reptiles
endangered	herbivores	yards

names of dinosaur species, such as
triceratops, apatosaurus, velociraptor,
and T. rex

Children's Books
Dinosaurs A–Z by Simon Mugford
Dinosaur Roar! by Paul and Henrietta Stickland
Harry and the Bucketful of Dinosaurs
    by Ian Whybrow
How Do Dinosaurs Say Goodnight?
    by Jane Yolen

Materials
masking tape
measuring tape
scissors
yarn

Preparation
- Research in books or on the Internet to find out the sizes of the mouth and the body of your group's favorite dinosaur or dinosaurs.
- Use masking tape to mark on the floor of your group-time area the shape and size of the dinosaur's mouth.
- With the measuring tape and yarn, premeasure the length of their favorite dinosaur from nose to tip of tail. Use different colored yarn for the individual dinosaurs. Write the name of each dinosaur on masking tape and use this masking tape to label the appropriate length of yarn.
- Create a strip of yarn that is the length of an elephant (approximately 11 feet) for comparison.

What to Do
1. Ask a group of children to stand inside the mouth of the dinosaur you have marked on the floor. They will be amazed how many of them can fit into the mouth!
2. Take the lengths of yarn and go inside or outside to the largest area.
3. Divide the class into groups and give each group one length of yarn. As the children unroll the lengths of yarn, identify the dinosaurs that each length of yarn measures. Make sure one group has the elephant ball of yarn. Many children have seen elephants, and this will help them absorb just how big some dinosaurs were.

Assessment
1. What did the child learn about dinosaurs? Does the child want to learn more about dinosaurs or measure more dinosaurs?
2. What did the child learn about measuring and comparing sizes?

Sharon Ness, Chestermere, AB, Canada

Another Encyclopedia of Theme Activities

Number Puzzles

Learning Objectives

Children will:

1. Use critical thinking skills.
2. Identify numbers.

Vocabulary

numbers   puzzle piece

Children's Books

How Many Bugs in a Box? by David A. Carter
Mother Goose Numbers on the Loose by Leo and Diane Dillon
Numbers by Henry Arthur Pluckrose

Materials

bold line black marker
8" x 11" sheets of card stock in different colors
resealable freezer bags
scissors

What to Do

1. Invite a group of children or an individual child to select a bag of puzzle pieces.
2. The children remove the pieces from the bag and then place the pieces together to form the number.
3. Ask the children to say the number aloud.
4. The children can continue until all the number puzzles are done.
5. Ask the children to place each set of pieces back in the bag so the game is ready for the next person.

Assessment

1. Does the child use critical thinking skills?
2. Does the child learn to identify numbers?

Mary Murray, Mazomanie, WI

Preparation

- Draw a large numeral, 1 through 10 (or 1 through 5, depending on the ages and abilities of the children in your class), on each piece of card stock. Use a different color for each number.
- Cut out the numbers, keeping the black outline intact on each number.
- Cut each number into four or five pieces to create a puzzle. Use a different cut, such as zigzag, straight, or rounded, for each piece of the puzzle.
- Place each set of puzzle pieces in a separate resealable freezer bag.

Number Towers

AGES
4+

Learning Objectives

Children will:

1. Learn about numbers.
2. Develop thinking skills.
3. Sort and classify blocks.
4. Improve their fine motor skills.

Vocabulary

bottom
build
numbers
top
tower

What to Do

1. Ask the children to sort the blocks into groups by numbers.
2. After they sort the blocks by numbers, suggest that the children build a tower using all the blocks with the same number.
3. Encourage the children to create five towers with the five sets of blocks, and then create larger or taller towers or buildings using two or three sets of blocks.

Children's Books

10 Black Dots by Paul Giganti
12 Ways to Get to Eleven by Eve Merriam
Each Orange Had 8 Slices by Paul Giganti

Materials

50 or more building blocks of varying sizes and types
number stickers (or use masking tape and marker)

Preparation

Attach a number sticker between one and five to each building block so there are at least five blocks with *1*s, five blocks with *2*s, and so on.

sticker with number

Assessment

1. Is the child able to sort the blocks by number?
2. How well does the child use his fine motor skills to build with the blocks?

Mary Murray, Mazomanie, WI

Sorting and Classifying

AGES 4+

Learning Objectives

Children will:

1. Learn about numbers.
2. Practice sorting, classifying, and identifying and creating patterns.
3. Identify colors and shapes.

Vocabulary

| group | numbers | pattern |
| number line | order | sort |

Children's Books

A-B-A-B-A: A Book of Pattern Play by Brian P. Cleary
Growing Patterns by Sarah C. Campbell

Numbers by Henry Arthur Pluckrose
Pattern Fish by Trudy Harris
Patterns by Henry Arthur Pluckrose
Patterns Outside by Daniel Nunn
Sorting by Henry Arthur Pluckrose

Materials

large index cards
markers

Preparation

Prepare number cards. Write one numeral from 1 through 5 (or 1 through 10 if appropriate for the children in your class) on an index card.

What to Do

1. Read books about patterns and then ask the children to identify patterns that they see in the classroom, on their clothes, and other places. Suggest that the children practice sorting and classifying the manipulatives in the classroom.
2. Create a human pattern by lining up four to six children in different ways and then asking the remaining children to identify the pattern, which could be *boy, girl, boy, girl* or *short pants, long pants, short pants, long pants*.
3. Do a human sorting activity by asking all of the children who are wearing red shoes to stand in one area, all of the children who are wearing white shoes to stand in another area, and so on. Ask the children to suggest other ways they can sort themselves.
4. If appropriate for the children in your class, talk about what a number line is (numbers placed in order).
5. Select a group of five children and give each child a number card. Ask them to make a human number line by lining up in order of their numbers. Help them figure out how to line up in numerical order. When they have made a line, have them call out their numbers to see if they lined up in order. If they have, they give themselves applause! If they have not, help them to make corrections.

Assessment

1. What did the child learn about numbers and the order of numbers?
2. Is the child able to sort and classify manipulatives?
3. Is the child able to use color and shape identification skills to create patterns?

Robin Frisch, Naperville, IL

Animal Counting Jars

AGES
5+

Learning Objectives

Children will:
1. Improve counting skills.
2. Practice one-to-one correspondence.
3. Develop fine motor skills.

Vocabulary

| animals | estimate | jar |
| count | guess | number |

Children's Books

1-2-3: A Child's First Counting Book by Alison Jay
Best Counting Book Ever by Richard Scarry
Count by Denise Fleming
Counting Crocodiles by Judy Sierra
Pizza Counting by Christina Dobson

Materials

chart paper and marker
many small plastic animals
various sizes of clear plastic jars with lids

Preparation

- Fill each jar with plastic animals, then cover tightly.
- Display the jars of animals on a table.

What to Do

1. Show the class one jar of animals.
2. Ask the children in the class to each guess how many animals are inside.
3. Record their guesses on a piece of chart paper.
4. Help one child count the animals from the jar. Note who came closest to estimating the correct number of animals.
5. Repeat the activity so children can have lots of practice estimating numbers of animals in jars of varying sizes.
6. Extend the activity by inviting one child to sit at the table with three or more jars of animals. Ask the child to select a jar and estimate or guess how many animal toys are inside the jar.
7. Help the child remove the lid, spill out the animals, and count them aloud.
8. Have the child place the collection of animals back in its jar and screw the lid on tight.
9. Repeat the activity of estimating and counting as he opens and counts the animals inside each jar.

Assessment

1. Is the child developing and improving counting skills?
2. Are the child's estimating skills improving?
3. Is the child developing fine motor skills as she counts the animals in each jar?

Mary Murray, Mazomanie, WI

Number Tunnel

Learning Objectives
Children will:
1. Improve gross motor skills.
2. Enhance number recognition skills.

Vocabulary
crawl   through   tunnel

Children's Books
Hockey Numbers by Matt Napier
I Like to Learn Numbers: Hungry Chameleon by Alex A. Lluch
Missing Mittens by Stuart J. Murphy
My Even Day by Doris Fisher
Numbers by Henry Arthur Pluckrose
Odds and Evens: A Number Book by Heidi Goennel
One Odd Day by Doris Fisher

Materials
beanbag pal
gross motor tunnel
index cards
markers
tape

Preparation
- Use the index cards and marker to create number cards. Write one numeral and the corresponding number of dots on each card.
- Tape the numeral cards randomly about the walls and ceiling inside the tunnel.

What to Do

1. Ask the children to form a single-file line at one end of the tunnel. Display the beanbag pal at the end of the tunnel. Explain to the children that there are several numbers displayed inside the tunnel.
2. Invite children to crawl through and say the numbers aloud or count the number of dots on each card.
3. When each child reaches the end of the tunnel, she picks up the toy animal and counts to five (or ten, depending on the ages and abilities of the children) by whispering in the beanbag animal's ear.
4. The child can wait for another turn or play elsewhere in the classroom.

Assessment

1. Is the child able to crawl easily through the tunnel?

2. Is the child improving her number recognition skills?

Mary Murray, Mazomanie, WI

Tactile Numbers

AGES 5+

Learning Objectives

Children will:

1. Identify numbers.

2. Improve their fine motor skills.

Vocabulary

crayon	marker	pen
feel	number	write
hand	paper	

Children's Book

I Like to Learn Numbers: Hungry Chameleon by Alex A. Lluch

My Even Day by Doris Fisher

Numbers by Henry Arthur Pluckrose

Odds and Evens: A Number Book by Heidi Goennel

One Odd Day by Doris Fisher

Materials

glue

large index cards

markers

sand, glitter, or another tactile material

Preparation

Write one large block number and the corresponding number of dots on separate index cards. Select numbers that are familiar to the children in your class.

What to Do

1. Invite the children to select one number card. If necessary, help individual children identify the number or count the dots.

2. Suggest that the children cover the number with glue and then sprinkle sand, glitter, or another tactile material onto the index card. Shake off the excess and let the index cards dry.

3. Encourage the children to feel the shape of the number.

Assessment

1. Is the child able to identify the numbers on the index cards?

2. Is the child improving his fine motor skills as he creates tactile numbers?

Mary Murray, Mazomanie, WI

Recycle and Save the Earth

AGES 3+

Learning Objectives
Children will:
1. Learn the meaning of recycling.
2. Begin to understand that we must care for the world.
3. Improve their language skills.

Vocabulary
conserve   landfill   reuse
Earth   recycle   trash

Children's Books
I Can Save the Earth! by Alison Inches
Michael Recycle by Ellie Bethel

Materials
none

What to Do
1. Talk with the children about what the word *recycling* means. Tell them how good things can be made from what we might otherwise put into the trash.
2. Read a book about recycling. Let the children help you point out all of the things we can do to help the Earth.
3. Teach the children the following song. (**Note:** Sing the word *once* as though it had two syllables.)

"Recycle and Save the Earth" by Anne Adeney
(sung to the tune of "Frère Jacques")

Let's recycle! Let's recycle!
You and me! You and me!
Use stuff more than once! Use stuff more than once!
Save the Earth! Save the Earth!

Assessment
1. Can the child tell you what *recycling* means?
2. Can the child name something that can be used more than once?

Anne Adeney, Plymouth, UK

Ocean Drawings

AGES 4+

Learning Objectives
Children will:
1. Learn about ocean creatures.
2. Draw or paint an ocean ecosystem.

Vocabulary
animals   plant
ecosystem
fish
ocean

Children's Books

Commotion in the Ocean by Giles Andreae
Eye Wonder: Ocean by Mary Ling
Follow the Water from Brook to Ocean by Arthur Dorros
Oceans by Seymour Simon
Somewhere in the Ocean by Jennifer Ward and T. J. Marsh

Materials

blue tempera paint, thinned with water (or blue watercolor paint)
chart paper and marker or whiteboard and dry-erase marker
crayons
paintbrushes
small bowls of water
white construction paper

What to Do

1. Read a few of the books to the children, and then place the books where the children can look at them independently.
2. Ask the children to name animals that live in the ocean. Write their answers on chart paper or a whiteboard.
3. Read another book about the ocean to the class. Have them also notice the plants that live in the ocean. Add to the chart more animals or plants that the children noticed from the book.
4. Provide crayons and paper for the children to make drawings of ocean animals and plants. Encourage them to fill the paper with colorful drawings but not to draw the water. When the children are finished drawing with crayons, have them use the blue paint and paint the ocean water on top of their drawings. The paint will reveal their colorful animals and plants!

Assessment

1. What did the child learn about ocean creatures?
2. Ask the child to tell you about her picture.

Fingerplays, Songs, and Poems

"Octopus" on *10 Carrot Diamond* CD by Charlotte Diamond

Tina Cho, Newton, IA

Maps!

AGES 4+

Learning Objectives

Children will:
1. Learn about maps.
2. Identify various cities, states, or countries with help.
3. Become aware of geography and map-reading skills.

Vocabulary

city	country	state
code	map	symbols

Children's Books

Follow That Map! A First Look at Mapping Skills by Scot Ritchie
Maps and Globes by Jack Knowlton
Me on the Map by Joan Sweeney
My Map Book by Sara Fanelli
Walk on Maps by Mel Campbell
Where Do I Live? by Neil Chesanow

Materials

six or more large maps

Preparation
- Invite five parent volunteers to come in for this learning activity.
- Display one large map at each table in the classroom.

What to Do
1. Introduce the parent helpers for this activity.
2. Tell the children they will be able to walk around the room and learn about different types of maps and different places in our world.
3. Divide the class into six groups. Have each group go to a table and learn from the parent as they explore the map together. Invite the parent helper to read various words such as city names, highway numbers, countries, and continents aloud. Have the helper show the children how to locate and identify various symbols on the map.
4. If time allows and the children are interested, let the groups change tables and look at another map.
5. Set or display one of the maps in the classroom so children can continue to examine and learn from the map.

Assessment
1. Ask the child to tell you one thing he learned about maps.
2. Is the child able to identify various cities, states, or countries with or without help?
3. Did the child learn map-reading skills?

Mary Murray, Mazomanie, WI

My Planet

AGES 4+

Learning Objectives
Children will:
1. Learn sponge-painting technique.
2. Identify colors.
3. Develop an appreciation for our planet.

Vocabulary
blue	Earth	planet
brown	green	white

Children's Books
Earth, revised edition, by Thomas K. Adamson
Our Home Planet: Earth by Nancy Loewen
This Is Our Earth by Laura Lee Benson

Materials
paint trays
photograph of Earth from space (the Internet is a good source)
round pieces of white construction paper
sponge pieces
tempera paint in blue, green, brown, and white

Preparation
Moisten the sponge pieces until they are slightly damp, and fill the paint trays with tempera paint. Place the paint trays and sponge pieces in the art center.

What to Do

1. Display a photograph of Earth taken from space.
2. Ask the children to describe Earth. What shape is it? What colors do they see? Discuss the features and beauty of our planet.
3. Provide each child with a round piece of white construction paper. Ask the children to paint a planet of their creation or pictures of Earth.
4. The children can dip the sponge pieces in the tempera paint and use them to paint their pictures. Let their paintings dry.

Assessment

1. Can the child identify the colors he used in his painting?
2. Are the children able to paint pictures of a planet of their own creation or of Earth?
3. Does the child have the fine motor control to do the sponge painting?

Laura D. Wynkoop, San Dimas, CA

> **Teacher-to-Teacher Tip**
>
> Cover a classroom bulletin board with black butcher paper. Paint white dots on the black paper to create a "space" look, and display the children's paintings in space.

Rain Forest

AGES 4+

Learning Objectives

Children will:

1. Learn the importance of rain forests.
2. Develop communication skills.

Vocabulary

damp	rain forest	water
ecosystem	trees	
moisture	warm	

Children's Books

The Great Kapok Tree by Lynne Cherry
Here Is the Tropical Rain Forest by Madeleine Dunphy
Rain Forest by Elinor Greenwood
Rain Forest by Jinny Johnson
Tropical Rain Forest by Donald Silver

Materials

child-safe scissors
globe of Earth
glue or paste
large maps of Earth (National Geographic has some excellent ones)
magazines
poster board or similar materials

Preparation

- About a week before this lesson, if you don't have all the materials, send home a note to parents and caregivers, requesting the materials you need. Also ask fellow teachers.
- The day of the activity, place the globe and maps on the floor where you will be sitting.

What to Do

1. Sit together on the floor in a circle, with the globe in the center.
2. Ask the children what they know about a rain forest. Have any of them been in a rain forest?
3. Point to areas on the globe where there are rain forests. Show the children the large maps.

4. Read one or two of the books and talk with the children about what makes a rain forest different from a regular forest.
5. Suggest that the children cut out pictures at the work tables and make collages of a rain forest.

Assessment
1. What can the child tell you about the importance of rain forests?
2. What communication skills did the child develop?

Shirley Anne Ramaley, Sun City, AZ

Learn about Lakes

AGES
5+

Learning Objectives
Children will:
1. Learn about an ecosystem.
2. Learn that a lake is one kind of ecosystem.
3. Develop an appreciation for the importance of lakes.

Vocabulary
algae	fish	reeds
beach	lake	shore
biome	nature	water
ecosystem	plants	

Children's Books
101 Facts About Lakes by Julia Barnes
Biomes and Ecosystems by Barbara J. Davis
Earth's Ecosystems by Jim Pipe
Great Lakes by Kim Valzania
Lakes by Aaron Frisch
Lakes and Ponds by Cassie Mayer
The Lost Lake by Allen Say
Morning on the Lake by Jan Bourdeau Waboose

What to Do
1. Show the children pictures in several books about lakes and ecosystems, reading appropriate pages.

Materials
books
child-safe scissors
glue or paste
magazine pictures of lakes
poster paper or other paper for each child

Preparation
Place magazines and other supplies on the work tables, with scissors and paper for each child.

2. Talk with the children about lakes and explain that they are one kind of ecosystem. Talk about ecosystems, what this means, and the importance of healthy ecosystems. Ecosystems, which can be small or large, include plants, trees, animals, people, water, and soil. When all the elements are in balance, the system is healthy. A healthy lake ecosystem has clean water and living organisms, such as fish, dragonflies, plants, and more.

3. Provide magazines for the children to cut out pictures and paste them onto their papers to make healthy lake ecosystem collages. Post the collages for a week for all to see, before letting the children take their collages home.

Assessment

1. Is the child able to describe an ecosystem?
2. What can the child tell you about lakes?

Fingerplays, Songs, and Poems

The Lake
by Shirley Anne Ramaley
A fish swims in the lake.
The water is clean and blue.
We look around and like what we see
As we paddle in our canoe.

Shirley Anne Ramaley, Sun City, AZ

> **Teacher-to-Teacher Tip**
> If you don't have enough magazines, send a note home the week before, and ask parents and caregivers to contribute any appropriate magazines they are willing to give to the class.

Making a Terrarium

AGES 5+

Learning Objectives
Children will:
1. Learn about an ecosystem and that it can be small.
2. Cooperate and work together.
3. Develop a beginning interest in Earth science.

Vocabulary

artificial	fertilizer	small
big	natural	soil
climate	plants	terrarium
Earth	rock	
ecosystem	science	

Children's Book
Plant Secrets by Emily Goodman

Materials
dirt and/or fertilizer
glass containers for terrariums (select one that suits the needs of the class)
plants of appropriate size
small bowls
small rocks and/or sticks

What to Do

1. Work with a small group of children. Explain to the children that a terrarium is a small ecosystem, a garden of plants growing in a clear container.

2. Read a book about plants or information from the Internet about making a terrarium.

3. Talk with the children about ecosystems and how it is important for each ecosystem to be healthy. Explain how they will make terrariums with the help of an adult. While you will be working on an artificial ecosystem, be sure the children understand that this is similar to natural ecosystems.

4. When the project is completed, keep the terrariums in the classroom for the children to observe over time.

Assessment

1. What did the child learn about a small ecosystem?

2. Did the child cooperate and work together to build a terrarium?

Shirley Anne Ramaley, Sun City, AZ

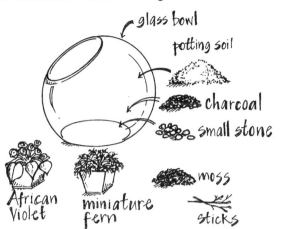

glass bowl
potting soil
charcoal
small stone
moss
sticks
African Violet
miniature fern

Teacher-to-Teacher Tips

● This project works best with up to four children at a time working with one adult.

● It may be helpful to have a finished terrarium in the class for the children to see before starting their own.

Recycling Fun

AGES 5+

Learning Objectives

Children will:

1. Identify which objects are plastic.

2. Learn that plastic can be recycled and used again.

3. Identify colors.

Vocabulary

carry   plastic   reuse
colors   recycle   save

Children's Books

The Adventures of a Plastic Bottle by Alison Inches

Stuff! Reduce, Reuse, Recycle by Steven Kroll
Where Do Recyclable Materials Go? by Sabbithry Persad
Why Should I Recycle? by Jen Green

Materials

20 assorted plastic jugs and containers, cleaned and dry
craft foam or colored construction paper
permanent marker
plastic recycling bin
safety pins
scissors

Preparation

- Place the plastic containers randomly about the room or in the dramatic play area.

- Create four I Will Recycle! badges as follows: Cut four 4" circles from craft foam or colored construction paper. Use a bold permanent marker to write *I Will Recycle!* on each badge.

What to Do

1. Talk with the children about the importance of recycling plastic materials. Each day select three or four children to be the class recyclers. Attach a recycling badge to each child's shirt.

2. Invite the three to four children to work together to collect the plastic containers displayed around the room and bring them to the recycling bin.

3. Encourage the children to describe each plastic container by color, size, shape, and use, and then place each item in the recycling bin. Once the bin is filled with plastic items, have the four children push the recycling container to the door.

4. At the end of the day, return the materials to their starting place so another group of children may practice recycling the following morning.

Assessment

1. Display 10 objects in a row—some plastic, some not. Is the child able to identify the objects that are plastic?

2. What has the child learned about plastic being recycled and used again?

3. Is the child able to identify the color of the plastic bottles and containers?

Mary Murray, Mazomanie, WI

Teacher-to-Teacher Tips

- Display the badges on a special bulletin board along with a list of names detailing which children will be the recyclers each day of the week. For extra fun, make enough badges so the children can take them home after wearing them on their designated days.

- Begin saving colorful laundry soap containers, food containers, and other plastic recyclables in advance of this activity, or invite each child to bring in one or more colorful plastic containers from home.

Bean Garden

Learning Objectives

Children will:

1. Observe seeds and spouts.
2. Learn how things grow.

Vocabulary

bean	seed
grow	sprout
observe	water
plant	

Children's Books

From Seed to Plant by Gail Gibbons
From Seed to Plant by Allan Fowler
How a Seed Grows by Helene J. Jordan
One Bean by Anne Rockwell
Planting a Rainbow by Lois Ehlert
The Tiny Seed by Eric Carle

Materials

assortment of bean seeds
ice cube trays
permanent marker
water

What to Do

1. Have the children look at and compare the bean seeds. Each child should choose a bean.
2. Mark the ice cube tray on the inside of each cell with a child's name so that the children can see their names. Let each child put her bean in her cell.
3. Move the trays to a place in the room that receives sunlight.
4. Have each child fill her cell with water.
5. Observe the sprouting and growing of each bean. (You need to keep each cell filled with water at all times.)
6. Plant the sprouts in a garden or individual cups for the child to take home.

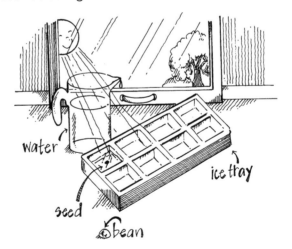

Assessment

1. Did the child observe the seeds growing and sprouting?
2. What did the child learn about how things grow?
3. Can the child explain what happened to her seed?

Sandy L. Scott, Meridian, ID

Plant Race

AGES
3+

Learning Objectives
Children will:
1. Learn what a plant needs to grow.
2. Develop observation skills.

Vocabulary

compare	root
germinate	seed
grow	soil
plant	sprout
predict	water

Children's Books
How a Seed Grows by Helen J. Jordan
How a Seed Grows into a Sunflower by David Stewart
How Flowers Grow by Emma Helbrough

Materials
2–3 types of beans
clear plastic cups
craft sticks
magnifying glasses
newspaper
poster board or chart paper
potting soil
scoop or shovel

What to Do
1. Gather the children. Show them the bean seeds you have chosen. You can give them magnifying glasses to explore, if desired.
2. Tell the children that they are going to plant the seeds. Ask the children what they think the seeds need to grow
3. Give each child a cup and have them choose which seed they would like to plant. (Make sure there are some of each bean represented.)
4. Have the children scoop the soil into the cups, place the seed into the soil, water the seed, and label the cup with the craft stick.
5. Ask the children to make predictions as to which seed will grow first.
6. Help the children record their observations each day. See whose predictions were right and why.

Assessment
1. Did the child understand what a plant needs to grow?
2. Did the child use his observation skills and note the changes each day?

Shelley Hoster, Norcross, GA

Flower Delivery

AGES 4+

Learning Objectives
Children will:
1. Learn about colors.
2. Improve oral language skills.

Vocabulary
colors	numbers
flowers	petals
leaf	pick

Children's Books
Eating the Alphabet by Lois Ehlert
The Flower Alphabet Book by Jerry Pallotta
Planting a Rainbow by Lois Ehlert

Materials
2–3 aprons
artificial flowers
plastic vases

What to Do
1. Display the materials at the dramatic play center.
2. Invite the children to put on the aprons and pretend to be working in a floral shop, creating flower arrangements by placing several artificial flowers in the vases.
3. Encourage the children to describe the flowers that they are putting in each vase.
4. Suggest that the children deliver a vase of flowers to another classmate.
5. When the children are finished playing, they return the materials to the center so other children can play.

Assessment
1. What did the children learn about colors?
2. How well did the child describe the flowers?

Mary Murray, Mazomanie, WI

> **Teacher-to-Teacher Tip**
> Purchase inexpensive flowers at a local craft shop or a secondhand store.

Growing and Changing

AGES 4+

Learning Objectives
Children will:
1. Develop communication skills.
2. Learn about the world around them.

Vocabulary
acorn	egg	pine tree
bulb	frog	pinecone
butterfly	grow	radish
caterpillar	match	seed
change	oak tree	tadpole
chick	pair	tulip

PLANTS

Children's Books

Animals Grow and Change by Bobbie Kalman
From Caterpillar to Butterfly
    by Deborah Heiligman
From Egg to Chicken by Gerald Legg
From Little Acorns: A First Look at the Life Cycle
    of a Tree by Sam Godwin
From Pinecone to Pine Tree by Ellen Weiss
From Tadpole to Frog by Wendy Pfeffer
How Tulips Grow by Joanne Mattern
The Oak Inside the Acorn by Max Lucado
Where Do Chicks Come From?
    by Amy E. Slansky

Materials

card stock, cut into cards of the desired size
glue stick
laminating materials or clear contact paper
pictures of plants and animals
scissors

Preparation

- Locate pictures showing the changes in growth of various plants and animals. For example, find pictures of radish seeds and a radish, an egg and a chick, a tadpole and a frog, a pinecone and a pine tree, an acorn and an oak tree, a tulip bulb and a tulip, a caterpillar and a butterfly. Magazines, catalogs, and the Internet are good sources for these pictures.
- Cut out the pictures and glue each to a separate card. Laminate the cards for durability.

What to Do

1. Talk to the children about how things grow and change. Tell them that lots of things start out from a seed. Some flowers start from a seed, some start from a bulb. Some acorns are the beginning of big oak trees.
2. Show the cards to a group of children. Ask the children to match the cards into pairs—the beginning of a plant and what it grew into.

Assessment

1. Can the child identify some of the plants and animals in the pictures?
2. Can he pair the mates correctly?
3. Did the child develop communication skills?
4. What did the child learn about the world around him?

Jackie Wright, Enid, OK

How Many Ways Can You Make a Tree?

AGES 4+

Learning Objectives

Children will:
1. Learn about trees.
2. Develop fine motor skills.

Vocabulary

bark	leaf	trunk
branch	root	wood
grow	tree	

Another Encyclopedia of Theme Activities

Children's Books

Be a Friend to Trees by Patricia Lauber
The Gift of a Tree by Alvin Tresselt
Our Tree Named Steve by Alan Zweibel
A Tree for All Seasons by Robin Bernard
A Tree Is Nice by Janice May Udry

Materials

blocks
fabric squares
glue or tape
pieces of green tissue paper and green
    construction paper

What to Do

1. Read one or two books about trees to the children. Place the other books where the children can look at them independently.
2. Invite the children to create a forest of trees by standing blocks on end and attaching to the top of each block a green treetop of paper or fabric.
3. Encourage children to try different ways to make their treetops, such as attaching crumbled tissue paper or folded green paper, draping green fabric squares over the blocks, or another way that they would like to try.

Assessment

1. What did the child learn about trees?
2. How well did the child use her fine motor skills to create the wood-block trees?

Mary Murray, Mazomanie, WI

green crunched tissue paper

block

Sensational Sunflowers

AGES 4+

Learning Objectives

Children will:
1. Learn about sunflowers.
2. Develop listening skills.

Vocabulary

grow	seed	sunflower
leaves	stem	tall

Children's Books

From Seed to Sunflower by Gerald Legg
How a Seed Grows into a Sunflower
    by David Stewart
Sunflower House by Eve Bunting
The Sunflower Parable by Liz Curtis Higgs

Materials

15' thin strip of green paper
picture of a sunflower
sunflower seeds
vase of sunflowers and dried sunflower head
    (if available)
xylophone and mallet
yellow paper sunflower head

What to Do

1. Show the children the sunflower picture, vase, and seeds. Explain that the sunflower is a tall flower that can grow up to 15 feet high. Unroll the strip of green paper to show how long 15 feet is. Set the paper flower head at one end of the green paper stem.

2. Give each child a seed and tell the children how the plant starts from a tiny seed like the one they are holding. Then share these sunflower facts.

   - Birds and people like to eat the seeds.
   - One sunflower produces many seeds.
   - The stem and leaves of sunflowers are very large.
   - Sunflowers come in many colors.
   - Sunflowers need soil, air, water, and sun to grow.
   - A sunflower can grow to be 15 feet tall.

3. Invite the children to curl up into a tiny ball on the floor, pretend to be a sunflower seed, and then "grow" up tall into a giant sunflower as you play the xylophone from the lowest note to the highest note.

4. Play a melody on the xylophone as the sunflowers stand up tall and blow in the wind. Then have the children return to a seed, all curled up on the floor.

5. Repeat the musical activity several times, or for as long as is appropriate for the children in your class.

Assessment

1. What did the child learn about sunflowers?
2. Was the child able to listen to the xylophone and unfold from a seed to a tall sunflower?

Mary Murray, Mazomanie, WI

A Tree House of Our Own

AGES 4+

Learning Objectives

Children will:

1. Learn about trees.
2. Enjoy looking at and "reading" books about trees.

Vocabulary

branches
build
construction
tree house

Children's Books

Be a Friend to Trees by Patricia Lauber
Tell Me, Tree: All About Trees for Kids by Gail Gibbons
Tree House in a Storm by Rachelle Burk
A Tree Is a Plant by Clyde Robert Bulla
A Tree Is Nice by Janice May Udry

Another Encyclopedia of Theme Activities

Materials

books about trees
box cutter (adults only)
crayons and markers
large refrigerator box
paper
pictures of trees
tape
tree branches with leaves

Preparation

Create a tree house from the box by cutting holes for windows and a door. (This is an adult-only step.)

What to Do

1. Help the children place several tree branches on and around the house, inserting part of a branch and some leaves through each window.
2. Attach the tree pictures to the inside and outside walls of the house. If children want to, supply them with materials to draw pictures of trees for their tree house.
3. Display the books inside the tree house.
4. Invite children to sit in the tree house, look at the pictures on the walls, and "read" a variety of books about trees.

Assessment

1. What did the child learn about trees?
2. Did the child enjoy sitting in the tree house and looking at books?
3. How did the child help create the tree house?

Mary Murray, Mazomanie, WI

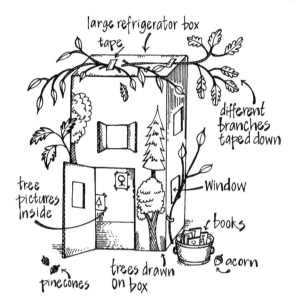

large refrigerator box
tape
different branches taped down
Window
books
acorn
tree pictures inside
trees drawn on box
pinecones

Desert Plants

AGES 5+

Learning Objectives

Children will:
1. Learn about cacti.
2. Learn how animals use cacti to survive in the desert.

Vocabulary

cactus   elf owl
desert   heat
names of animals that live in the desert, such as *elf owl, rattlesnake, tarantula, scorpion, butterfly, roadrunner, coyote, gila monster, hummingbird, rabbit,* and so on
names of different types of cacti, such as *saguaro, ocotillo, cholla, barrel, prickly pear,* and so on

Children's Books
101 Questions About Desert Life
  by Alice Jablonsky
Cactus Hotel by Brenda Z. Guiberson
Creatures of the Desert World by National
  Geographic Society
Desert Giant: The World of the Saguaro Cactus
  by Barbara Bash
Way Out in the Desert by Jennifer Ward and
  T. J. Marsh

Materials
green tempera paint
paintbrushes
pictures of desert animals
pictures of the desert
Styrofoam shapes
toothpicks

Preparation
Bring in different types of cacti for the children
to see, and ask parents to bring any examples
they may have.

What to Do
1. Show the children the pictures of the desert and read one or two books about the desert.
2. Talk about how the animals in the desert use plants to survive.
3. Show the children the live cacti that you have brought in, and talk to them about how cacti store water inside and how animals can eat the cacti. Tell the children that elf owls live inside cacti, and how they all need each other to survive.
4. Let the children go to the art table and create their own cactus with the Styrofoam pieces, paint, and toothpicks.

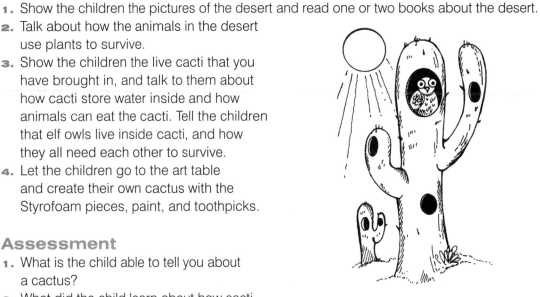

Assessment
1. What is the child able to tell you about a cactus?
2. What did the child learn about how cacti and animals survive in the desert?

Holly Dzierzanowski, Bastrop, TX

Teacher-to-Teacher Tip
Consider having a classroom cacti garden and make a graph of how long you go without watering the garden.

Edible Plant Parts Snack

AGES 5+

Learning Objectives
Children will:
1. Learn about different parts of a plant.
2. Learn about healthy foods.

Vocabulary
flower   plant   sprout
fruit   root   stem
leaf   seed   vegetable

Children's Books
Eating the Alphabet by Lois Ehlert
From Seed to Plant by Gail Gibbons
*Kids in the Garden: Growing Plants for Food and
Fun* by Elizabeth McCorquodale

Materials
an assortment of food to eat, such as carrots,
radishes, celery, bamboo shoots, lettuce,
spinach, broccoli, cauliflower, apples,
dates, tomatoes, nuts, rhubarb, sunflower
seeds, pumpkin seeds, and peas
chart paper and markers

Preparation
● Create a chart with five columns: roots,
stems, leaves, flowers, fruits, and seeds.
Write the word and add a picture at the top
of each column.
● Wash and prepare the food.

What to Do
1. Engage the children in a discussion about plants and growing food to eat. Ask the children
to name plants that they eat.
2. Display the chart with the parts of the
plant. Add the following foods to each
column, and then add the children's
answers.
     Roots: carrots, radishes
     Stem: celery, rhubarb, bamboo shoots
     Leaves: lettuce, spinach
     Flowers: broccoli, cauliflower
     Fruits: apples, dates, tomatoes
     Seeds: nuts, sunflower seeds,
       pumpkin seeds, and peas
3. Place samples of the foods that the
children eat for all the children to taste, or
combine a few foods into a healthy salad
for all to enjoy!

Assessment
1. What did the child learn about the different
parts of a plant?
2. What did the child learn about
healthy foods?

Teacher-to-Teacher Tip
Before serving food to children, check
for food allergies or restrictions.

Fingerplays, Songs, and Poems

"Oats, Peas, Beans, and Barley Grow" (Traditional)

Chorus:
Oats, peas, beans, and barley grow,
Oats, peas, beans, and barley grow,
Can you or I or anyone know
How oats, peas, beans, and barley grow?

First the farmer sows his seed,
Stands erect and takes his ease,
He stamps his foot and claps his hands,
And turns around to view his lands.
    (Chorus)

Next the farmer waters the seed,
Stands erect and takes his ease,
He stamps his foot and claps his hands,
And turns around to view his lands.
    (Chorus)

Next the farmer hoes the weeds,
Stands erect and takes his ease,
He stamps his foot and claps his hands,
And turns around to view his lands.
    (Chorus)

Last the farmer harvests his seed,
Stands erect and takes his ease,
He stamps his foot and claps his hands,
And turns around to view his lands.
    (Chorus)

Kaethe J. Lewandowski, Centreville, VA

Flower Power!

AGES 5+

Learning Objectives
Children will:
1. Learn about flowers.
2. Develop fine motor skills.

Vocabulary
flowers
nature
plants
pressed flowers
wildflowers

Children's Books
Flowers by Lynn Stone
Flowers Bloom! by Mary Dodson Wade
Why Do Plants Have Flowers? by Louise and
    Richard Spilsbury

Materials
card stock
flowers or wildflowers
glue sticks
heavy books or flower press
markers
paper towels

What to Do
1. Either have children gather wildflowers or bring flowers from home. Flowers can be purchased if necessary. The best flowers for this activity are daisies, cosmos, Queen Anne's Lace, or flowers that can be spread out in one semi-flat layer.

2. If you are using a flower press, follow the directions for it. If you are using heavy books, use the following directions:
   - Place a paper towel in book.
   - Spread flower out as flat as possible, and cover with another paper towel.
   - Close book and let flowers dry about a week.
3. When the flowers are dry, allow children to place flowers on card stock and think about a design for their picture.
4. Help the children to carefully lift the flowers and glue them where they want to place the flowers.
5. Help the children press the flower into the glue. Let dry.
6. When the glue is dry, the children can draw designs around flowers to decorate picture.

Assessment
1. What did the child learn about flowers?
2. Was the child able to use his fine motor skills to glue and arrange the flower successfully?

Fingerplays, Songs, and Poems

"Flowers All Around"
by Donna Alice Patton
(Tune: "Twinkle, Twinkle, Little Star")

Flowers, flowers all around
Pretty flowers dot the ground.
We will pick them and you'll see
A flower picture made by ME!

Donna Alice Patton, Hillsboro, OH

Teacher-to-Teacher Tip

If possible, encourage children to bring vines, leaves, and other interesting plants to dry.

A Plant's Life

AGES 5+

Learning Objectives
Children will:
1. Identify the growing cycle (from seed to sprout to plant).
2. Develop observation skills.

Vocabulary
cycle seed
germination seedling
plant sprout

Children's Books
Curious George Plants a Tree by H. A. Rey
From Seed to Plant by Gail Gibbons
A Fruit Is a Suitcase for Seeds by Jean Richards
How a Seed Grows by Helene J. Jordan
How Do Plants Grow? by Melissa Stewart

Materials
illustration of plant life cycle
paper and crayons for each child
The Tiny Seed by Eric Carle

Preparation

Find or create an illustrated plant life cycle.

What to Do

1. Gather children on a carpet and read *The Tiny Seed* by Eric Carle, or another book about seeds and plants. Pause as needed to discuss and answer questions. Explain that just as people grow up from babies to adults, plants have life cycles, too. How did the tiny seed in the story change? What did it become?
2. Show the children illustrations of the plant life cycle and discuss each stage: seed, sprout, seedling, plant.
3. Help the children divide their papers, label the plant life cycle, and draw each step of the plant life cycle.

Assessment

1. Is the child able to explain what happens as a seed begins to grow into a plant?
2. Did the child use her observation and listening skills to learn about the life cycle of a plant?

Kathryn Hake, Lebanon, OR

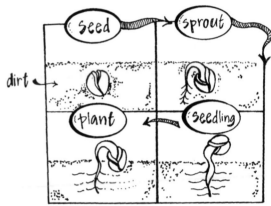

Teacher-to-Teacher Tip

Let children glue a real seed in the first box of their illustrated plant life cycle.

We Planted a Tree

AGES 5+

Learning Objectives

Children will:
1. Discover that trees are important to the environment.
2. Plant a tree.

Vocabulary

grow   plant   tree
oxygen   sapling

Children's Books

Be a Friend to Trees by Patricia Lauber
Tell Me, Tree: All About Trees for Kids by Gail Gibbons
A Tree Is a Plant by Clyde Robert Bulla
We Planted a Tree by Diane Muldrow

Materials

chart paper
markers
shovel
sand
soil
tree sapling
water source

Preparation

Select a planting location in close proximity to a water source.

What to Do

1. Ask the children to sit in a circle. Place the sapling in the center of the circle.
2. Say, "Today we are learning about something that is important to our environment—trees. In the center of our circle is a sapling, a young tree. As I read this book, listen and look for important things trees do that help people."
3. Read *We Planted a Tree,* and show the illustrations to the children.
4. Title a sheet of chart paper "Trees." Ask, "Why are trees important to people?" (Possible answers: Trees provide food, shade, homes for animals, and so on.) Add each idea to the chart. If children have difficulty thinking of ways trees help people, look back at the pictures in the book for clues.
5. Say, "Trees also help our environment in many ways. Trees provide oxygen in the air we breathe and help make the air cleaner and better to breathe. Add the word *oxygen* to the chart and define the word.
6. Tell the children that they are going to plant a tree sapling today. Carry the planting supplies to the predetermined location. Let the children take turns digging the hole, providing assistance as needed.
7. Place a few handfuls of sand in the bottom of the hole for drainage, place the sapling root ball in the hole, fill in with dirt, pat down the soil, and water thoroughly.
8. Ask the children to stand around the tree. Say, "On the count of three, let's shout, 'We planted a tree!' Ready? One. Two. Three!"

Assessments

1. What did the child learn about how trees are important to the environment?
2. How did the child help plant the tree?

Rob Sanders, Brandon, FL

Teacher-to-Teacher Tips

● Arrange the planting site with your school ahead of time.

● Ask a parent volunteer or two to help you with the planting.

Dinosaur Dig

AGES 3+

Learning Objective
Children will:
1. Learn about colors.
2. Learn about paleontologists.

Vocabulary
bones	dinosaur	fossil
dig	discover	paleontologist

Children's Books
The Big Book of Dinosaurs by DK Publishing
Digging Up Dinosaurs by Aliki
Dinosaur Roar! by Paul and Henrietta Stickland
Edwina, The Dinosaur Who Didn't Know She Was Extinct by Mo Willems
Stone Girl, Bone Girl: The Story of Mary Anning by Laurence Anholt

Materials
laminating machine or clear contact paper
paper in different colors
sand in a large tub or sand table
scissors

Preparation
- Cut dinosaur shapes out of different colors of paper. Laminate or cover with clear contact paper.
- Hide the paper dinosaurs in the sand.

What to Do
1. Read one of the suggested books and then tell the children that they are going to be a special kind of scientist called a *paleontologist*. Explain that paleontologists study the history of life on Earth.
2. Select a few children to be the paleontologists who are going to study the sand table.
3. If appropriate, ask each child to find a certain color dinosaur.
4. Offer an additional challenge by cutting the dinosaur shapes into puzzle pieces that the children find and then put together, just as *paleontologists* put together the bones they find to re-create the bone structure of animals that once lived on our planet.

Assessment
1. What did the child learn about colors?
2. What did the child learn about paleontologists?

Fingerplays, Songs, and Poems

Paleontologists
by Kristen Peters
(Tune: "Here We Go 'Round the Mulberry Bush")

Here I go digging,
Digging, digging
Here I go digging
To find my dinosaur.

I found a dinosaur piece
Dinosaur piece, dinosaur piece
I found a dinosaur piece
I'm a paleontologist!

Kristen Peters, Mattituck, NY

Green, Green, Green

AGES 3+

Learning Objectives
Children will:
1. Learn about the color green.
2. Practice observation skills.

Vocabulary
color	grass	leaf
flower	green	vegetable
fruit	insect	

Children's Books
Green by Laura Vaccaro Seeger
Green Eggs and Ham by Dr. Seuss
My Many Colored Days by Dr. Seuss

Materials
chart paper or whiteboard
green flowers, such as bells of Ireland, hydrangea, chrysanthemum, or zinnia
green fruit, such as apple, pear, or a cut kiwi fruit
green leaves in a variety of shapes
green marker or dry-erase pen
green vegetables, such as sweet peppers, zucchini, or celery
magnifying glasses

Preparation
In the discovery science area, provide a variety of green items from nature for the children to examine with magnifying glasses.

What to Do
1. Hold up an example of a green leaf. Ask the children to name the color. Ask the children to name other green things that can be found in nature. Let the children offer a variety of examples. They may offer ideas such as insects, inchworms, frogs, flowers, grass, rocks, and so on. List their ideas on chart paper or a whiteboard.
2. Read a book about the color green with the children (see list of suggested titles). Let them point out the green items in the story.
3. In the discovery science area, give the children magnifying glasses and encourage them to examine a green item, such as a flower. Ask the children to notice the details: How many petals do they see? Help them try to count the petals.
4. Encourage them to examine other green items in the center. What do they notice? Which is darker in color—the zucchini or the pear? Which is lighter in color—the celery or the kiwi fruit? Do they see the little veins in the green leaves? Encourage them to verbalize the details they notice.

Assessment
1. Can the child recognize and name the color green?
2. Can the child tell you the names of some green items found in nature?

Teacher-to-Teacher Tips
- When the children have finished examining the fruit, wash it and use it to make a yummy fruit salad.
- Adapt this activity for an examination of other colors found in nature, such as orange or purple or blue.

SCIENCE and NATURE

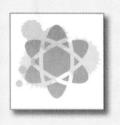

Fingerplays, Songs, and Poems

"The Green Grass Grows All Around" (Traditional)

(*Note:* This song is quite long and can be shortened to fit the needs and abilities of the children in your class. Or, sing with a partner and let the children clap and dance along.)

There was a tree
(There was a tree)
All in the wood
(All in the wood)
The prettiest tree
(The prettiest tree)
That you ever did see
(That you ever did see)

The tree in a hole
And the hole in the ground
And the green grass grows all around, all
  around
The green grass grows all around

And on that tree
(And on that tree)
There was a branch
(There was a branch)
The prettiest branch
(The prettiest branch)
That you ever did see
(That you ever did see)

The branch on the tree,
And the tree in a hole,
And the hole in the ground
And the green grass grows all around, all
  around
The green grass grows all around.

Continue, adding as many verses as you wish:

And on that branch was a nest...
And in that nest was an egg...
And in that egg was a bird...

Ending with:

Yes! The green grass grows all around, all
  around.
The green grass grows all around.

Mary Murray, Mazomanie, WI

Hello, Fish!

Learning Objectives

Children will:
1. Learn about fish.
2. Take care of fish.

Vocabulary

black molly	fishbowl	guppy
eyes	food	mouth
feed	gills	tail
fin	goldfish	

Children's Books

About Fish: A Guide for Children by Cathryn P. Sill
Fish Eyes: A Book You Can Count On
  by Lois Ehlert
Fish Faces by Norbert Wu
Fish Wish by Bob Barnes
The Rainbow Fish by Marcus Pfister
Swimmy by Leo Lionni
What's It Like to Be a Fish? by Wendy Pfeffer

Materials

fish, such as goldfish, guppies, or black mollies
fish food
fishbowl
water

What to Do

1. Display a fishbowl containing two or more different fish, such as goldfish, guppy, and black molly.
2. Read a few books about fish.
3. Ask the children to observe the fish and to identify the various parts of the fish, such as the fins, gills, tail, eyes, and mouth.
4. Show the children how much to feed the fish each day; select a different child to feed the fish each day.

Assessment

1. What did the child learn about fish?
2. Did the child learn to take care of fish?

Mary Murray, Mazomanie, WI

Guppy (brown with a blue tail)
Goldfish (gold)
Black Molly (black)

Teacher-to-Teacher Tip

Invite a person from your local department of natural resources to come in and talk about the various fish that can be found in the lakes, rivers, or ocean in your area.

Footprints and Fossils

AGES 4+

Learning Objectives

Children will:
1. Develop fine motor skills.
2. Identify dinosaurs.

Vocabulary

clay
dinosaur
footprint
fossil
imprint
press

Children's Books

Barnum Brown: Dinosaur Hunter by David Sheldon
The Big Dinosaur Dig by Esther Ripley
Digging Up Dinosaurs by Aliki
Fossil Factory: A Kid's Guide to Dinosaurs, Exploring Evolution, and Finding Fossils by Niles Eldredge and Douglas Eldredge
Fossils Tell of Long Ago by Aliki

Materials

magnifying glass
modeling dough
rolling pin (optional)
small plastic dinosaur toys
soft-bristle paintbrushes

What to Do

1. Share with the children some basic information about fossils, using one or more of the suggested books.
2. Invite the children to roll out or flatten a portion of the modeling dough and then to select various plastic dinosaurs and press them into the flattened dough one at a time.
3. Have the children lift the dinosaur toy from the dough to see the imprint or "fossil" in the clay.
4. Suggest that the children "walk" a dinosaur through another piece of flattened clay to make a trail of footprints.
5. The children can use the magnifying glass to observe each fossil more closely.
6. The children can use the soft bush to pretend to brush sand and dirt off the fossils, just like fossil hunters do.
7. Encourage the children to talk about what they are doing as they work.

Assessment

1. Is the child improving the use of his fine motor skills by doing this activity?
2. Is the child able to identify and describe the characteristics of different dinosaurs?

Mary Murray, Mazomanie, WI

Teacher-to-Teacher Tip

Most large department stores and dollar stores carry bags of small plastic dinosaurs that work well for this activity.

Ramps and Marbles

AGES 4+

Learning Objectives

Children will:
1. Create ramps.
2. Use problem-solving skills.

Vocabulary

movement   trajectory
path   turn
ramp
roll

Children's Books

Ramps and Wedges by Chris Oxlade
Roll, Slope, and Slide: A Book About Ramps by Michael Dahl
What Is a Plane? by Lloyd G. Douglas

Materials

marbles
unit blocks, including pieces that can be used as ramps

What to Do

1. Place a marble on the floor, and ask the children how to get the marble to move.
2. Allow the children to try out their ideas in the block area. Challenge the children to try to get the marble from one place to another using ramps and unit blocks.
3. Allow the children to interact with the materials freely during exploratory time, observing, challenging, and scaffolding where needed. Introduce the idea of a ramp if the children do not create one on their own.
4. If possible, allow the children to work in a large area such as the hallway. Ask the children questions about their ramps and pathways and what they are trying to accomplish with them, and encourage the children to use language to describe spatial relationships.

5. If appropriate, challenge the children to try to use the ramps to roll marbles into buckets to experiment with trajectory.

Assessment
1. Did the child create a ramp or ramps?
2. What problem-solving skills did the child use?

Rachael Partain, Mechanicsburg, PA

Sink or Float?

AGES
4+

Learning Objective
Children will:
1. Practice making predictions.
2. Learn new vocabulary.

Vocabulary
float   predict   sink

Children's Books
Geoffrey Groundhog Predicts the Weather by Bruce Koscielniak
Will It Float or Sink? by Melissa Stewart

Materials
items to sink or float, such as large plastic toys, blocks, plastic bowls, large marbles, ball of playdough, crayons, wooden beads, and a ball
large dishpan or water table

Preparation
Fill the dishpan or water table with water.

What to Do
1. Read *Will It Float or Sink?* by Melissa Stewart. Explain the meaning of the vocabulary words *float, sink,* and *predict.*
2. Ask the group to choose one of the items and to guess or predict whether it will float on top or sink to the bottom.
3. Choose a child to gently place the item into the water. Observe the result.
4. Continue with the other objects.

Assessment
Have an additional set of smaller objects (block, crayon, toy car) to ask children to predict individually.
1. What did the child learn about making predictions?
2. Which new words did the child learn?

Susan Oldham Hill, Lakeland, FL

SCIENCE and NATURE

Star Gazing

AGES 4+

Learning Objective

Children will:

1. Learn that a star is made up of burning gases.
2. Learn that stars are very far away.
3. Improve fine motor skills.
4. Enhance oral language development.

Vocabulary

galaxy	planet	star
gas	sky	sun
hot	space	

Children's Books

Our Solar System by Seymour Simon
The Solar System by Emily Bone
Stars by Jennifer Dussling
What's Out There? A Book about Space by Lynn Wilson

Materials

black construction paper, one per child
black mural paper, one sheet
colored paper stars in red, orange, yellow, blue, white
colored paper sun shape (same size as the stars)
flashlight
shallow paint trays
star-shaped sponges, one per child
tape
tempera paint in red, orange, yellow, blue, and white

Preparation

- Cut out stars and the sun from the colored paper, and place them on the black mural paper.
- In the art center, set out the sponges along with paint trays that are filled with star colors.

What to Do

1. Gather the children around and display the stars on the black sky as you introduce the topic. Read a book about stars and our solar system to the children.
2. Explain some basic facts about stars:
   - Stars are very far away, and our sun is actually a star, too. It is the closest star to Earth. The sun appears to be the biggest star, but it actually isn't; it's just closer to us so it seems big.
   - Stars are very large balls of burning hot gases.
   - Stars are actually different colors, depending on how hot they are. They can be red, orange, yellow, blue, or white. The blue stars are the hottest, and the red stars are the coolest.
3. Turn the lights down in the room. Teach the children this chant:
   Star light, star bright, first star I see tonight.
   Go ahead and shine your light.
4. Shine your flashlight on a specific star, and invite the children to name the color: red, orange, yellow, white, or blue. Repeat the chant and continue the activity as you shine your light on a variety of colors of stars.
5. Invite the children to move to the art center, where they can create their own star paintings.
6. Invite the children to dip star-shaped sponges into shallow trays of paint and make several stars on their black paper galaxies. If they wish, they can add a sun as well.

Assessment

1. What did the child learn about stars?
2. What did the child learn about our sun?

Fingerplays, Songs, and Poems

Star Light, Star Bright
(Traditional)
Star light, star bright,
First star I see tonight.
I wish I may, I wish I might
Have the wish I wish tonight.

"Twinkle Twinkle, Little Star" (Traditional)
Twinkle, twinkle, little star.
How I wonder what you are.
Up above the world so high,
Like a diamond in the sky.
Twinkle, twinkle, little star.
How I wonder what you are.

Mary Murray, Mazomanie, WI

Will It or Won't It?

AGES 4+

Learning Objectives
Children will:
1. Learn about gravity.
2. Practice predicting what will happen.

Vocabulary
bigger
cause and effect
down
experiment
fast
gravity
heavy
light
prediction
rolling
slow
smaller
up

Children's Books
Forces Make Things Move by Kimberly Brubaker Bradley
Gravity by Robin Nelson
Gravity Is a Mystery by Franklyn M. Branley
I Fall Down by Vicki Cobb
Up, Down, All Around: A Story of Gravity by Jacqui Bailey

Materials
5–6 long rectangular unit blocks
18" piece of heavy cardboard
items to test, such as a paper towel tube, crayon, glue stick, empty tissue box, notepad, and car

What to Do
1. Read one of the book suggestions.
2. Show the children how to build a ramp using the unit blocks and cardboard. Bend one end of the cardboard and position it on the stacked blocks to make a ramp.
3. Show the children the paper towel tube, crayon, glue stick, empty tissue box, notepad, and car. Ask them which of the items

they think will slide fastest down the ramp. Try all the items and talk about the results.
4. Ask the children to look around the room and suggest things that they could test on the ramp. Help the children to classify the items into groups, such as rolling, sliding/flat, with wheels, and so on.
5. Give each child the opportunity to test one of the items.
6. Remove or add a unit block to increase or decrease the incline of the cardboard. Retest the items. Now let the children experiment in the center.

SCIENCE and NATURE

Assessment

1. What did the child learn about gravity?
2. What did the child learn about predicting what will happen?

LuAnn Carrig, Falls Church, VA

Full Moon Fest

AGES 5+

Learning Objectives

1. Learn about the phases of the moon.
2. Make a moon lantern.

Vocabulary

crescent   gibbous   phase
eclipse   moon   wane
full moon   new moon   wax

Children's Books

Lin Yi's Lantern: A Moon Festival Tale
   by Brenda Williams
The Moon Book by Gail Gibbons
The Moon Lady by Amy Tan
The Moon Seems to Change
   by Franklyn M. Branley
Thanking the Moon: Celebrating the
   Mid-Autumn Moon Festival by Grace Lin

Materials

12" piece of string
chart of moon phases
glue stick or stapler
markers or crayons (optional)
paper
scissors

The Chinese Moon Festival is on the fifteenth day of the eighth lunar month. It is a traditional festival that is also known as the Mid-Autumn Festival. Although the traditional festival occurs at a specific time, it is fun to use some of the traditions to celebrate any time the moon reaches its full moon phase.

What to Do

Learn about moon phases:

1. Read a book about phases of the moon and look at a moon chart with the children.
2. Engage the children in a discussion about the different phases of the moon.

Make moon lanterns:

1. Each child colors or decorates a piece of paper and then folds it in half lengthwise.
2. Cut strips into the paper, stopping about 2" from the edge at the top, and then unfold the paper.
3. Glue or staple the sides together to create a cylinder. Add a string to the top and hang.

Assessment

1. What did the child learn about the phases of the moon?
2. Was the child able to make a moon lantern?

Brandy Bergenstock, Newport News, VA

Teacher-to-Teacher Tip

When the children learn about the moon phases, start with a full moon. This is to illustrate that the moon is always round, even when it looks different at different times of the month.

Moonlight Madness

AGES
5+

Learning Objectives

Children will:

1. Learn about moonlight.
2. Learn how light reflects.

Vocabulary

astronaut	light	sun
bounce	moon	surface
flashlight	moonlight	
galaxy	reflect	

Children's Books

I Want to Be an Astronaut by Byron Barton
Long Night Moon by Cynthia Rylant
Me and My Place in Space by Joan Sweeney
The Moon Book by Gail Gibbons
Roaring Rockets by Tony Mitton

Materials

unit blocks
aluminum foil
flashlights

Preparation

Cover a few unit blocks with aluminum foil. Before class center time, place the foil-covered blocks in the block area.

What to Do

1. At morning circle, read one of the suggested books to the children.
2. Tell the children that they will find flashlights and blocks covered in foil in the block area.
3. Let the children build with regular blocks and with foil-covered blocks.
4. Show the children how to shine a flashlight on the foil-covered blocks so the light reflects off the blocks. If possible, darken the room so that the children can see more clearly the light reflected off their structures.
5. Explain to the children that the foil-covered blocks are like the moon, which does not produce its own light. Moonlight is sunlight that has bounced off the moon! When light hits a surface, some of it bounces off or is reflected.

Assessment

1. What did the child learn about moonlight?
2. What did the child learn about how light reflects?

LuAnn Carrig, Falls Church, VA

Four Seasons Walkway

AGES 3+

Learning Objectives

Children will:

1. Learn about the four seasons.
2. Improve their understanding of how seasons change.

Vocabulary

change	spring	weather
fall	summer	winter

Children's Books

Four Seasons Make a Year by Anne Rockwell
The Reasons for Seasons by Gail Gibbons
Sunshine Makes the Seasons
    by Franklyn M. Branley
To Everything There Is a Season by Leo and
    Diane Dillon
A Tree for All Seasons by Robin Bernard

Materials

12 carpet squares or pieces of felt, three of
    each color: white, green, blue, and brown
items or pictures of items to represent the four
    seasons in your area:
    summer: grass, flowers, sun, child's
        lawnmower, swimming pool, gardening
        tools, insects, bugs, plastic bug house
    spring: raindrops, umbrella, puddles of
        water, kite, birds, robin, birds' nests
    fall: leaf rake, leaves, pumpkin, cornstalk,
        gourds, football, acorns, squirrels,
        pinecones
    winter: snow shovel, snowflakes, snowman,
        mittens, gloves, winter outerwear, sled,
        icicles, animals hibernating

Preparation

- Create a secluded seasonal pathway for the children to enjoy by placing the 12 carpet squares in a row (with a foot of space between) near a wall.
- Move two or three bookshelves or toy shelves to the other side of the carpet squares, parallel with the wall, creating an enclosed tunnel effect.
- Lay out the carpet squares to correspond with seasons: Begin with white for winter, blue for spring puddles, green for summer grass, and brown for fall. Then get creative! Display a variety of objects, stuffed animals, and pictures in, on, around, and above the walkway, creating a fun seasonal walkway. Children will enjoy passing through winter, moving on to spring, experiencing summer, and appreciating fall as they transition to another activity.

What to Do

1. When it's time to transition from one activity to another, invite the children to walk to the entrance of the seasonal walkway.
2. Have the children move slowly through the walkway one at a time and experience the various seasons by observing their surroundings, touching objects, and enjoying reminders of how the seasons change.

3. When the children reach the other side, they move on to the next activity.

Assessment
1. What did the child learn about the four seasons?
2. What did the child learn about how seasons change?
3. Is the child able to describe her favorite season?

Mary Murray, Mazomanie, WI

Leaves Are Falling Down

AGES
3+

Learning Objectives:
Children will:
1. Practice visual discrimination and pre-math and pre-science skills.
2. Practice sorting and classification skills.

Vocabulary
autumn   leaves
brown   orange
fall   red
green   yellow

Children's Books
Red Leaf, Yellow Leaf by Lois Ehlert
Why Do Leaves Change Color? by Betsy Maestro

Materials
10 leaves of each color: orange, brown, red, yellow, and green
basket to hold the leaves

Preparation
Place the leaves in a basket.

What to Do
1. Let the children discover and explore the leaves.
2. After the children have had time for free exploration of the leaves, explain that you would like the children to sort and count the leaves. Help the children determine how they will sort the leaves, which could be by color, by size, by type, or any other characteristic.
3. For older children, extend the activity by asking the children to create different patterns with the leaves.

Assessment
1. Is the child able to use visual discrimination to sort the leaves?
2. Is the child able to sort the leaves by a characteristic of her choosing?

LuAnn Carrig, Falls Church, VA

> **Teacher-to-Teacher Tip**
> For older children, this activity can be used to practice patterning. Create several pattern charts and place them in the center—encourage children to extend the patterns.

Snowman's Face

AGES
3+

Learning Objectives
Children will:
1. Learn to recognize facial features.
2. Develop fine motor skills.
3. Learn about healthy snacks.

Children's Books
All You Need for a Snowman by Alice Schertle
The Biggest, Best Snowman by Margery Cuyler
The Biggest Snowman Ever by Stephen Kroll
Snowmen at Night by Caralyn Buehner

Vocabulary
circle	snowman
face	spread
recipe	winter
snow	

Materials
baby carrots
cream cheese, plain, in a tub
large round rice cakes
plastic knives
raisins
small paper plates

What to Do
1. Provide a sufficient quantity so each child has all the ingredients she needs.
2. Ask the children to wash their hands before they come to the table.
3. Give each child one large rice cake on an individual paper plate.
4. Provide a small container of cream cheese and a plastic knife for each child. Each child spreads the cream cheese onto the rice cake.
5. Ask each child to create a snowman's face, using the raisins for eyes and a mouth and a baby carrot for the nose.
6. Ask the children if they are making a sad or a happy snowman's face.
7. Enjoy eating the snowman face!

Assessment
1. Did the child learn to recognize facial features?
2. Did the child develop fine motor skills?
3. What did the child learn about healthy snacks?

Kaethe J. Lewandowski, Centreville, VA

Teacher-to-Teacher Tip
Check for food allergies or restrictions before serving any food.

A Time for Planting

AGES 3+

Learning Objectives
Children will:
1. Learn that spring is a time of planting.
2. Develop their vocabulary.
3. Practice social skills.

Vocabulary

beans	harvest	soil
corn	plant	sow
crops	rows	tractor
field	seeds	

Children's Books
The Farmer by Mark Ludy
Farmer Duck by Martin Waddell
This Is the Farmer by Nancy Tafuri

What to Do
1. Read to the children one or more of the suggested books or other information about farmers and spring planting.
2. Use the toy tractor in the sand to demonstrate how a farmer drives a tractor through the field to turn over the soil and prepare it for planting.
3. Show the children the seed packets and explain how the farmer then uses machines to plant various crops in the warm soil.
4. Place the materials in the sand table so a small group of children can use the tractors as they pretend to turn over the soil and then pretend plant various crops.
5. Encourage the children to verbalize as they work. Teach the children "Old MacDonald," "Oats, Peas, Beans, and Barley," or any other song about farms or farming, and invite the children to sing as they work with the materials. When children are finished, ask them to label the crop they "planted" in each field by inserting the seed packets into the sand.

Materials
clean, empty margarine tubs
sand table
seed packets of corn, beans, cucumbers, and so on
soil
tape
toy tractors
wooden craft sticks

Preparation
Attach each seed packet to a wooden craft stick with tape so that it can be inserted into the sand or soil.

toy tractor
sand table

Assessment
1. What did the child learn about spring being a time of planting?
2. Did the child increase her vocabulary?
3. Did the child learn how to work cooperatively?

Mary Murray, Mazomanie, WI

> **Teacher-to-Teacher Tip**
> Prepare several shallow tubs of soil. Open a packet, show the children the seeds, and plant a few seeds in the soil. Let the children observe the growing plants over time.

S E A S O N S

Clay Snowmen

AGES 4+

Learning Objectives
Children will:
1. Create snowmen from clay.
2. Learn about size.
3. Develop fine motor skills.

Vocabulary

arms	biggest	snowman
ball	nose	toothpick
big	roll	
bigger	scarf	

Children's Books
All You Need for a Snowman by Alice Schertle
The Biggest Snowman Ever by Stephen Kroll
The Snowman by Raymond Briggs

Materials
blue construction paper
fleece fabric scrap
orange toothpicks
small pieces of twigs
toothpicks
white chalk
white felt or fabric
white modeling clay

Preparation
- Break each orange toothpick into two or three pieces for snowman noses.
- Cut the twigs into small 2" pieces.
- Cut ¼" x 5" strips from the fleece to make snowmen scarves.

What to Do
1. Provide each child with three lumps of clay, small, medium, and large.
2. Invite the children to use the modeling dough to create a snowman sculpture. If necessary, demonstrate how to roll clay into a ball shape using the palms of your hands.
3. Show the children how to insert a toothpick between the large ball and the medium ball and between the medium ball and the small ball to connect the balls together, or how to press and smooth the clay balls together to create a snowman shape.
4. Suggest that the children use two small twigs to represent snowman arms and an orange toothpick to represent a nose. The children can use a pen or other object to poke two eyes and buttons into the snowman sculptures.
5. If the children are interested in adding scarves to their snowmen, provide a strip of material to wrap around the neck of the snowmen.
6. Display the snowmen sculptures in a prominent place in the classroom against a sheet of blue paper as a decorative backdrop.

Assessment
1. Is the child able to create a snowman from the clay?
2. What did the child learn about size?
3. Did the child develop his fine motor skills?

Mary Murray, Mazomanie, WI

Teacher-to-Teacher Tip
Display the snowman sculptures on a swatch of white fabric to represent a snowy landscape. Use chalk to draw snowflakes on the blue paper and display it behind the snowmen sculptures.

Another Encyclopedia of Theme Activities

Nesting Bags

AGES 4+

Learning Objectives
Children will:
1. Learn about how birds make nests.
2. Develop fine motor skills.

Vocabulary
bird   nest   straw

Children's Books
The Best Nest by Doris L. Mueller
Birds, Nests, and Eggs by Mel Boring
From Robin to Egg by Susan Canizares

How and Why Birds Build Nests
    by Elaine Pascoe
Owl Babies by Martin Waddell
Whose Nest Is This? by Heidi Roemer

Materials
colored wrapping paper
dryer lint
handful of straw
1–2 netted produce bags (mostly intact, such
    as ones used for onions, oranges, or
    potatoes)
shredded paper
yarn

What to Do
1. Read a few books about birds and how they make their nests. Make the books available to the children to look at independently.
2. Have the children cut the colored paper and yarn into strips and pull some of the shredded paper and lint apart into smaller sections.
3. Cut a few small slits on the sides of the bags for birds to retrieve the items after hanging the bags.
4. Have the children randomly place the lint, straw, paper, and yarn items into the bags.
5. Tie the bags at the top with a longer piece of yarn. Hang the bags from a nearby tree.
6. Watch for the birds to come and take some of the items out of the bags to make their spring nests. Dispose of bags after early spring is over.

Assessments
1. What did the child learn about how birds make nests?
2. Did the child develop his fine motor skills?

Tina R. Durham-Woehler, Lebanon, TN

Teacher-to-Teacher Tips
- Hang the gabs on a low but visible tree branch; this can be visible from either the outside play area or from a classroom window.
- Place clipboards and paper on the playground or in the window area for children to draw what kinds of birds take the items in the bags and what they take.

SEASONS

Pumpkin Panorama

Learning Objectives

Children will:
1. Learn about how pumpkins grow.
2. Explore the concepts of *heavy* and *light*.
3. Practice gross motor skills.

Vocabulary

compare	light
heavy	pumpkin

Children's Books

The Biggest Pumpkin Ever by Stephen Kroll
Pumpkins by Ken Robbins
Pumpkins: A Story for a Field by Mary Lyn Ray
Too Many Pumpkins by Linda White

What to do

1. Draw the children's attention to the pumpkin patch as you read one or more books about pumpkins to the children.
2. Teach the children how pumpkins grow from tiny seeds into great big heavy pumpkins.
3. Suggest that each child take a turn picking up one of the pumpkins to see how heavy it is.
4. Play the Pumpkin Pass game as follows: The children pass the miniature pumpkin around the circle as the class chants, "Pumpkin, pumpkin who's got the pumpkin?" Whoever is holding the pumpkin when the verse ends says, "I've got the pumpkin now," and then passes it to the next person. Encourage the children to clap as they keep the beat of the chant as they wait for their turn to pass the pumpkin. Continue until the pumpkin goes around the circle several times.

Materials

brown paper or blanket
green yarn with paper leaves attached
paper sun shape
pumpkin seeds
several large pumpkins
small pumpkin
watering can

Preparation

Arrange the pumpkins on the brown paper. Connect the pumpkin with the green yarn and paper leaf vine. Display the other items in the "pumpkin patch."

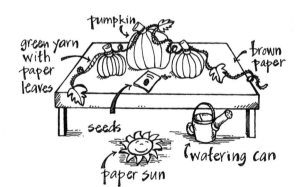

Assessment

1. What did the child learn about how pumpkins grow?
2. What did the child learn about the concepts of *heavy* and *light*?

Mary Murray, Mazomanie, WI

Winter Dress and Play

AGES 4+

Learning Objectives
Children will:
1. Improve fine and gross motor skills.
2. Identify numbers 1 to 5.

Vocabulary
boots	mittens	sled
coat	pull	snowpants
hat	scarf	snowsuit

Children's Books
All Kinds of Clothes by Jeri S. Cipriano
The Jacket I Wear in the Snow by Shirley Neitzel
Warm Clothes by Gail Saunders-Smith

Materials
baskets
dolls or stuffed animal toys
marker
paper snowflakes
plastic sled
winter clothing items for children to try on and wear

Preparation
- Number the snowflakes from 1 to 5 and add the corresponding number of dots to each numbered snowflake. Display the snowflakes in order, creating a trail of snowflakes to follow.
- Place the winter clothing in a basket.

What to Do
1. Read one or more books about winter clothing. Place the books in a basket near the basket of winter clothes.
2. One child at a time chooses an assortment of winter clothing to try on and also places one or more dolls or stuffed toys in the sled.
3. This child pulls the sled around the room, following the trail of snowflakes from 1 to 5.
4. After the child completes the pathway, she removes the winter clothing and places it in the basket, and removes the dolls from the sled so the activity is ready for the next child.

Assessment
1. Did the child improve his fine and gross motor skills?
2. Is the child able to identify numbers 1 to 5?

Mary Murray, Mazomanie, WI

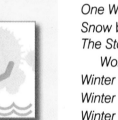

Winter Reading Fun

AGES
4+

Learning Objectives

Children will:
1. Develop an appreciation for books and reading.
2. Learn about winter.

Vocabulary

books	scarf	snowman
cold	sled	winter
read	snow	

Children's Books

It's Winter by Susan Swan
One Winter's Day by M. Christina Butler
Snow by Cynthia Rylant
The Story of Snow: The Science of Winter's Wonder by Mark Cassino
Winter by Nuria Roca
Winter Eyes by Douglas Florian
Winter Lullaby by Barbara Seuling

Materials

colorful winter scarves and other winter- or snow-related objects
paper snowflakes
plastic child's sled or large adult-size wooden sled
snowman picture
strings of colorful mittens
stuffed snowmen
white bedsheet
winter-themed pillows

Preparation

Set up a fun winter reading area in your classroom. Decorate the area with books about winter, a sled, winter scarves, snowmen, colorful winter clothing articles, paper snowflakes, and other appropriate items. Place one or more winter-themed pillows in the sled or reading corner.

What to Do

1. Talk with the class about the characteristics of winter weather.
2. Show the children the winter reading corner.
3. Invite one or more children to put on a colorful winter scarf, and then sit in a sled and read quietly.
4. Allow time each day for various groups of children to enjoy the winter reading corner.

Assessment

1. Is the child developing an appreciation for books and reading?
2. What did the child learn about winter?

Mary Murray, Mazomanie, WI

Teacher-to-Teacher Tips

Ask a parent to bring in a sled from home or purchase one at a rummage sale or secondhand shop.

Birds in Spring

Learning Objectives

Children will:

1. Learn about the habits of birds in spring.
2. Understand the term *migration*.

Vocabulary

birds	fly	perch
build	insects	worms
eat	migration	
eggs	nest	

Children's Books

Flute's Journey: The Life of a Wood Thrush
    by Lynne Cherry
How Do Birds Find Their Way? by Roma Gans
The Journey of a Swallow by Carolyn Scrace
Migration by Robin Nelson
Moonshadow's Journey by Gillian Lobel
The Peregrine's Journey: A Story of Migration
    by Madeleine Dunphy

Materials

plastic toy birds
paper bags
rocks or stones
scissors
2' tree branch
yarn
yellow paper sun

Preparation

- Attach the tree branch and the yellow paper sun to a bulletin board at a child's level.
- Cut yarn into 1" segments to represent worms and ¼" pieces to represent insects.
- Display all the items near the tree branch to create a bird-themed dramatic play area with toy birds, the tree branch, stones, and yarn insects and worms.
- Create "birds' nests" by rolling down and crumpling the sides of a lunch bag until you have a rounded nest shape. Set the nests in the tree branch or near the other items.

What to Do

1. Use one or more of the book suggestions to introduce the topic of bird migration or birds in spring. Talk about migration and how birds fly south for the winter and then return to warmer weather in the spring.
2. To help the children understand the concept of migration, ask several children to stand on the far side of the room holding a toy bird and then to move (migrate) to the front of the room.
3. Remind the children that spring is a time for birds to build nests and lay eggs. Show the children the area you set up, and let the children work with the materials to learn about migration and birds in spring.

Assessment

1. What did the child learn about the habits of birds in spring?
2. Does the child understand the term *migration*?

Mary Murray, Mazomanie, WI

My House All Year Long

AGES 5+

Learning Objectives
Children will:
1. Learn about and identify seasonal changes.
2. Learn new vocabulary.

Vocabulary

fall	house	spring
flowers	leaves	summer
grass	snow	winter

Children's Books
Changing Seasons by Sian Smith
Four Seasons Make a Year by Anne Rockwell
Our Seasons by Grace Lin and Ranida T. McKneally
The Reasons for Seasons by Gail Gibbons
Seasons by Blexbolex
The Seasons of Arnold's Apple Tree by Gail Gibbons
To Everything There Is a Season by Leo and Diane Dillon
A Tree for All Seasons by Robin Bernard

Materials
books about seasons (see suggestions)

What to Do
1. Read a few of the books about the changing seasons and then engage the children in a discussion about the seasons and how they change.
2. Ask the children questions about things they notice about each season. For example, do they notice the following?
   - spring rainstorms
   - colorful spring flowers
   - windy spring days
   - warm summer days
   - long, sunny summer days
   - colorful leaves
   - falling leaves in autumn
   - raking leaves in the fall
   - cold days in winter
   - snow and other precipitation in winter

Assessment
1. What did the child learn about seasonal changes?
2. What new words did the child learn?

Mary Murray, Mazomanie, WI

Pumpkin Numbers

AGES 5+

Learning Objectives
Children will:
1. Develop counting skills.
2. Improve their fine motor skills.

Vocabulary
circumference
compare
measure
numbers: *one*, *two*, *three*, and so on

Children's Books
The Biggest Pumpkin Ever by Stephen Kroll
Pumpkins by Ken Robbins
Pumpkins: A Story for a Field by Mary Lyn Ray
Too Many Pumpkins by Linda White

Materials
masking tape
miniature pumpkins
paper
pumpkin shapes and glue or pumpkin stamps
  and stamp pad
scale
string
yardstick

What to Do
1. Wrap a piece of masking tape around the widest part of each pumpkin.
2. Invite children to hold a string around the pumpkin at the taped line and then lay the string next to the yardstick to measure the pumpkin's circumference.
3. Suggest that the children place the pumpkins on the scale and weigh them.
4. After measuring and weighing the pumpkins, suggest that the children make pumpkin counting books by gluing pumpkin shapes or stamping pumpkins onto the pages of a blank book.

Assessment
1. What counting skills did the child develop?
2. Did the child improve her fine motor skills?

Mary Murray, Mazomanie, WI

S E A S O N S

Body Shapes

AGES 3+

Learning Objectives
Children will:
1. Make a variety of shapes using their bodies.
2. Work in pairs to create these shapes.

Children's Books
Body Parts by Bev Schumacher
Shape by Shape by Suse Macdonald
Shapes, Shapes, Shapes by Tana Hoban

Vocabulary
arm	hand	rectangle
circle	head	square
foot	leg	triangle

Materials
examples of each shape

What to Do
1. Show the children the examples of each shape one at a time. Ask which shape it is. How do they know?
2. Demonstrate making one shape with a part of your body. For example, you can make a triangle with your thumbs and index fingers or by putting one foot on the other knee.
3. Call out shape names to allow the children to practice individually. Divide the group into pairs and have the pairs spread out around the classroom. Tell the children that you will call out a shape and body parts. They are to work together to make the shape with those parts of the body. (It is often easier for young children to do this lying down.) Help the children as needed.

Assessment
1. Was the child able to make shapes with his body?
2. Was the child able to work with another child to create shapes?

Debbie Vilardi, Commack, NY

Teacher-to-Teacher Tip
Expand this activity by asking the children to form letters or numbers.

Cookie Cutter Animals

AGES 4+

Learning Objectives
Children will:
1. Develop fine motor skills.
2. Recognize various animals.

Vocabulary
animal names	modeling dough
clay	press
cookie cutter	

Another Encyclopedia of Theme Activities

Children's Books

Animal Babies by Bobbie Hamsa
Snakes and Their Homes
    by Deborah Chase Gibson

Materials

animal-shaped plastic cookie cutters
modeling dough (see recipe at right)
rolling pins

Preparation

Make basic modeling dough.
½ cup cornstarch
2 cups salt
1 cup boiling water
1/3 cup cold water
waxed paper
Combine the salt and 1 cup of water in a saucepan over medium-high heat. Heat until boiling, and stir until the salt is dissolved. Remove from heat and add the cornstarch and cold water. Stir thoroughly. Set aside until cool enough to handle safely. Knead on waxed paper. Place in an airtight container to keep it moist until ready to use. This recipe can be doubled or tripled. The dough will air dry and can be painted when dry.

What to Do

1. Invite children to use a rolling pin or their hands to smooth out a handful of modeling dough.
2. Have the children choose a cookie cutter and cut an animal shape in the dough. Invite children to identify the type of animal and tell about its physical features.
3. Let the clay animal creations dry, and allow the children to paint them if desired.

Assessment

1. Is the child improving her fine motor skills?
2. Is the child able to recognize and describe the features of various animals?

Mary Murray, Mazomanie, WI

Find a Shape Song

AGES
4+

Learning Objectives

Children will:
1. Identify colors and shapes.
2. Follow directions.

Vocabulary

friend
names of colors and shapes
pass
sing

Children's Books

Shape by Shape by Suse Macdonald
Shapes, Shapes, Shapes by Tana Hoban

Materials

basket or a container that is easy for the
    children to pass around
set of attribute blocks

Preparation

Put the attribute blocks in the basket or container of your choice.

What to Do

1. Explain that you are going to sing a song.
2. As you begin to sing the following song, give the basket to the first child. This child picks out the described shape and holds it up for the class to see before returning the shape to the container and passing the basket to the next child.

"Find a Shape"
by Jackie Wright
(Tune: "Mary Had a Little Lamb")

Find a red square. Hold it up,
Hold it up, hold it up.
Find a red square. Hold it up,
Now pass it to a friend.

3. Change the color and shape with each verse as the children pass the container around the circle. Encourage the children to sing along.

Assessment

1. What did the child learn about colors and shapes?
2. Is the child able to follow directions?

Jackie Wright, Enid, OK

Shaker Eggs

AGES
4+

Learning Objectives
Children will:
1. Develop listening skills.
2. Identify shapes.

Vocabulary

beans	listen	shapes
eggs	shake	

Children's Books

Mouse Shapes by Ellen Stoll Walsh
Round Is a Mooncake: A Book of Shapes by Roseanne Thong
A Star in My Orange: Looking for Nature's Shapes by Dana Meachen Rau
When a Line Bends . . . A Shape Begins by Rhonda Gowler Greene

Materials
colorful plastic eggs
glue
paper clips, pebbles, or other small objects
permanent marker
strong tape
transparent tape

Preparation
Use permanent marker to draw one shape on each plastic egg. You can create more than one egg for each shape.

Another Encyclopedia of Theme Activities

What to Do

1. Invite the children to create a rhythm instrument called a shaker egg, and then have some fun using the shaker egg to improve their shape recognition skills.
2. Help the children count out 10 paper clips or pebbles. Have them place the paper clips or pebbles inside one half of an egg.
3. Help children place the other half of the egg on top, snap it shut, and seal the egg tightly with glue and tape.
4. Help the children identify the shapes on their eggs.
5. Encourage the children to explore the sound and feel of their eggs. Invite the children to listen to the sounds of their classmates' eggs as each child takes turns shaking his egg.
6. Instruct the children to listen carefully as you read a book or tell a story that has shape words, such as *circle, square, triangle, rectangle, diamond,* or *oval,* in the story. Each time a shape is mentioned in the story, the children are to shake their eggs. When the story is finished, everyone shakes their eggs high above their heads and shouts, "The end!"

Assessment

1. Is the child developing listening skills?
2. What did the child learn about shapes?

Mary Murray, Mazomanie, WI

> **Teacher-to-Teacher Tip**
> Keep the shaker eggs handy for music and rhythm activities.

Shape Dinosaurs

AGES 4+

Learning Objectives

Children will:

1. Identify shapes.
2. Create dinosaurs from felt shapes.

Vocabulary

apatosaurus	stegosaurus
felt	T. rex
flannel board	triangle
rectangle	triceratops
square	

Children's Books

Dinosaurs! by Gail Gibbons
Dinosaurs A–Z: For Kids Who Really Love Dinosaurs by Simon Mugford
Dinosaur Roar! by Paul and Henrietta Stickland
Drawing and Learning About Dinosaurs: Using Shapes and Lines by Amy Bailey Muehlenhardt
Let's Draw a Dinosaur with Shapes by Joanne Randolph

Materials

dinosaur pictures
felt shapes
flannel board

What to Do

1. Display the dinosaur pictures, the felt shapes, and the felt board. Look at the different shapes of felt and describe and name all the shapes.
2. Invite the children to identify each dinosaur and describe its characteristics.
3. Demonstrate how to adhere the felt shapes to the board to create dinosaurs.

4. Place the felt shapes and the felt board in one of the centers for the children to use to create shape dinosaurs or a creation of their choosing.
5. As a variation, cut shapes from craft foam and let the children create with the foam shapes.

Assessment

1. Is the child able to identify different shapes?
2. Is the child able to create a dinosaur from the felt shapes?

Mary Murray, Mazomanie, WI

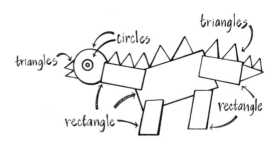

Teacher-to-Teacher Tip

Make your own flannel board by wrapping a thick piece of cardboard or wood with flannel. Tack or staple the flannel to the back, and cover the tack or staples with duct tape. You can easily cut your own set of shapes from felt purchased at a department store or craft store.

Wagon Walk

Learning Objectives
Children will:
1. Improve gross motor skills.
2. Identify shapes.

Vocabulary
pull   wagon
shapes   walk

Children's Books
Friday My Radio Flyer Flew by Zachary Pullen
Red Wagon by Renata Liwska

What to Do
1. Invite the child to pull the wagon around the room and look for the four shapes to collect.
2. When the child finds a shape, he names the shape and puts it in the wagon.

Materials
4 or more plastic or paper shapes
child's toy wagon (or create your own wagon by adding a string handle to a large shoe or boot box)

Preparation
Randomly display the assortment of shapes around the room and within a child's reach.

Another Encyclopedia of Theme Activities

3. After the child has found all four shapes he may return the wagon "home" (the place in the classroom where he found the wagon) with the shapes.

4. Invite the child to place the four shapes randomly about the room for the next child's turn.

5. Invite pairs or small groups of children to walk together so more than one child can play this game at any given time. Children waiting their turn can watch and talk about the shapes as they observe their classmate collecting shapes around the room.

Assessment

1. Walk with a child as she pulls the wagon around the room and collects shapes. Does the child know the names of the shapes?

2. Is the child able to skillfully pull the wagon around the classroom?

Fingerplays, Songs, and Poems

Teach the children this song sung to the familiar tune of "Bumping Up and Down in My Little Red Wagon." Have the children sing as they look for shapes in the room.

"Little Red Wagon"
I'm looking for shapes with my little red wagon,
Looking for shapes with my little red wagon.
I'm looking for shapes with my little red wagon.
I hope that I can find some.

Mary Murray, Mazomanie, WI

Wall of Shapes

AGES 4+

Learning Objectives

Children will:

1. Identify shapes.
2. Develop oral language skills.

Vocabulary

circle	oval	square
diamond	rectangle	triangle

Children's Books

Circles by Dana Meachen Rau
I Spy Shapes in Art by Lucy Micklethwait
Museum Shapes by the NY Metropolitan Museum of Art
Shapes, Shapes, Shapes by Tana Hoban

Materials

black paper
glue stick
marker
pictures of shapes in our world (sources: magazines, the Internet)
tape

Preparation

● Glue each picture to a sheet of black paper to give it a framed look.
● Display the pictures at the children's eye level on one wall in the classroom. Use a marker to highlight one or more shapes in each framed picture.

What to Do

1. Invite the children to look at the display of pictures.
2. Suggest that the children walk along the wall and observe the shapes in each picture.
3. Encourage the children to talk about the shapes in the pictures.
4. After the children finish the "shape walk," engage the children in a discussion about shapes in their world. Also ask the children to recall and comment on what they saw in the pictures.

Assessment

1. Is the child able to identify shapes in the pictures?
2. Is the child able to describe the shapes in the pictures and the shapes found in the world?

Mary Murray, Mazomanie, WI

Teacher-to-Teacher Tip

Take your class on a shape walk in and around your school. Bring along a digital camera. Look for shapes in the world and take photographs of the children near the various shapes. Display these photos in a photo album and invite children to "read" the book and identify shapes within the pages of photos.

But It Wasn't a Butterfly

AGES 5+

Learning Objectives

Children will:

1. Create symmetrical clouds using the "ink blot" method.
2. Imagine what a cloud looks like.

Vocabulary

clouds	shape
imagine	symmetry

What to Do

1. Talk about how things look different to different people. Show children *The Cloud Book*.
2. Work with a small group of children to create a class *Cloud Book*. If there are clouds in the sky, take a walk outside to look at the clouds and discuss what the clouds look like.
3. Show the children how to drizzle white paint onto the dark blue construction paper, fold the paper, and gently rub to make a unique, symmetrical shape. Discuss that the shapes are symmetrical.

Children's Books

The Cloud Book by Tomie dePaola
It Looked Like Spilt Milk by Charles Shaw
Little Cloud by Eric Carle

Materials

dark blue construction paper
plastic spoons
white paint in small bowls

paint on half of paper

white paint

spoon

cloud

4. Help each child fill in the following sentence for his page: "My cloud looks like a _____.
5. Bind all the children's pictures to create a class book. Share the book at circle time before putting it in the library. If you would like, send the book home with each child to share with her parents.

Assessment
1. Does the child understand the meaning of *symmetry*?
2. Can the child use her imagination to determine what a cloud looks like?

Rachael Partain, Mechanicsburg, PA

Cut and Carry Shapes

Learning Objectives
Children will:
1. Improve their oral communication skills.
2. Identify shapes.

Vocabulary
carry   fold
cut   shapes

Children's Books
Mouse Shapes by Ellen Stoll Walsh
Shapes, Shapes, Shapes by Tana Hoban

Materials
basket
glue
large paper (for class collage)
magazines
poster board
scissors

Preparation
Cut a variety of shapes from poster board and place them in a basket.

What to Do
1. Invite the children to pick up a shape, identify it, and describe it. Continue until all the shapes have been identified and described by the children.
2. Suggest that the children select a shape and carry it around the classroom as they look for objects in the classroom that are the same shape as the poster board shape they are holding.
3. Provide the children with magazine pages. Invite the children to cut shapes on the pages and glue the shapes to a class collage as they learn to identify various shapes in the world.

Assessment
1. Is the child able to describe the shapes?
2. Is the child able to identify and name the shapes?

Mary Murray, Mazomanie, WI

Shopping for Shapes

Learning Objectives
Children will:
1. Improve their shape recognition skills.
2. Develop their language skills.

Vocabulary
bag	cost	shapes
buy	money	shop

Children's Books
Mouse Shapes by Ellen Stoll Walsh
Shapes, Shapes, Shapes by Tana Hoban

Materials
cash register (optional)
common objects of varying shapes: balls, plates, birthday hat, books, and so on (or use a collection of plastic shapes)
decorative gift bags
play money
sign that reads "Store"

Preparation
Create a department store in the dramatic play center by displaying the items on shelves and tables for the shoppers to view. Add a price tag to each item. Display the store sign, cash register, and gift bags near the entrance to the dramatic play center.

What to Do
1. Invite the children to help you set up the department store.
2. The children can take turns shopping at the store. Have the children select and purchase items using the play money.
3. Encourage the children to verbalize as they play, talking about the shapes of the items on display. Invite the clerk to place each customer's items in a gift bag so he can carry them home.

Assessment
1. Is the child able to recognize different shapes?
2. Did the child develop her language skills?

Mary Murray, Mazomanie, WI

Teacher-to-Teacher Tips
- At another time, create a grocery store at the dramatic play center. Simply replace the objects that are certain shapes with foods and food containers that are certain shapes, and add a stack of grocery bags. Invite the children to grocery shop for foods of varying shapes.
- Observe the children as they play at the center. Identify children who may have difficulty naming the various shapes. Invite one or more children to go shopping for you. Tell them specifically what you would like them to purchase. When they return with the bag of items, help them identify the shape of each item you requested.

What Can You Do with a Dot?

AGES 5+

Learning Objectives

Children will:
1. Use dots to make a work of art.
2. Draw and cut out circles in various sizes.

Vocabulary

balance   circle   dot   overlap

Children's Books

Dot by Patricia Intriago
Little Blue and Little Yellow by Leo Lionni
So Many Circles, So Many Squares
    by Tana Hoban

Materials

construction paper
cotton swabs
The Dot by Peter H. Reynolds
glue
markers
paint
paint dotters (similar to Bingo markers), pencils
scissors

What to Do

1. Read *The Dot,* and then discuss the book with the children.
2. Make a dot on a piece of paper. Ask the children what it is. Ask them to imagine the dot bigger. What would it be? A larger dot would be a circle.
3. Show the children how to draw and cut out circles. Show how circles can be small, medium, large, extra large, or super-duper tiny.
4. Demonstrate how to place the circles on top of each other and overlap them to make them more interesting.
5. Let the children use the materials to draw and cut out circles, and create their own arrangements of circles on pieces of paper. When they are satisfied with their arrangements, they can glue the circles to the paper.
6. The children can also add dots, circles, and other designs to the paper. If you have paint dotters, the children can use these to add dots of paint to their pictures. They can also use cotton swabs or the eraser on a pencil dipped in paint to make dots.

Assessment

1. Is the child able to use dots to create a work of art?
2. Is the child able to trace, draw, and cut out circles?

Marcia Beckett, Madison, WI

Teacher-to-Teacher Tip

If you have prints of artworks that use dots (Aboriginal Australian, Georges Seurat), you can show these to the children. Gather circular items that the children can trace (circle templates, plastic lids, masking tape rolls). Depending on the abilities of the children in your class, consider precutting circles or helping children who need assistance.

SHAPES

Each and Every Day

AGES  3+

Learning Objectives
Children will:
1. Learn about the different times of day—morning, afternoon, evening, and night.
2. Discuss the activities that are done each time of day.

Vocabulary
afternoon   evening   night

day   morning

Children's Books
The Best Time of Day by Eileen Spinelli
My Day: Morning, Noon, and Night
    by Lisa Bullard
Time to Get Up, Time to Go by David Milgrim

Materials
glue or tape
markers
pictures depicting different times of the day
poster board

Preparation
Divide the poster board into four sections. Label one "morning," another "afternoon," the third "evening," and the last "night." Glue or tape the appropriate photo to each time of day.

What to Do
1. Explain to the children that you are going to talk about different times of day. Ask the children to name the things they do in the morning before coming to school.
2. As the children name the things they do, make simple drawings—a toothbrush for brushing their teeth, a bowl for eating cereal, and so on—to the poster board.
3. Ask the children, "What do you do in the morning at school?" Add these things to the poster board.
4. Repeat with afternoon, evening, and night.
5. If appropriate for the children in your class, ask them if there things that they do only at one time of day. What are things they can do any time of day?

Assessment
1. Did the child learn about the different times of the day?
2. What did the child learn about things that he does at different times of the day?

Sue Bradford Edwards, Florissant, MO

My Day

Learning Objectives

Children will:

1. Learn sequencing skills.
2. Recognize numbers on a clock.
3. Begin to realize how we use clocks.

Vocabulary

analog	clock face	schedule
big hand	digital	second hand
clock	little hand	time

Children's Books

Clocks and More Clocks by Pat Hutchins
Telling Time by Jules Older
Time to Get Up, Time to Go by David Milgrim

Materials

camera and printer
clock with numbers and face
glue
markers
poster board

Preparation

- Take a photo of each part of your day. For example, morning greeting, center time, circle time, outdoor time, snack, playground, and so on.
- Place the clock where the children can see it.

What to Do

1. Gather the children for circle time and show them the photos that you've taken and show them the clock. Talk to them about the purpose of the clock and identify the parts of the clock.
2. Tell the children that they are going to make a schedule of their day by helping you put the photos in order of the day's events.
3. With the children's help, glue the photos on the poster board from top to bottom, starting with the first thing that you do each day to the last thing that you do each day.
4. Beside each photo, write a small description of what you are doing, and then draw a clock face with the time on it.
5. Post the schedule on the wall with the clock beside it. Throughout the day, point out the schedule and the clock.

Assessment

1. What does the child understand about the sequence of the school day?
2. Does the child recognize the numbers on the clock?
3. Is the child beginning to understand how we use clocks?

Holly Dzierzanowski, Bastrop, TX

Around the Clock

AGES 5+

Learning Objectives
Children will:
1. Identify numbers 1 through 12.
2. Count in order from 1 to 12.

Vocabulary
clock	order	time
numbers	sequence	
o'clock	ticktock	

Children's Books
Clocks and More Clocks by Pat Hutchins
Telling Time by Jules Older
Time to Get Up, Time to Go by David Milgrim

Materials
assortment of clocks and watches that no longer work
bell
number cards, 1–12
plastic game cone

Preparation
Display the number cards in a large circle on the floor in clock formation from 1 to 12.

What to Do
1. Display an assortment of clocks and watches that no longer work. Let the children explore the watches and identify the numbers on each one.
2. Invite 12 children to line up around the numbers.
3. Ask the class to chant the following several times until you ring a bell: "Ticktock, ticktock, ticktock around the clock." When the bell rings, each of the 12 children stands near a number card. Set the plastic game cone near the number 1. The class then recites "What time is it, _____?" filling in the name of the child standing near the number 1. The child replies by saying "one o'clock."
4. Move the plastic game cone from number to number as the chanting question and response continues until all the children name their number to tell what time it is.
5. Invite a different set of children to stand around the clock and repeat the activity.

Assessment
1. Is the child able to identify numbers 1 through 12?
2. Is the child able to count in order from 1 to 12?

Mary Murray, Mazomanie, WI

My Favorite Time

Learning Objectives
Children will:
1. Understand the concept of time.
2. Learn the numbers 1–12 found on the clock.
3. Develop fine motor skills.

Vocabulary
favorite   lock   time

Children's Books
Bats Around the Clock by Kathi Appelt
Clocks and More Clocks by Pat Hutchins

Telling Time by Jules Older
Time to Get Up, Time to Go by David Milgrim

Materials
clock
crayons
paper

Preparation
Draw the outline of a clock with the numbers written on it. At the bottom of the clock, write the words "My favorite time is _____." Make one copy for each child.

What to Do
1. Show the children a clock and discuss the daily schedule of the children at school from the time they arrive until the time they leave.
2. Distribute the copies of the clock, and ask the children to name their favorite time at school. Help every child to complete the sentence "My favorite time is _____." Help the children draw on the clock the correct time for their favorite activity.

Assessment
1. What does the child understand about the concept of time?
2. Does the child know that the numbers 1 through 12 are the numbers on a clock?

Fingerplays, Songs, and Poems

Time by Shyamala Shanmugasundaram
Time to play,
Time to read,
Time to eat,
And time to sleep,

From morning till evening
I find time to do everything.

Shyamala Shanmugasundaram, Annanagar East, Chennai, India

Travel Song

AGES 3+

Learning Objectives
Children will:
1. Make up verses to a new song.
2. Learn the names of various forms of transportation.

Vocabulary

bike	car	taxi
boat	plane	van
bus	sing	verse

Children's Books
The Adventures of Taxi Dog by Debra and Sal Barracca
Airport by Byron Barton
Harbor by Donald Crews
Planes by Anne Rockwell
The Wheels on the Bus by Paul Zelinsky

Materials
pictures of various forms of transportation
card stock
scissors

Preparation
Glue images of various forms of transportation onto card stock.

What to Do
1. Read the children's favorite books about transportation. (Use the list provided for suggestions.) Sing the following song and display the vehicle pictures with the appropriate verses:

   "Travel Song"
   by Jackie Wright
   (Tune: "Here We Go 'Round the Mulberry Bush")

   This is the way I like to travel,
   Like to travel, like to travel.
   This is the way I like to travel:
   I like to go by plane.

2. Make up additional verses for *bike, car, bus, taxi, van, boat,* and other kinds of transportation.

Assessment
1. Is the child able to sing the song?
2. Can the child name different kinds of transportation?

Jackie Wright, Enid, OK

All about Cars

AGES
4+

Learning Objectives
Children will:
1. Learn basic facts about cars.
2. Explore the concepts of *speed* and *motion*.

Vocabulary

battery	steering wheel
engine	tires
gas tank	trunk

Children's Books
Cars and Trucks and Things That Go
   by Richard Scarry
First Discovery: Cars and Trucks by Scholastic
If I Built a Car by Chris Van Dusen

Materials
3 hand towels or carpet squares
hard-surface floor
pictures of various cars

What to Do
1. Introduce the topic of cars as you show the children an assortment of car pictures and read a book about cars.
2. Invite the children to comment on the characteristics of the various cars. Talk about the basic components that all cars have, such as tires, engine, steering wheel, battery, windows, door, trunk, gas tank, and so on.
3. If appropriate for the children in your class, invite the children to have a "car(pet) race." Three children kneel on a carpet square at the starting line, with their hands placed on the floor. On the command, "On your mark, get set, go," the children leave the starting line and pull themselves along the floor with their hands as they race to the finish line on the opposite side of the room. The children's classmates can observe the race as spectators and cheer each racer as she crosses the finish line.
4. Invite a new set of children to begin a new race. Play several times until the children have had numerous opportunities to race across the room.

Assessment
1. Did the child learn about the parts of a car?
2. What did the child learn about *speed* and *motion*?

Mary Murray, Mazomanie, WI

Teacher-to-Teacher Tip
If possible, invite a mechanic to come in and talk with the children about his job. Allow time for children to ask questions.

TRANSPORTATION

Build-a-Boat Workshop

Learning Objectives
Children will:
1. Identify and name at least three shapes.
2. Identify and name at least three colors.

Vocabulary

blue	orange	square
circle	oval	star
diamond	purple	triangle
green	rectangle	yellow
heart	red	
octagon	semicircle	

Children's Books
Ship Shapes by Stella Blackstone
So Many Circles, So Many Squares
    by Tana Hoban

What to Do
1. Give each child a piece of blue construction paper.
2. Place the construction paper shapes in a central location. Review the names of the shapes with the children.
3. Explain that the children will be constructing a boat from these shapes. Let the children use glue and the shapes of their choice to create a boat. Let dry completely.

Assessment
1. Is the child able to identify and name the shapes in his boat?
2. Is the child able to identify and name the colors of the shapes in her boat?

Tomi Anne Lessaris, Greenwood, IN

Materials
construction paper in blue and other colors
glue
scissors

Preparation
- Each child will need one full sheet of blue construction paper.
- Cut the other colors of construction paper into a variety of shapes, including large semicircles, circles, triangles, squares, ovals, rectangles, diamonds, stars, hearts, and octagons.

Teacher-to-Teacher Tip
Ask each child if she would like to name the boat. If so, write "S.S." and the name the child chooses on the child's boat.

Delivery Time!

Learning Objectives
Children will:
1. Learn about delivery trucks.
2. Match colors.

Vocabulary
deliver
package
trucks

Children's Books
Cars and Trucks and Things That Go
by Richard Scarry
First Discovery: Cars and Trucks by Scholastic

Materials
2 chairs
5 or more boxes
5 or more colored door-shaped pieces of paper
bedsheet or drop cloth
construction paper

Preparation
- Glue colored pieces of paper onto the sides of the boxes so that one box matches each door-shaped piece of paper.
- Draw a window and doorknob on each door-shaped piece of paper.
- Place the two chairs at the front of the bedsheet to create the cab of the truck. Stack the color-coded boxes on the sheet behind the chairs to represent the trailer portion of the truck.
- Display the colored "doors" randomly about the room.

What to Do
1. Engage the children in a discussion about delivery trucks and delivery drivers.
2. Invite children to pretend to drive the delivery truck and stop to make deliveries by delivering the color box that matches each color door displayed in the classroom.
3. The children pick up the packages from the trailer and deliver them to each door according to color.

Assessment
1. What did the child learn about deliveries and delivery trucks?
2. Is the child able to match the color package to the same color door?

Mary Murray, Mazomanie, WI

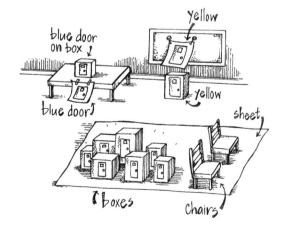

Families on the Go

AGES 4+

Learning Objectives
Children will:
1. Identify various modes of transportation.
2. Improve their oral language skills.

Vocabulary

airplane	horse
bicycle	tricycle
boat	truck
bus	van
car	wagon

Children's Books
All Aboard Airplanes by Frank Evans and George Guzzi
Amazing Airplanes by Tony Mitton and Ant Parker
The Bicycle Book by Gail Gibbons
Busy Boats by Tony Mitton and Ant Parker
Cars and Trucks and Things That Go by Richard Scarry
School Bus by Donald Crews
The Wheels on the Bus by Paul O. Zelincky

Materials
toy vehicles of the vehicles on the vocabulary list
small toy people

What to Do
1. Gather the children together in the large group area. Display the various vehicles and modes of transportation at a table along with the toy people.
2. Select each item and hold it high so the children can see it. Ask the children to name each type of transportation. Remind the children that families often travel together, sometimes in a car, sometimes on bicycles, sometimes on an airplane, or in a variety of other ways.
3. Invite children to work independently with the materials. The children identify the various modes of transportation and then place people in or on the different modes of transportation, including a horse. The children might move "families" about the table or floor area as they talk about how each family is traveling and where they may be going.
4. When the children are finished playing, ask them to line up the vehicles so the activity is ready for another group of children.

Assessment
1. Is the child able to name the different modes of transportation?
2. Is the child able to use verbal communication skills to describe different modes of transportation and what the families are doing as they travel in the vehicles?

Mary Murray, Mazomanie, WI

Teacher-to-Teacher Tip
If you don't have small toy people, display photographs of families at the table for children to talk about as they move the vehicles from place to place.

Five Little Cars

AGES 4+

Learning Objectives

Children will:

1. Identify colors and numbers.
2. Develop listening skills.

Vocabulary

bright	left	store
car	new	tree
drive	shiny	turn

number names, *one, two, three, four, five*

Children's Books

Cars by Anne Rockwell
My Car by Byron Barton

Materials

flannel board
felt (blue, yellow, red, green, and purple)
scissors

Preparation

Cut five car shapes from the five colors of felt.

What to Do

1. Distribute the five cars to five different children.
2. Teach the poem "Five Little Cars" to the class.

Five Little Cars
by Jackie Wright

One little blue car,
All shiny and new,
Met a bright red car,
Now there are two.

Two little cars
Driving past a tree,
A yellow car turned left,
Now there are three.

Three little cars
Driving to the store,
A green car pulled out,
Now there are four.

Four little cars
Going for a drive,
A purple car joined them,
Now there are five.

3. As the class says the poem, the child with the appropriate color car puts it on the flannel board as that color car is mentioned in the poem.
4. Give the felt cars to five different children, and repeat the rhyme until each child has had a turn placing a car on the flannel board.

Assessment

1. Did the child put the correct color car on the flannel board at the correct time?
2. Was the child able to listen to and learn the poem?

Jackie Wright, Enid, OK

TRANSPORTATION

Forward Motion

AGES
4+

Learning Objectives
Children will:
1. Explore the concepts of *speed* and *motion*.
2. Learn about estimating.

Vocabulary
angle   measure
distance   speed
incline   steep

Children's Books
Cars and Trucks and Things That Go
   by Richard Scarry
First Discovery: Cars and Trucks by Scholastic

Materials
racetracks or ramps
ruler or measuring tape
toy cars

What to Do
1. Help the children set up three racetrack pieces or ramps in a row, so that the second one has a steeper incline than the first and the third one has a steeper incline than the second.
2. Invite children to estimate how far a car will go once it travels down each ramp, off the edge, and onto the floor.
3. If the children want to, invite them to use the ruler or measuring tape to measure the distance the cars travel.
4. Suggest that the children experiment with various cars on different ramps.

Assessment
1. Did the accuracy of the child's estimations increase over time?
2. Did the child build other ramps to explore *speed* and *motion*?

Mary Murray, Mazomanie, WI

Horse Play

AGES
4+

Learning Objectives
Children will:
1. Learn about horse-drawn transportation.
2. Practice the directions *left* and *right* while pretending to drive a horse and cart.

Vocabulary
left   right   whoa
rein   turn

Children's Books

Barney's Horse by Syd Hoff
Clara and the Book Wagon
    by Nancy Smiler Levinson
Daily Life in a Covered Wagon by
    Paul A. Erickson

Materials

cotton rope
large building blocks or large sturdy
    cardboard box
pictures of horses hitched to wagons, carts, or
    buggies
rocking horse

What to Do

1. Show the children pictures of horse-drawn transportation. Show how the driving reins go right up to the horses' mouths and attach to metal bits. Discuss how tugging hard on the reins might hurt the horse and why it's important to be gentle when steering a horse.

2. Let the children help build a "cart" from blocks or use a sturdy cardboard box. Tie the cotton rope around the nose of the rocking horse.

3. Demonstrate driving skills by showing how to ask the horse to pull forward by flicking both reins and saying, "Walk on," and to turn right or left by gently pulling the right or left rein. To stop, pull both reins straight back as you say, "Whoa."

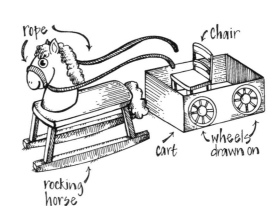

4. Invite the children to take turns driving or riding in the cart. While the passengers are waiting their turns to drive, encourage imagination by pretending to wave to other people who are also in carts or pointing out places of interest that you are passing on your trip.

Assessment

1. Does the child pull left to go left and pull right to go right?
2. What has the child learned about horses and horse-drawn vehicles?

Kay Flowers, Summerfield, OH

Road Signs Matching Game

AGES
4+

Learning Objectives

Children will:
1. Learn about road signs in their community.
2. Learn the color and shape of road signs.

Vocabulary

caution	railroad crossing
color	road construction
curve	shape
deer crossing	sign
detour	stop
pedestrian	yield

Children's Books
City Signs by Zoran Milich
I Read Signs by Tana Hoban
Road Signs by JoAnn Early Macken
Signs on the Road by Autumn Leigh
Signs on the Road by Mary Hill

Materials
computer and printer
laminating machine or clear contact paper
pictures of road signs (the Internet is
    a good source)
small container to hold photos
white card stock

What to Do
1. Show the children the photos during group time and discuss what each sign means. Tell the children that the photos will be in the block area (or another center of your choosing).
2. Tell the children that they can match the pictures to one another. The children can associate the meaning, name, color, shape, and words on each sign. Allow the children to play the game as long as they are interested.

Assessment
1. What did the child learn about the road signs in his community?
2. Is the child able to describe the shape and color of each sign?

Tina R. Durham-Woehler, Lebanon, TN

Preparation
● Locate pictures of various road signs that the children might see in your immediate community. Print two of each road sign on white card stock.
● Cut out each photo and laminate it or cover it with clear contact paper.
● Place the photos in a small container labeled "Road Signs Matching Game."

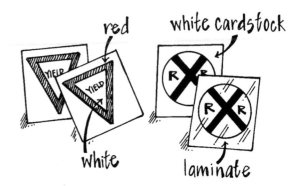

Teacher-to-Teacher Tip
Allow the children to use road signs in the block center with cars to make a roadway.

Taxiing Down the Runway

AGES 4+

Learning Objectives
Children will:
1. Learn about different types of air transportation.
2. Learn vocabulary associated with aircraft and airports.

Vocabulary

air traffic controllers	land
airplane	luggage
airport	passengers
bathroom	pilot
briefcase	runway
captain	seat
cargo	steps
carry-on	suitcase
cart	takeoff
clouds	ticket
door	ticket attendant
flight attendant	ticket booth
fly	tray
helicopter	uniform
jet	wings

Children's Books

Airplane Flight! A Lift-the-Flap Adventure by
   Susanna Leonard Hill
All Aboard Airplanes by Frank Evans and
   George Guzzi
Amazing Airplanes by Tony Mitton and Ant Parker
DK Big Book of Airplanes by Caroline Bingham
The Noisy Airplane Ride by Mike Downs

Materials

Airport by Byron Barton
block people
large white bulletin board paper
crayons and markers
glue sticks
paper, cut into cloud shapes
pictures of airplanes
pictures of airports
toy airplanes, helicopters, choppers, and jets
travel posters
unit blocks

Preparation

- If possible, set up a trip to a small or large airport, runway, or hangar. If a trip to an airport is not possible, read one or more books about airports to the children.
- Gather the materials listed and set up the block area for the children to create an airport.
- Create an airport Word Splash. On a large white bulletin board paper, draw a picture of an airplane in the middle of the paper. Write "things in an airport" on the airplane.

What to Do

1. Read *Airport* by Byron Barton to the children, and then show the children a picture of the inside of an airport. Discuss what they see. Ask the children if anyone has been to an airport for a trip or to pick up a relative or friend. Ask these children to describe their experiences.
2. Give each child a cloud-shaped paper, and ask them to draw a picture of something that is associated with airports.
3. Glue the children's drawings to the Word Splash bulletin board paper.
4. Ask the children to describe their drawings, and as they do, write the words they associate with airports under their drawings.
5. Suggest that the children use the materials in the block area to build an airport.

Assessment

1. What words has the child learned about airports and airplanes?
2. Is the child able to describe different types of planes?

Quazonia J. Quarles, Newark, DE

All Aboard the Alphabet Train

AGES 5+

Learning Objectives
Children will:
1. Name things that begin with the letters of the alphabet.
2. Recognize the letters of the alphabet and the sound of each letter.

Vocabulary
alphabet	boxcar	sound	train
begin	letter	ticket	

Children's Books
Alphabet Book by Audrey and Bruce Wood
Alphabet City by Stephen T. Johnson
The Alphabet from A to Y with Bonus Letter Z! by Steve Martin
Eric Carle's ABC by Eric Carle
Q Is for Duck: An Alphabet Guessing Game by Mary Elting and Michael Folson

Materials
alphabet book
items that start with each letter of the alphabet
large appliance box
paint and paintbrush
plastic alphabet letters
Velcro

Preparation
- Paint a large appliance box, creating windows, a door, and wheels to resemble a train engine. Create a sign: The Alphabet Train.
- Paint large lowercase or uppercase letters of the alphabet on the train or attach plastic alphabet letters with Velcro.
- Gather a collection of small items that start with each letter of each alphabet.

What to Do
1. Read an alphabet book to the children to introduce and view letters.
2. Introduce the Alphabet Train. Point to one of the letters on the train. Ask the children to say the letter.
3. Place a few of the items in the middle of the floor. Say the name for each item. Ask the children to find one of the items on the floor that could take a ride on the train because it starts with the letter you pointed to on the train.
4. Repeat with another letter.
5. When the children are familiar with this activity, let the children pick a letter as well as an item that could take a ride on the train.

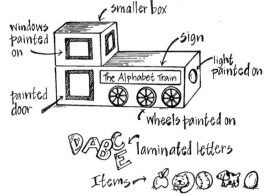

Assessment
1. Is the child able to recognize the letters of the alphabet?
2. Is the child able to name things that begin with each letter of the alphabet?

Quazonia J. Quarles, Newark, DE

Another Encyclopedia of Theme Activities

Down the Tracks

AGES 5+

Learning Objectives
Children will:
1. Name the parts of a train.
2. Describe where trains travel.
3. Learn and properly use new vocabulary words.

Vocabulary
baggage car
boxcar
caboose
cargo
cave
city
conductor
country
engine
flat car
hopper car
mountain
passenger car
railroad
tank car
tickets
tracks
train
train station
trestles

Children's Books
Caboose Who Got Loose by Bill Peet
Freight Train by Donald Crews
I've Been Working on the Railroad by Laura G. Gates
Tracks by David Galef
Train Song by Diane Siebert
Trains by Gail Gibbons

Materials
audio recording of train sounds
chart paper
construction paper
crayons
Freight Train by Donald Crews
markers
paper

Preparation
Make a web graphic organizer. Draw a large circle in the middle of a piece of chart paper. In the circle, write the word *train*. Draw lines extending out from the circle to create a web.

What to Do
1. Begin by playing an audio recording of train sounds. See if the children can recognize the sounds. Ask children if they have ever been on a train or have seen a train.
2. Read *Freight Train* by Donald Crews. Using the graphic organizer, write on the web what the children have learned about trains.
3. Remind the children that in the story the train was going different places, different directions, and in different kinds of weather. Encourage the children to retell the story.
4. Provide paper, crayons, and markers for the children to make pictures of train stories or to make a series of pictures that retells the story of *Freight Train*, or any other train story they know or can imagine. If the children make a series of pictures that retells a story, ask the children to dictate captions for each picture, and then bind the pictures together to make class books.

Assessment
1. Did the child learn the names of the parts of a train?
2. What did the child learn about train travel?
3. Did the child learn new vocabulary words?

Teacher-To-Teacher Tip
This activity may take more than one day to complete. You may also need a parent helper or another volunteer to help the children complete the activity.

TRANSPORTATION

Fingerplays, Songs, and Poems

"I've Been Working on the Railroad" (Traditional)

I've been workin' on the railroad,
All the livelong day.
I've been workin' on the railroad,
Just to pass the time away.
Don't you hear the whistle blowing?
Rise up so early in the morn.
Don't you hear the captain shouting
"Dinah, blow your horn?"

Dinah, won't you blow,
Dinah, won't you blow,
Dinah, won't you blow your horn?
Dinah, won't you blow,
Dinah, won't you blow,
Dinah, won't you blow your horn?

Someone's in the kitchen with Dinah.
Someone's in the kitchen, I know.
Someone's in the kitchen with Dinah
Strumming on the old banjo.

Fee, fie, fiddle-e-i-o.
Fee, fie, fiddle-e-i-o-o-o-o.
Fee, fie, fiddle-e-i-o.
Strumming on the old banjo.

Quazonia J. Quarles, Newark, DE

Driving Words

AGES 5+

Learning Objectives
Children will:
1. Learn words related to cars and driving.
2. Improve fine motor skills.

Vocabulary

car	gas	speed
drive	ride	steer

What to Do
1. Display the large word cards. Tell the children about the meaning of each word.
2. Invite the children to "drive" a mini car along the letters of the words as you help the children identify the letters in each word and then say each word together.

Assessment
1. Did the child learn new words related to cars and driving?
2. Is the child able to follow the shape of each letter as she drives a car along each letter?

Mary Murray, Mazomanie, WI

Children's Books
Cars and Trucks and Things That Go by Richard Scarry
First Discovery: Cars and Trucks by Scholastic

Materials
4 small toy cars
large 12" x 18" word cards of *drive, car, gas, speed, steer, ride*

On the Road Again

AGES
5+

Learning Objectives
Children will:
1. Learn about the roads in their own community.
2. Learn about traffic signs.

Vocabulary
community   signs
road   street

Children's Books
Along a Long Road by Frank Viva
City Signs by Zoran Milich
I Read Signs by Tana Hoban
Road Work Ahead by Anastasia Suen

Materials
4" x 6" (or larger) flannel-backed vinyl upholstery fabric
block people
plastic cars
small street signs
white, blue, and yellow medium-point paint pens

Preparation
- Place the fabric on a flat, smooth surface. This will be the map of your community.
- Make road outlines using the white and yellow paint pens. Make straight roads, curved roads, and intersections to resemble your town.
- Use the blue pen to draw rivers, creeks, ponds, lakes, and other water features on the map.

What to Do
1. Engage the children in a discussion about the roads in your community: how they look, their colors, the signs on the roads, how to drive on the roads, and any other appropriate information.
2. If appropriate, discuss that in some countries they drive on the left instead of the right as we do in the United States.
3. Add the road mat to the block area. Add plastic cars, small street signs, people, and other materials to the center. Allow the children to drive their cars on the mat, pretending to drive around town.

Assessment
1. What did the child learn about her community?
2. What did the child learn about street signs and their meaning?

Tina R. Durham-Woehler, Lebanon, TN

Teacher-to-Teacher Tip
Discuss street safety with the children: cross the street with an adult, look both ways, wait for street crossing signs, and so on. Discuss street signs the children may see on their way to and from school.

TRANSPORTATION

Transportation over the Years

AGES 5+

Learning Objectives

Children will:

1. Learn about the history of transportation.
2. Learn what transportation looked like in the past.

Vocabulary

airplane	Model T
boat	stagecoach
cars	train
horse and buggy	

Children's Books

Boats by Anne Rockwell
Boats: Speeding! Sailing! Cruising! by Patricia Hubbell
Daily Life in a Covered Wagon by Paul Erickson
Freight Train by Donald Crews
They're Off! The Story of the Pony Express by Cheryl Harness
Tin Lizzie by Allan Drummond

Materials

crayons
markers
paper
pictures of different types of transportation, from the present day and the past

What to Do

1. Ask the children to name as many different ways to travel as they can. Next, explain that there were not always cars, planes, and other types of motorized transportation.
2. Show the children pictures of present-day transportation and transportation in the past. What similarities and differences do the children notice? Discuss where each form of transportation is or was used. Can a boat sail down a road? Can a car go on a railroad track?
3. Read some of the books listed to the children and leave the books in the reading area for the children to look at independently.
4. Suggest that the children draw pictures of ways to get around now and/or ways to get around long ago.

Assessment

1. What did the child learn about the history of transportation?
2. What does the child know about what transportation looked like in the past?

Hilary Romig, Ruidoso, NM

Yellow School Bus

AGES 5+

Learning Objectives
Children will:
1. Learn about traffic safety and how to board and leave a school bus.
2. Begin to prepare for attending a primary school.

Vocabulary
bus	ride	traffic
bus driver	rules	watchful
caution	safety	
quiet	school	

Children's Books
The Little School Bus by Carol Roth
School Bus by Donald Crews
Staying Safe on the School Bus
   by Joanne Mattern

Materials
classroom chairs

Preparation
Arrange the children's chairs in rows, two on each side of an aisle, similar to the seating in a bus. Put one chair up front for the bus driver.

What to Do
1. Read *Staying Safe on the School Bus* by Joanne Mattern or a similar book.
2. Ask the children if any of them have ridden on or seen a yellow school bus. Do they know any rules of safety when going to a bus and riding the bus? Discuss some important rules with them:
   - Walk to the bus; don't run.
   - Walk quietly to a seat.
   - Sit quietly while the bus is moving.
   - Do what the bus driver tells you.
   - Don't stand up until the bus stops.
3. Ask one of the children to volunteer to be the bus driver. Have her sit in the driver's seat. The other children practice walking to the bus, getting on, and then sitting while the bus is moving. The driver can say when they are moving. When the bus stops, they walk off.
4. Repeat the activity, letting other children be the bus driver.
5. Recite the poem "Going to the School Bus" together.

> ### Going to the School Bus
> **by Shirley Anne Ramaley**
> *I'm going to ride the bus today.*
> *I know it will be fun.*
> *I'll follow rules and to be safe,*
> *I'll walk and I won't run.*

Assessment
1. What did the child learn about traffic safety and how to board and get off a school bus?
2. What did the child learn about preparing to ride a bus to primary school?

Shirley Anne Ramaley, Sun City, AZ

TRANSPORTATION

Bubble, Bubble

AGES  3+

Learning Objectives
Children will:
1. Make bubbles using a simple recipe.
2. Learn how common objects can be used to make different shapes of bubbles.

Vocabulary
air   bubbles   recipe
blow   liquid

Children's Books
Bubble Trouble by Margaret Mahy
How to Make Bubbles by Erika L. Shores
Pop! A Book About Bubbles
    by Kimberly Brubaker Bradley
The Unbelievable Bubble Book by John Cassidy

What to Do
1. Help the children make one of the following bubble recipes:
   - 2/3 cup dish soap, 1 gallon water, 3 tablespoons glycerin (available at most pharmacies)
   - 6 parts water, 2 parts dish soap, 3/4 parts corn syrup
2. Pour a small amount of bubble mix into the shallow pans.
3. Let children experiment with each bubble wand or object. What kind of bubble is formed with each object?

Assessment
1. Did the child learn how to blow bubbles?
2. Was the child able to understand how the shape of each bubble-maker creates a bubble that is roughly the same shape, at least until it leaves the bubble-maker?
3. What did the child learn about how bubbles are formed?

Donna Alice Patton, Hillsboro, OH

Materials
bubble wands and other objects to make bubbles: chenille craft stems (pipe cleaners) formed into shapes, strawberry baskets, straws, coat hangers, and cookie cutters
glycerin or corn syrup
measuring cups and spoons
shallow pans
dish soap
water

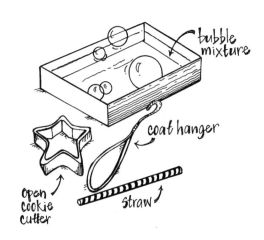

bubble mixture
coat hanger
open cookie cutter
straw

Teacher-to-Teacher Tip
This activity is best done outside.

Fill and Pour

Learning Objectives
Children will:
1. Compare the amount of water that will fill each container.
2. Learn fine motor skills of filling and pouring.

Vocabulary

compare	least	most
different	less	pour
fill	more	same

What to Do
1. Place several containers in the water table and allow the children to explore.
2. Fill one container with water with the children's help. Pick another container and ask the children if the second container will hold all the water from the first container. Let the children make a prediction, and then pour the water while the children observe what happens.
3. Continue comparing different containers with the same process. Have the children line up the containers from the one that holds the most water to the one that holds the least.
4. Use a small container, such as a 1-cup measure, and ask how many it will take to fill a specific container. Write down the children's predictions. Have the children fill the container with the 1-cup measure and mark each cup. Finally, help the children count the number of cups used.

Assessment
1. Is the child able to compare the sizes of containers?
2. With practice, is the child able to estimate how many cups it will take to fill another container?

Sandy L. Scott, Meridian, ID

Children's Book
One Giant Splash by Michael Dahl

Materials
containers of different sizes
sand and water table
water

Preparation
Fill the table with water before the children arrive.

water table

tall pitcher

little pot

measuring cup

small bowl

How Do We Use Water?

Learning Objective
Children will:
1. Recognize ways water is used.
2. Learn to wash and dry dishes.

Vocabulary
clean	dry	wash
cool	splash	water
dishes	swim	
drink	warm	

Children's Books
A Drop of Water: A Book of Science and Wonder
   by Walter Wick
Water by Frank Asch

What to Do
1. Let the children feel the cool water. Ask them what can be done with cool water. (Drink it, swim in a pool, give it to their pet, run in a sprinkler, splash in a fountain, and so on.)
2. Have the children feel the warm water in the container. What can be done with warm water? (Wash dishes, clothes, hands, themselves, and so on.)
3. Show the children the plate with the dried marker on it. Ask a few of the children to take the dry towel and wipe the mark off. When it doesn't come off, ask them how to get the mark off. (Wash the dish.)
4. Help the children add dish soap to the container of warm water, swish it around to form suds, and then put the plate in the water and rub it. What could the soap and water do that the towel couldn't?

Assessment
1. Is the child able to describe the uses of cool and warm water?
2. Does the child understand that the warm water and soap can remove things that simple rubbing cannot?

Terry Callahan, Easton, MD

Materials
containers of cool water and warm water
dish soap
dry towel
plastic plate
washable marker

Preparation
- Scribble marks on the plastic plate with a washable marker and let the marks dry thoroughly. Test to make sure the marks will wash off. If not, use a thin coat of dried food.
- Place warm water in one container and cool water in another.

Another Encyclopedia of Theme Activities

How Does Water Change Sand?

Learning Objectives

Children will:

1. Learn about the properties of water and dry sand.
2. Notice how sand changes when water is added.

Vocabulary

change	properties	water
dry	sand	wet

Children's Books

Jump into Science: Sand by Ellen J. Prager
Sea, Sand, and Me! by Patricia Hubbell

Materials

2 clear plastic glasses
chart paper or a whiteboard
containers of water and dry sand
larger container to mix sand and water (large
    enough so children can touch the mixture)
measuring cups and/or sand molds
shallow tray
small paper cups
wooden spoon to mix sand and water
    (optional)

What to Do

1. Show the children a glass of water. Ask them, "What does water look like? What does it feel like? How does it move? Where do you find it?" If appropriate, list their responses on chart paper or a whiteboard.
2. Pour the water out on a flat surface. Does it stay in one place?
3. Using the sand, repeat steps one and two.
4. Mix enough water into the sand in the large container so the sand is wet enough to mold into shapes. Let the children scoop and mold the sand.

Assessment

1. Is the child able to see the differences between the properties of sand and water?
2. What does the child notice about how sand and water change when mixed together?

Terry Callahan, Easton, MD

Teacher-to-Teacher Tip

Show some pictures of sand castles and discuss children's knowledge of them.

The Water Goes Up!

AGES
4+

Learning Objectives

Children will:
1. Observe how water levels change based on the weight of objects placed in the water.
2. Learn about the concepts of *heavy* and *light*.

Vocabulary

displace	light	objects
heavy	lightweight	water level

Children's Books

Heavy or Light by Charlotte Guillain
How Much, How Many, How Far, How Heavy, How Long, How Tall Is 1000? by Helen Nolan

Materials

large tub or sink with water
objects of varying weights (plastic cup or plate, a large wooden block, and a large jar of tempera paint)
marker or crayon

Preparation

- Make sure that a mark made by the crayon or marker can be seen by the children as the water in the tub or sink rises.
- Make sure the objects that you have chosen show varying displacement levels.

What to Do

1. Tell the children they are going to see what happens when things are added to a tub of water. First, use the marking tool to show the original water level.
2. Pass around the lightest object, such as a plastic cup or plate. Let the children tell you if it is heavy or light. Put this object in the water. Draw a line for the new water level, which may not have visibly changed.
3. Ask the children about the original line that showed the water level and the new line. Why do they think the level changed very little or not at all?
4. Remove the weight. Pass around the object of medium weight, such as a large wooden block. Ask the children how it differs from the first object. Put it in the water and draw a new line. What do the children observe? Remove the weight.
5. Pass around the heaviest object, such as a large jar of tempera paint. (Help the children hold it, if necessary.) How does it compare to the previous weights? What do they think the water level will do? Add the object and mark the water level. Were they right about the water level?
6. Explain that the objects move the water out of the way—they *displace* it.

Assessment

1. Is the child able to understand why the water levels changed?
2. Is the child able to predict correctly what will happen to the water level for each object?

Terry Callahan, Easton, MD

The Importance of Water

AGES
5+

Learning Objectives

Children will:

1. Learn about the importance of water to the earth.
2. Communicate and share their ideas with others.

Vocabulary

earth	pond	surface
importance	river	water
lakes	science	world
ocean	stream	
percent	study	

Children's Books

All the Water in the World by George Ella Lyon
A Drop of Water by Walter Wick
Keeping Water Clean by Helen Frost
Our Earth: Saving Water by Peggy Hock
Our World of Water by Beatrice Hollyer
The Water Cycle by Rebecca Olien

Materials

children's books about water and the water cycle
globe
large maps of the world

What to Do

1. Sit in a circle with the globe in the center. Ask the children if they can point out the water on the globe. What do they think of so much water? Explain that about 70 percent of Earth's surface is covered in water. Demonstrate this on the globe and explain *percent*.

2. Spread the maps on the floor. See if the children can point to the water on the maps. Ask the children to fill in the blank: "When I think of Earth, I think of _____." Be sure each child has a turn and participates.

3. Read one or more of the books about water, and then talk with the children about the importance of water. Explain that the water in our world is all the water we will ever have, and that not all people in the world have clean water. Ask the children for ideas about how to help keep our water supply clean.

Assessment

1. Is the child able to point to the water on the globe and maps?
2. What can the child tell you about water and Earth?
3. Is the child able to understand the importance of water?

Shirley Anne Ramaley, Sun City, AZ

Teacher-to-Teacher Tip

If there is time, talk with the children about the water they drink and how important it is to their health.

W
A
T
E
R

Blowing Leaves

AGES
3+

Learning Objectives

Children will:

1. Move around the room in creative ways.
2. Listen to directions, including when to move and when to stop.
3. Imagine what it is like to be a leaf blowing in the wind.

Vocabulary

blow	freeze	twirl
fall	leaf	wind
float	roll	
flutter	scatter	

Children's Books

Feel the Wind by Arthur Dorros
Like a Windy Day by Frank and Devin Asch
One Windy Wednesday by Phyllis Root
The Wind Blew by Pat Hutchins

Materials

none needed

What to Do

1. Tell the children that they are going to be leaves and you are going to be the wind. They may move around the room as you blow, and when you stop, they will fall to the ground until you begin to blow again.
2. Make blowing sounds and tell the children to float and scatter. Stop blowing and see how quickly they drop to the floor.
3. Blow again and repeat the process. You can suggest that the children flutter, float, twirl, or roll to keep them interested in this game.
4. Once the children understand how to play, let one of the children be the wind.

Assessment

1. How easily can the child move?
2. Did the child show creativity in his movements?
3. Did the child listen and follow directions?
4. Did the child show impulse control when you stopped blowing?

Shelley Hoster, Norcross, GA

Make Thunder

Learning Objectives

Children will:
1. Learn the cause of thunder.
2. Discover that thunder isn't as scary as it sounds.
3. Experiment with making sounds.

Vocabulary

boom	lightning	thunder
crash	rumble	vibration
flash	sound	

Children's Books

Flash, Crash, Rumble, and Roll by Franklyn M. Branley
Thunder-Boomer! by Shutta Crum
Thunder Cake by Patricia Polacco

Materials

aluminum pie plates (one per child)

What to Do

1. Gather the children for circle or group time.
2. Explain that the big—sometimes scary—sounds that thunder makes happen because lightning causes the air to move (or vibrate) when it strikes. Explain that the same thing happens when we make sounds. When we talk or clap our hands, we cause the air to vibrate too.
3. Demonstrate that shaking a pie plate makes sounds that are very similar to the rumbling sounds that thunder makes.
4. Invite the children to make their own thunder sounds with the pie plates. After they have had a few minutes to play, refocus their attention by explaining that thunder can make both soft sounds and loud sounds. Show them that shaking their pie plates slowly results in a small sound, while shaking their pie plates quickly results in a big sound. Give them an opportunity to practice both.

Assessment

1. Is the child able to name things that make big sounds?
2. Is the child able to make soft sounds and loud sounds with the pie plate?

Erin Huffstetler, Maryville, TN

Rainy Day Fun

Learning Objectives
Children will:
1. Learn that rain comes from clouds in the sky.
2. Develop oral language skills.
3. Improve fine and gross motor skills.

Vocabulary
clouds   rainy
rain   umbrella

What to Do
1. Engage the children in a discussion about rain. Explain that rain falls from clouds.
2. Teach the children the American Sign Language sign for rain: Wiggle your fingers as you move your hands from up in the air in a downward direction.
3. Invite children to practice the sign as they make a pitter-patter raindrop sound.

Assessment
1. Does the child understand that rain comes from the sky?
2. Can the child make the sign for rain?

Mary Murray, Mazomanie, WI

Children's Books
Come On, Rain! by Karen Hesse
Down Comes the Rain by Franklyn M. Branley
Rain by Robert Kalan
The Rain Came Down by David Shannon
Who Likes Rain? by Wong Herbert Yee

Materials
none needed

Story for a Rainy Day

Learning Objectives
Children will:
1. Improve their oral language skills.
2. Develop vocabulary.

Vocabulary
blue   storm
clouds   sun
gray   sunshine
rain   white
sky   yellow

Children's Books

Come On, Rain! by Karen Hesse
Down Comes the Rain by Franklyn M. Branley
The Rain Came Down by David Shannon
Who Likes Rain? by Wong Herbert Yee

What to Do

1. Display the book *Rain* by Robert Kalan. Read the book to the children to help them become familiar with the text.
2. Ask the children to draw different aspects of the story on large index cards. If appropriate, write a word on each index card that relates to each child's picture.
3. Read the book again and invite the children to hold up their picture card at the appropriate place in the story.

Assessment

1. Has the child learned new vocabulary?
2. Does the child understand the meaning of the weather words?

Mary Murray, Mazomanie, WI

Materials

crayons and markers
large index cards
Rain by Robert Kalan

Weather Cards

Learning Objectives

The children will:

1. Learn weather-related vocabulary.
2. Develop fine motor skills by matching pictures to words.

Vocabulary

circle	picture	sunny
cloudy	rainy	windy
match	snowy	

Materials

card stock, cut into five 3" x 11" cards, or large index cards
glue or tape
images representing five different types of weather (the Internet is a good source)
laminating materials or clear contact paper
scissors

Children's Books

Flash, Crash, Rumble, and Roll
    by Franklyn M. Branley
Oh Say Can You Say What's the Weather Today? All About Weather by Tish Rabe
Weather by Seymour Simon
Weather Words and What They Mean
    by Gail Gibbons
What Will the Weather Be? by Lynda DeWitt

Preparation

- On card stock or index cards, print or glue images representing five different types of weather—sunny, cloudy, windy, rainy, and snowy—and write the corresponding weather word.
- On separate cards, print one weather word on each card: *sunny, cloudy, windy, rainy,* and *snowy.*
- Laminate all the cards for durability.

What to Do

1. Put the weather word cards, along with the picture cards, in a center.
2. Talk with the children about five different types of weather—sunny, cloudy, windy, rainy, and snowy.
3. Encourage the children to match the card with the image and word to the card with the corresponding weather word.

Assessment

1. Is the child able to understand the different types of weather?
2. Is the child able to match the weather picture with the correct weather word?

Fingerplays, Songs, and Poems

"What's the Weather?"
(Traditional)

(Tune: chorus of "Bingo")

S-U-N-N-Y
S-U-N-N-Y
S-U-N-N-Y
And sunny was the weather.*

* *Change the spelling, and sing a verse for* cloudy, windy, rainy, *and* snowy.

Jackie Wright, Enid, OK

The Weather Center

AGES
4+

Learning Objectives

Children will:
1. Learn about various types of weather.
2. Practice making predictions.
3. Practice making observations.

Vocabulary

days of the school week
names of various weather conditions: *snowy, rainy, windy, sunny, cloudy,* and so on
observation
prediction
today
tomorrow
weather
yesterday

Children's Books

Flash, Crash, Rumble, and Roll
by Franklyn M. Branley
*Oh Say Can You Say What's the Weather Today?
All About Weather* by Tish Rabe
Weather by Seymour Simon
Weather Words and What They Mean
by Gail Gibbons
What Will the Weather Be? by Lynda DeWitt

Materials

card stock cut into 5" x 7" pieces or large index cards
chart paper and markers
images of a variety of weather conditions
tape

Preparation

- On chart paper, make a five-columned chart titled "Weather Observations." Write one day of the week at the top of each column.
- Glue or draw weather symbols for sunny, windy, snowy, rainy, and cloudy on card stock or index cards. Make a few cards for each type of weather.

What to Do

1. Talk with the children about different kinds of weather.
2. On Monday, have the children discuss the weather for the day and determine which weather symbol(s) best represents the weather for the day. Tape the appropriate card or cards in the column for Monday. Write under that card "Monday's weather observation."
3. Ask the children to guess tomorrow's weather. Place the appropriate card underneath Monday's weather observation card in the Monday column. Underneath the prediction card, write "Our prediction for tomorrow's weather."
4. Continue for the rest of the week, discussing the actual weather and the children's predictions. Were the children right in their predictions?

Assessment

1. Can the child identify the weather conditions represented on the weather symbol cards?
2. Does the child understand the concept of guessing or predicting what he thinks the weather will be the next day?

Jackie Wright, Enid, OK

Clouds

Learning Objectives

Children will:

1. Understand and recognize the different types of clouds.
2. Create a cotton-ball cloud picture.

Vocabulary

cirrus	gray	stratus
clouds	high	white
cumulus	low	wide
feathery	puffy	

Children's Books
The Cloud Book by Tomie dePaola
Hi, Clouds by Carol Greene
Little Cloud by Eric Carle
Weather Words and What They Mean
    by Gail Gibbons

Materials
book about clouds
cotton balls
glue
light blue construction paper
marker
photographs of clouds (the Internet is a good
    source)

What to Do
1. Show the children photos of the three main kinds of clouds: cirrus, cumulus, and stratus. Discuss the appearances of the different types of clouds and the weather they bring:
   - Cirrus: white, feathery, high clouds (in Latin means "curl")
   - Cumulus: puffy, low clouds (in Latin means "heap")
   - Stratus: wide, gray, low clouds (in Latin means "covering" or "blanket")

2. Read *Little Cloud* or another book about clouds. Discuss what the children observed in the story.

3. Give each child a sheet of construction paper, glue, and cotton balls. Have the children create the types of cloud they want by pulling the cotton balls into their desired shapes and gluing the shapes on the paper.

4. Label each cotton-ball cloud picture with the Latin names and the name of the child who created the cloud picture.

Assessment
1. Can the child identify and classify the three main types of clouds?
2. Can the child create a cloud picture with cotton balls?

Sandy L. Scott, Meridian, ID

Experimenting with Evaporation

AGES
5+

Learning Objectives
Children will:
1. Make predictions.
2. Learn about evaporation.

Vocabulary
evaporation   prediction
puddles   rain

Children's Books

Down Comes the Rain by Franklyn M. Bernley
A Drop Around the World by Barbara McKinney
Puddles by Jonathan London
Why Does Water Evaporate? by Rob Moore

Materials

chalk
chart paper and marker
puddles of water

What to Do

1. After a rainfall, talk to the children about what evaporation means or read books about rain, puddles, and evaporation.
2. Go outside and have the children find a large puddle. (**Note:** If you live in an area with little rainfall, just create your own puddle with a garden hose or bucket of water.) Have one child use the chalk to trace around the puddle. Look for other puddles and have the children trace around them.
3. Ask the children to make predictions about what will happen to the puddles and how long it will take for them to change. Write down their predictions on a large sheet of paper.
4. A little later, return to the puddles and talk about the changes. Have the children draw a line around the new, smaller puddles. Ask children to make more predictions.
5. Return often to see the changes.

Assessment

1. Is the child able to make predictions about evaporation?
2. Is the child able to trace the puddle shapes?

Sandra Ryan, Buffalo, NY

Pinwheels in the Wind!

AGES 5+

Learning Objectives

Children will:
1. Make pinwheels to study wind direction.
2. Learn about the wind.

Vocabulary

diagonal
pinwheels
weather
wind

Children's Books

Watching the Wind by Edana Eckart
Wind by Terry Jennings

Materials

construction paper cut into squares (other papers work too—you can even glue two colors of paper together to make a cool pattern), one for each child
hole punches
paper fasteners (also called *brads*)
pencil
ruler
scissors
stapler (optional)
straws—the nonbendable ones are best

Preparation

- Draw two straight diagonal lines from the top corners to the bottom corners of the construction paper.
- Punch a hole in the very center, where the diagonal lines cross.
- Cut along all the lines, but stop about two-thirds of the distance from the hole.
  Tip: If the children are using two colors of paper, glue the pieces of paper together and allow to dry before marking and cutting.

What to Do

1. Read books about the wind and how wind is part of the weather.
2. Give each child a square of construction paper. The children fold each section of the paper toward the hole. The ends should all line up, one on top of each other. (You might need to hold the sections in place or staple them in place.)
3. Help the children push a paper fastener through all the folds and the hole, and then push the paper fastener sticking out of the pinwheel through the side of the straw. Fold open the ends of the paper fastener to hold the straw in place against the paper pinwheel.
4. Use the pinwheel to test the direction of the wind. Stand in different places and see where the pinwheel spins the fastest or slowest.

Assessment

1. What did the child learn about the wind?
2. Can the child explain how the wind makes the pinwheel spin?
3. Was the child able to make a pinwheel?

Donna Alice Patton, Hillsboro, OH

Teacher-to-Teacher Tip
Ask for parent volunteers to help the children with this activity.

Simple Sun Catcher

Learning Objectives
Children will:
1. Develop fine motor skills.
2. Learn about sunshine.

Vocabulary

decoration	star	sunshine
glitter	sticky	tissue
light	sun	warm
plastic	sun catcher	weather
shine		

Children's Books
Sunshine Makes the Seasons by
   Franklyn M. Branley
Sunshine, Moonshine by Jennifer Armstrong

Materials
clear contact paper
hole punch
pencils
scissors
string or shiny thread
tissue paper

What to Do
1. Help the children cut out two identical circles of clear contact paper, peel the backing off one circle, and place this circle sticky-side-up on the table.
2. Tell the children to tear tissue paper into small pieces and then press the pieces of torn tissue onto the sticky surface, alternating between colors to create a stained-glass effect.
   Tip: Ask the children not to place tissue paper all the way to the edge of the contact paper circle. The second circle will stick better is there is a little clear space at the edge.
3. When the children have filled the circle with torn tissue, help them peel the backing off the second circle and press and smooth this circle onto the tissue-paper-filled circle.
4. Help the children make a hole at the top and thread a length of string or shiny thread through the hole.
5. Hang the finished sun catchers near a bright window or glass door.

Assessment
1. Does the child have the fine motor skills to cut the circles of contact paper and pieces of tissue paper?
2. Does the child notice the sun shining through the colors of tissue paper in the sun catchers?

Kirsty Neale, Orpington, Kent, UK

Weather Wheels

Learning Objectives
Children will:
1. Identify the weather outside.
2. Practice cutting skills.

Vocabulary
cloudy   snowy   weather
rainy   sunny   windy

Children's Books
Weather Words and What They Mean
    by Gail Gibbons
What Will the Weather Be? by Lynda DeWitt

Materials
brass fasteners (also called *brads*)
construction paper or tagboard
crayons or markers
scissors

Preparation
● Trace two 12" circles on construction paper or tagboard
● Draw lines on the circles to divide them into five pie-shaped slices.
● Search the Internet to find photographs or illustrations of the five weather words in the vocabulary list (*cloudy, rainy, snowy, sunny,* and *windy*). Make enough copies for each child to have one of each picture depicting the five weather words.

What to Do
1. Ask each child to cut out two circles. Help the children who need it.
2. Have the children glue one weather picture into each wedge on one of the circles.
3. Show the children how to cut one wedge slice out of the remaining circle.
4. Help the children place the circle without pictures over the circle with pictures and attach with a brass fastener through the middle of the two circles. (The children should be able to turn the top circle so that the open wedge displays one of the weather pictures on the circle below.)
5. Ask one child to look outside, describe the weather, and then turn her weather wheel to display the appropriate picture that matches the weather outside.
6. Challenge the children to turn their weather wheels to display different weather words you name. Say, for example, "Show me windy," or "Show me snowy."

Assessment
1. Can each child describe the weather pictures?
2. Is each child able to cut straight lines and circles?

Sandra Ryan, Buffalo, NY

Index

following directions, 32, 40, 63, 101–102, 118–119, 129–130, 172–173, 178–179, 203–204, 215, 277–278

gardening activities, 119–120, 242

gross motor skills, 31–32, 36–37, 42, 64, 81, 88, 95, 98–99, 100–101, 113–115, 118–119, 129– 130, 171, 173, 206, 224, 270, 271, 280–281

health/nutrition, 118–123, 308

kindness, 140–145, 204–205

language skills, 17–18, 30, 34–40, 62, 65–66, 83–84, 94, 96–1004, 102–103, 110–115, 135–136, 140–141, 173–174, 176–177, 185–189, 191, 214, 216, 219, 225, 236–237, 243–244, 259–261, 280–281, 294, 298–299, 314–316

listening skills, 150–151, 178, 187–188, 214, 219, 245–246, 278–279, 295

literacy skills, 39–40, 69–70, 94, 102–103, 150–151, 177, 234–235, 246–247, 272

mapping skills, 69–70, 234–235

matching games, 37–40, 132, 188, 190, 203–204, 215, 243–244, 293, 297–298, 315–316

math skills, 17–18, 82–84, 97, 150–164, 188, 202–203, 224–230, 287

measuring skills, 128–129, 157–158, 163–164, 226, 296, 307

memory skills, 38–39, 162–163, 214

music/movement activities, 33–34, 171–179

number activities, 81, 83, 153–160, 224–230, 271, 287, 295

observation skills, 85, 133, 152–153, 177, 316–317

one-to-one correspondence, 156–158, 161

outdoor activities, 114–115, 121–122, 127, 216

pattern activities, 160, 188, 229–230

phonemic awareness, 150–151

plants activities, 243–247

predicting skills, 259, 261–262, 316–317

problem-solving skills, 258–259

recycling activities, 233–237

rhyming skills, 128–129, 162–163, 176

school activities, 214–220

science/nature activities, 243–247, 257–262, 291, 309–310, 315–317

seasons, 268–272

self-concept, 17–19

sensory activities, 109–115, 224

shapes, 122–123, 141, 155–156, 204–205, 215, 229–230, 276–282, 292, 297–298

sizes, 80–81, 128–129, 157–158, 204–205, 226, 268

social/emotional development, 83, 95, 140–145, 205–206, 216, 219–220

sorting skills, 41, 121–122, 151–152, 155–156, 218, 228–230

space activities, 68–69, 260–261

spatial awareness, 65–66, 258–259

storytelling, 178–179

time activities, 287

transportation, 290–299

visual discrimination skills, 177

water play, 307–310

weather activities, 268–272, 315–317

writing skills, 94

Ages 5+

alike/different, 53–54

alphabet activities, 300

animal activities, 24, 44–55, 179–180

art activities, 70–74, 193–196, 262–263, 283, 285, 317–318

blocks/construction activities, 86

body awareness, 19–20, 71–72

classification skills, 48

colors, 103–107, 193–196, 239–240

community/neighborhood, 191–197

cooperative play, 54–55, 106, 193–196, 207, 238–239

counting activities, 90–91, 105, 164–166, 168, 230–231, 275, 288

creative expression, 54–55, 70–71, 87, 89–90, 137–138, 193–194, 282–283

critical thinking skills, 52–54, 86, 167, 222–223

dramatic play, 284

earth knowledge, 237–240

estimating skills, 167

fine motor skills, 71–74, 104–105, 146, 165–166, 230–232, 250–251, 262–263, 275, 283, 285, 289, 302, 321–322

following directions, 46–48, 73–74, 93, 107, 194–195, 210

gardening activities, 252–253

gross motor skills, 47–51, 104–107, 179–180, 231–232

health/nutrition, 123–124, 249–250, 311

kindness, 146–148, 194–195

INDEX

INDEX

INDEX